A Critique of the Study of Kinship

A Critique of the Study of Kinship

David M. Schneider

The University of Michigan Press   *Ann Arbor*

1987   1986   1985   4   3   2

Library of Congress Cataloging in Publication Data

Schneider, David Murray, 1918–
    A critique of the study of kinship.

    Bibliography: p.
    1. Kinship. I. Title.
GN487.S36   1984   306.8′3   84-5246
ISBN 0-472-10051-3
ISBN 0-472-08051-2 (pbk.)

To Addy

Preface

In a paper read to the Anthropological Society of Washington in 1971 I asserted that " 'kinship,' like totemism, the matrilineal complex and matriarchy, is a non-subject since it does not exist in any culture known to man" and " 'kinship' is an artifact of the anthropologists' analytic apparatus and has no concrete counterpart in the cultures of any of the societies we studied" (Schneider 1972:59). I also said that the notion of "kinship as an idiom" was sheer nonsense, and this too was a bald assertion. This book is an attempt to make the grounds for those assertions clear and to back them with reasoned argument.

Needham asserted a similar position at about the same time (1971). Though his reasoning differs from mine, we agree that there is no such thing as kinship. Needham's position is that since there is no unitary "thing" that *kinship* refers to, there can in the nature of the case be no theory about kinship, for there can be no legitimate theory about some "thing" which does not exist. Needham is thus relieved of the task of having to consider what other anthropologists, who believe that there is such a "thing," consider kinship theory. This obviously depends on the premise that there are objective "things" apart from an observer or an observer's relation to them and that their existence and nature can be objectively described.

My own view is that whether kinship exists or not depends on how it is defined by the observer, which in turn states the observer's conception of "it" and his relationship to "it." Needham seems to take the view that this is simply an empirical question; kinship is either an existential "thing" that is "there," or it is not. If it actually exists, it is there, whether we like it or not, no matter how we define it or how we conceive of it, and our problem is to discover its nature and characteristics and so describe and define it correctly. I do not share this view. For me its very existence is in significant part a consequence of how it is understood and defined, and the definition does not, nor can it, arise solely as a consequence of "its" real nature.

My second difference stems from the next step in Needham's argument. Despite the fact that he feels that there is no unitary thing which can be called "kinship" he affirms that "I am not denying, therefore, that the word 'kinship' is useful. . . . it has an immense variety of uses, in that all sorts of institutions and practices and ideas can be referred to by it" (p. 5) and "Let me simply adopt the minimal premise that kinship has to do with the allocation of rights and their transmission from one generation to the next" (p. 3). Needham justifies this position by invoking Wittgenstein: "the term 'kinship' is what Wittgenstein calls an 'odd-job' word'' (p. 5). In brief, despite the fact that there is no such thing as kinship, that there can be no such thing as kinship theory, it is nevertheless useful to use the word because all sorts of institutions and practices and ideas having to do with the allocation of rights and their transmission from one generation to the next can be referred to by it. Not only does the logic of this position escape me, but this only begs the question by shifting the problem onto the question of what *generation* means. For if we take *generation* in the sense in which it is usually used by anthropologists and in studies of kinship, then we are right back where we started—is there really such a ''thing''?

The primary objective of this book is a critical examination of the presuppositions that are part of the study of kinship and the whole idea of ''kinship'' as it has been pursued by anthropologists in recent decades. It is the theory of Radcliffe-Brown, Lowie, Fortes, Eggan, Murdock, and Needham before he saw the light, among others, their co-workers and students. It is the theory which is the conventional wisdom of today and can be found in textbooks, monographs, and papers by anthropologists dealing with the subject.

However, I will not deal systematically with ''kinship terms,'' ''descent,'' or ''marriage'' here although the discussion will necessarily have implications for these.

In part this critical examination is conducted by juxtaposing two ''descriptions'' of the ''kinship system'' of the island of Yap, West Caroline Islands. Another objective of the book, though a minor one, is to make clear the degree to which I can no longer support my writings on Yap on which the first description is based. This is, therefore, a published, public correction or reevaluation of those materials.

Many people have helped with this book. First, my debt to Dr. David Labby for his understanding of Yapese culture, based on a very fine piece of fieldwork, is great and obvious. As is evident, in the light of his fieldwork and interpretation I not only reformulated my own conception of Yapese culture, but was able to understand a host of problems that had effectively prevented me from producing a monograph of my own. My interpretation of Yapese culture, as embodied in the papers listed in the bibliography, was simply inadequate. Labby did, for me at least, really ''demystify Yap'' and I think his demystification has held up under close study.

Dr. Robert McKinley read the next to last draft of the book with great care, and in part as a result of his suggestions the book was largely rewritten and reorganized. I am most grateful for the care and attention he gave the manuscript and the many useful suggestions he made—not all of which I had the good sense to follow, of course. He can on no account be held responsible for the defects of the book—he tried his best. But he is responsible for some of its stronger points.

Dr. John Kirkpatrick was particularly helpful with the ethnographic accounts, for he had himself done fieldwork on Yap and knew the materials intimately. I regret not having had the benefit of his views on this last draft.

The penultimate draft was read by John Comaroff, Part I by Terrance Turner, and chapter 13 by Ward Goodenough. Their comments were appreciated even when we flatly disagreed. It is only fair to say that I doubt if any of these readers agrees with everything, or even most of the things, said in this book. I alone am responsible for its faults. D. D. Kaspin's editing helped immeasurably to make the book readable, where it is readable, that is.

Grateful acknowledgment is made to the National Endowment for the Humanities for the fellowship during which the first two drafts of the manuscript were written. I am also grateful for the support of the Lichtstern Fund of the Department of Anthropology of the University of Chicago.

Contents

232587

PART I

Introduction and the Two Descriptions

1   Introduction

The ideas of kinship, the kin-based society, the idiom of kinship, and the content of kinship are the received wisdom of today, as they have been almost from the beginnings of anthropology. This wisdom is entrenched in our thinking and especially in our theory, which derives closely from our own cultural notions. These are a very compelling set of ideas, for the doctrines seem self-evident, as well they should if they are essentially our own cultural conceptions. These doctrines seem to accord with all that we have experienced but also with all that we have learned as well as with what we find in the field and in reading the very finest monographs. Whether it is *The Web of Kinship among the Tallensi* (Fortes 1949), *The Nuer* (Evans-Pritchard 1940), *Pul Eliya* (Leach 1961), *We, The Tikopia* (Firth 1936), or *The Elementary Structures of Kinship* (Lévi-Strauss 1969), the facts seem clearly in accord with the theory. Fortes says quite clearly that for the Tallensi the ideology of kinship is so dominant that all other modes of relationship are assimilated to that ideology. Leach affirms that kinship is not a thing in itself but rather a way of thinking about the rights and usages with respect to land for the village of Pul Eliya. They were there. They saw it. They talked to the natives.

But just what did Fortes and Leach and Evans-Pritchard actually see and hear? What did the Nuer actually tell Evans-Pritchard? What did Fortes ask the Tallensi and what did they answer? And what did Fortes actually see them do? Just who was Leach listening to? Most important of all, how did Fortes, Leach, and Evans-Pritchard translate what they were told and what they saw?

Between the fieldwork and the monograph falls the shadow of translation. What is heard and seen is transformed by the field-worker. That transformation or translation depends on at least two things: (1) the input, and (2) the decoding, the machinery of translation. The machinery of translation in turn depends on sets of understandings and presuppositions, on a more or less explicit theory of what that which is being translated is all about. The problem of translation consists in the natives' saying and doing things and the anthropologist transforming that material into the raw material of the ethnography, and often directly into the ethnography itself.

Just how does the ethnographer transform what he sees and hears into the ethnography? He does it, to put it in the most condensed form, by refracting what he thinks he perceives the natives saying and doing through his own culture, modified by his "scientific" ideas of how people act, what social life is like, what forms of organizations he knows human society can take, what

3

his own aims and interests are—whether he is concerned with social order, the structure of the human mind, or the structure of meaning.

One intervening screen in translation that yields ethnographic accounts of kin-based societies is a particular definition of what kinship *is:* what the ethnographer knows as a member of his own culture, plus what he has learned in his study of, and in his reading about, other societies—his social theory in the most general terms.

Did the Tallensi say, "Our ideology of kinship is so pervasive. . ."? I doubt it. Did the Nuer say, "We have patrilineal lineages. . ."? I am quite sure that they did not. Nor do Fortes or Evans-Pritchard say that they said so in just those words. Did the villagers of Pul Eliya say in so many words that kinship was not a thing in itself but rather the way in which they thought and acted about rights and usages with respect to land? I am quite sure they did not. Nor does Leach claim that they did.

It is not news that theory guides the inquiry of fieldwork. It is hardly news that the capacity to see and to understand what one is seeing depends very much on the kind of training one has had. I am affirming no more than what we all know and accept (at this time—what we will believe in another decade or two I won't guess). Perception is guided and shaped by the instruments of perception as well as by the nature of what is perceived. I do not mean to say that we can *only* see what we are trained to see. I do not claim that once we have been taught to see only one thing we can never change, never alter our perceptual apparatus. But I am saying, and I think that it needs no extensive documentation, that anthropology has seen many things at one period only to decide later either that they were never there at all or that they were not what they were thought to be. The mention of such subjects as totemism, matriarchy, bride purchase, and the fact that Malinowski did not know that the Trobrianders were avunculocal, but that Kroeber had to explain it to him, should be enough to convince one that there may be some merit in what I say.

If what is seen and heard is transformed by passage through a perceptual screen of presuppositions, assumptions, and theories about what kinship is and how societies are constructed, then there is a sense in which it is not possible (let alone desirable) to see in pure uninterpreted form what is actually "out there" as it "actually is," undiminished and undistorted by the filter of the relationship and the perceptual apparatus. To put it simply, my criticisms of Fortes, Leach, et al. is *not* that they used a theory to screen what the natives said and to convert it into what they reported. I do the same thing. Everyone does the same thing. No one can do anything different. My complaint is that their theory is wrong; their theory leads them into error. But I should not be interpreted to mean that *I* "tell it like it is" while *they* distort reality. All analysis and all interpretation constructs reality. But there is another point which is vital to the argument I am presenting.

All theories of society are not equally valid; all presuppositions about how social systems work are not equally consistent either internally or with the evidence; all definitions of kinship, and in particular the very assumption that "kinship" can be identified and distinguished, are not equally logically consistent or equally in accord with the evidence.

Where the apparatus by which what the natives say and do is translated is itself theoretically faulty, the result is necessarily wrong. The point of this book is to show that the theoretical apparatus through which Fortes, Leach, Lévi-Strauss, and others who share their theory translated their field materials led them to false conclusions. The problem, in other words, is to make explicit and to evaluate the presuppositions and assumptions about kinship underlying what purport to be ethnographic facts.

It is important that the precise formulation of the problem be clear. One can draw a distinction between good kinship theory and bad kinship theory, between the skillful use of the concepts of kinship and their crude use or even misuse. This is not the problem that I am addressing in this book. The question at issue is the ideas of kinship, the theory of kinship itself, no matter how skillfully or crudely applied. The question is not whether Fortes, for example, did a finer, more productive analysis than some lesser craftsman. The question is whether the assumptions and presuppositions about kinship that both Fortes and the lesser craftsman shared are tenable in the first place.

I will deal with this problem in part by considering work that I did, beginning in 1947–48, on the island of Yap in the West Caroline Islands and wrote up as my doctoral dissertation in 1949 and continued later in a series of publications from 1953 to 1962. This description is compared with a quite different description, the key element of which was first developed by Dr. David Labby as a result of his work on Yap more than twenty years later. (Labby 1976a). I have also taken into account the work done at about the same time by Dr. Sherwood Lingenfelter (Lingenfelter 1975), as well as the work of Dr. John Kirkpatrick (Kirkpatrick and Broder 1976, Kirkpatrick 1977), Mr. Charles Broder (Broder 1972), and Dr. Richard Marksbury (1979).

The material I collected in 1947–48 is in general very much the same as the material which Labby, Lingenfelter, Kirkpatrick, Broder, and Marksbury collected. Yet two radically different descriptions can be drawn from what appears to be the same body of factual materials.

How can the same body of materials provide two radically different descriptions? Obviously, the theory and presuppositions which inform each description, the purposes of the descriptions, the implicit premises which guide the transformation of the field materials into descriptions must differ in order for the descriptions to differ.

The organization of this book is simple. The two descriptions of Yapese kinship and social organization follow. Then, point by point, the presuppositions and assumptions of the conventional wisdom of kinship underlying what purport to be the ethnographic facts of the first description are made explicit and evaluated. Before proceeding to the two descriptions a few words are necessary to place them in perspective.

The purpose of the first description is to provide concrete materials in terms of which the conventional wisdom about the study of kinship can be both exemplified and examined. The first description is given in the shorthand and relatively summarizing style common in contemporary ethnographic reports. There is talk of lineages, descent, residence, inheritance, succession, and so on. It cleaves as closely as possible to the standard anthropological forms, premises, theories, presumptions, presuppositions about kinship. It assumes kinship. It converts native cultural constructs into those of kinship. It assumes a kin-based society, or something very close to it. It does not question what a kin-based society is or what assumptions are embedded in it or whether they apply to this particular culture. It makes a complex series of implicit assumptions about the "idiom of kinship" which, because they are unstated, are not open to easy review or evaluation or to any appraisal of their relevance or applicability.

The second description has a specific and limited purpose and should be judged only in terms of this purpose. The purpose of the second description is to take roughly the same data and restate it insofar as possible without most of the assumptions or presuppositions about kinship that are in the first description. It thus recasts the material of the first description in terms which do not presuppose kinship. But this imposes certain restrictions on the second description.

The second description takes as its starting point the premise that the first problem of any ethnographic account is to comprehend the conceptions, ideas, beliefs, images, meanings of a culture, and that this is the material which must be the very substance of any statement of the "ethnographic facts." Nevertheless, the content of this second description must be limited by an entirely extraneous consideration. Since this second description is intended *only* as a foil for the first description, it invokes only those materials relevant to illuminating the problems and difficulties of the first description. Thus this second description must be understood as limited to its relevance as a corrective to the first. It is not an ideal description in its own right. It is not an example of what a proper description of Yapese culture should be as it stands.

The reason that this second description cannot be regarded as either complete or ideal is that the aim of the book is a critique of the theory underlying the first description. That being the case, the nature and content of the first description necessarily shapes much of what is present in the second description. For example, the first description is couched largely in jural terms, stating rights and duties. So the second description, in order to illuminate the problems and difficulties of the first description, necessarily casts much of its rhetoric in jural terms as well. Another example is that the first description is heavily concerned with group functions, group composition, and the rules for recruitment to groups and categories. The first description can be criticized as being unduly restrictive even in its attempt to follow accepted kinship usage, for it neglects the relational aspects of kinship. It can thus be viewed as an example of poor kinship work, the description too thin, too schematic, biased toward the jural and group membership aspects. But that is not the problem at issue here. Even if the description were better it would make no difference to the central problem of this book. But just because the first description stresses the jural and group structure aspects, the second description must necessarily address just those concerns and so cast much of its rhetoric in jural and group membership terms. The second description is thus itself far from ideal.

A further important point follows. The first description omits or skims lightly over certain materials which the second description dwells on. Crudely put, the first description seems to omit certain data which appear in the second description and which, if those data had been properly stressed in the first description, might well have changed it. I should explain why this is so.

The first reason why some new data appears in the second description which does not appear, or only appears in passing, in the first description, is that the theory in terms of which the first description was written made those data of minimal relevance, irrelevant, or put those data in an ambiguous or anomalous position. It is not that the data were obviously inconsistent with the first description. I do not believe that I fudged the data consciously or unconsciously when I wrote the first description either in its original form in the papers of 1953 to 1962 or in its present form. Rather, I had a fairly clear paradigm in mind of what kinship was and what a kinship system could be built like, and then sorted the Yapese materials to see which particular form, of all known forms, the Yapese form took. It is not that I failed to appreciate the significance or relevance of these materials; the paradigm of the traditional wisdom of kinship studies defined their significance for the task at hand for me.

The second reason why some new data appears in the second description is that Labby (1976a) provided a radically new understanding of the material, which then brought many things previously ignored or treated as irrelevant into a position of new significance. Labby's account showed that instead of land being transmitted in a patrilineal line, it was transmitted instead from one *genung* (crudely glossed here for the moment as a matriline) to another. This view then required a reconsideration of many other "facts" that had quite different significance in the first description. For example, in the first description the Yapese *genung* is treated simply as a dispersed ex-ogamous matrilineal clan with limited functions, even suggesting that it was a form of organization which was disappearing as the importance of the patrilin-eal lineage, father-son relations, and an abundance of land following rapid and radical depopulation gained in prominence. That is, *genung* was treated as one kind of clan, as this term is commonly understood in present-day anthropological studies of kinship. In the second description it turns out that this distorts the meaning of *genung*. Rather than treating it as a social unit, category, or membership group, it is better understood as a kind of rela-tionship that, when marked in different ways in different contexts of use, can yield different categories of greater or lesser scope. One such category is the *genung* that holds an estate and transmits it (not by inheritance at all) to another *genung*.

I must emphasize once again that the second description is far from what I would regard as ideal; it does not really explicate fully and in native terms the native conception of their universe. It is narrowly oriented to the "social organization" of Yap; it is too heavily laden with terms like *matriline* and jural considerations required to rectify the deficiencies in the first descrip-tion. As I have said elsewhere (Schneider [1968] 1980, 1972, 1976) and as I will say again later in this book, the arbitrary segregation of a rubric like "kinship," taken out of the context of the whole culture, is not a very good way to understand how a culture is structured.

The second description has a special job to do here; it is counterpoised to the first description even to the point, at times, of accepting the dubious premises and presuppositions of the first description in order to show that they are insufficient to the task set even by their own insufficient standards.

The descriptions are necessarily highly condensed. Limitations of space are such that I could not possibly reproduce more than the main features pertinent to the topic under discussion. On the other hand, the reference list is available for the interested reader to check and bring to bear material, the relevance of which I may have overlooked.

I have not cited the source of each element presented in the two descrip-tions, instead relying on the material listed in the reference list as well as on my own field notes. I have also used some of the unpublished papers of others which are listed in the reference list. These are available to any scholar who desires copies. I did not use the material from the Spanish, German, or Japanese periods and have omitted this literature from the reference list.

Finally, a note on the pronunciation of Yapese words. Although Jensen

(1977a, 1977b) has provided both a grammar and a dictionary of Yapese, I have chosen to stay with the spelling of Yapese words which I used in my earlier publications (for example, Schneider 1953, 1962) in part to maintain consistency with those reports, and in part because my spellings tend to reflect the pronunciation of the area in which I worked (Rumung) rather than the area from which Jensen drew his informants. But my spellings should not be used as a guide to the proper pronunciation of Yapese words. I have used the glottal stop (') sparingly and have not distinguished between long and short vowels, in order to facilitate reading.

If English pronunciation is used throughout, the reader will be able to follow the text. For example, -au, in the Yapese word *tabinau* is the same sound as the English *bough, now,* or *cow.*

There is one exception to ordinary English pronunciation. I have consistently used *c* for the *ch* sound of *child, chill,* and *chin.* The frequently encountered Yapese words *citamangen* and *citiningen* should therefore be pronounced as if the initial sound were *ch* as in *chicken.*

2   The First Description

The cultural unit on Yap called *tabinau* is made up of two kinds of groups. One is a patrilocal extended family, the other is a patrilineage. That is, seen as a domestic unit, which includes the in-marrying wives but excludes the out-marrying sisters and daughters (when they have married out and no longer live there), it is a patrilocal extended family. As a patrilineage, it includes the out-marrying sisters and daughters but not the in-marrying wives. However, it should be noted that the Yapese say that both out-marrying sisters and daughters and in-marrying wives are members of the *tabinau*. There is a clear difference, however, between out-marrying sisters and daughters and in-marrying wives in their rights in land and in their relations to the men of the patrilineage as well as to each other. In-marrying wives may leave at any time, which terminates their membership in the *tabinau* immediately and automatically; out-marrying sisters and daughters cannot lose membership in the *tabinau*. All those who are descended from a known, genealogically traceable ancestor (or putatively traceable), descent being traced through males alone, form the patrilineage. The localized males of the patrilineage form the core of the patrilocal extended family. The patrilineage has a clear structure of authority and this is supplemented by a clear set of rules for succession to the office of head of the *tabinau*. The rule is that succession goes from the oldest male to the next oldest in that generation, namely, those who are classed as his siblings (*wolagen*) who are members of the *tabinau*. (Some *wolagen* are not members of ego's patrilineage.) This set includes ego's father's children and his male patriparallel cousins. Only after that generation is exhausted does succession pass to the next generation, to the eldest of the set of children of the father, father's brothers and father's male patriparallel cousins and so on from generation to generation. The *tabinau* can be considered to be a corporate landholding unit, although land is said to be held by the head of the *tabinau*. Since the *tabinau* is a corporate landholding unit, there can be no inheritance since the corporation normally perseveres through time. There is only succession to the office of head of the *tabinau*, the nominal holder of the land. However, if the corporation is left with only female members, then the land passes to the female members and from them to their children. Whether this is regarded as a special case of succession or as inheritance of the land by members of a different *tabinau* seems immaterial. The female members to whom the land passes are first, the daughter, then the father's sisters, then father's sister's sons and daughters. The father's sister and her children are called *mafen* and we shall encounter them later. Ob-

11

viously, there may be a series of such lines starting with father's sister, then father's father's sister, then father's father's father's sister and so on. The first in line to inherit is the daughter in the absence of any male members of the lineage. Lacking the daughter, the next in line is the person who was the sister of the holder, i.e., a man's sister if he has no daughter.

Those who are children of the same father and mother, or the same father but different mothers, as well as the children of the male parallel cousins are *wolagen*. Those who are father, father's brothers, or father's male patriparallel cousins are *citamangen*. The children of *citamangen* are *fak*. (However, not all *citamangen* are father, father's brother, or father's male patriparallel cousins. Similarly, it is not only the children of father, father's brother, or father's male patriparallel cousins that are *fak*.)

It is appropriate at this point to introduce an interesting feature of the terminological system. The Yapese rarely use kinship terms in address except under very special formal and ritual circumstances. Normally only the name of the person addressed is used. Thus father, mother, and so on are addressed by their name and that name is used by everyone who talks to them.

But reference is restricted such that only the own real living relative is referred to by the kinship term. Thus if the own real *citamangen* (father, mother's husband) is alive, he and only he will be referred to as *citamangen*. If he dies, he is then succeeded—perhaps by his eldest surviving *wolag* (sibling; male in this case). At that point and not before, that person will be referred to as *citamangen*. Similarly if the own real *citiningen* (mother) is alive, she and only she will be referred to as *citiningen*. But if she dies, whoever takes her place (and that person alone) will be referred to as *citiningen*. If one asks a Yapese, "List for me all those who are your *citamangen*," one will receive only one name in reply. Inquiry may show that that person is alive and was his mother's husband at the time he was born and so his real father. Or it may show that it is a deceased father's brother who is now the head of the *tabinau*. Or it may even be someone who is an elder sibling or elder patriparallel cousin but who is the landholder and head of the *tabinau*. I have called this a "reservoir system" elsewhere (Schneider 1953) since, while only one person occupies the status marked by the kinship term at one time, there is a reservoir of persons ready to step into the position when that person dies. Furthermore, only one person can normally act as *citamangen* toward ego at any one time, and the person who plays the role of the *citamangen* is referred to by that term. Similarly although a father's brother, for example, may be in the reservoir and potentially a *citamangen,* he will not play that role until he formally occupies the proper status. Thus the reservoir system permits ego to have only one "mother" and one "father" (though many siblings) at any one time, but he is never without a father or mother since if either of these die they are replaced from the reservoir. The levirate articulates with this system very nicely. The levirate (or widow inheritance, to follow British usage) is optional on Yap. If a man's father dies, his mother may remain in the *tabinau* and is then regarded as married to the man who succeeds to the father's place.

Finally, if a *tabinau* is composed of two or more brothers and their wives and children, then normally each child refers to his own mother's husband as *citamangen* whether he is head of the *tabinau* or not. But where relations outside the *tabinau* occur then the head of the *tabinau* acts as *citamangen* for all the children.

There is no jural difference between children of the same father by the same mother or by different mothers, although informal bonds between children of the same mother may be stronger than those between children of the same father and different mothers, except where a woman holds property which she can leave to her own children and which is not shared by her husband's children by other wives.

The most important function of the patrilineage (*tabinau*) is that of a landholding corporation. The *tabinau* holds plots of land within a village (*binau*) and these are scattered and of various kinds: garden land, taro pits or portions of them, land on which stands of coconuts grow, land within the reef (though underwater), paths, plots on which house platforms are built, and so on. Plots of land are ranked and a particular plot which is ranked highest of all the plots within the estate usually has a carefully paved area, and within that, a stone and coral house platform, the facing of which is made of carefully fitted stones, where a house either stands or once stood. The spirits of all the ancestors of the *tabinau* live in that house platform. Along with rank, plots of land have associated with them certain offices and specialized statuses, such as elder of the village, chief of the village, chief of the young men, priest or magician (*tamerong*), leader of certain kinds of communal fishing, and so on. The *tabinau* which holds that land holds the office associated with it. The land of the *tabinau* thus provides its food—taro, yams, sweet potatoes, bananas, coconuts, fish, and so on, including the ubiquitous areca nut and pepper leaf for the betel nut chewed by everyone old enough to do so. It also provides the offices of the village (the *binau*), the district (the *bayang e nug*), and the three major alliances.

Thus landholding entails each patrilineage in the political system either as a low-ranking, but still to be counted, unit within the village (and a village—*binau*—is a geographically contiguous association of *tabinau*), or as a high-ranking chiefly lineage with chiefly office in the village, the district, or the alliance of districts. To put the matter simply, the *tabinau* is the basic political unit in Yapese social structure. For as different patrilineages are associated as a village, different contiguous districts are then associated into one or another of three major coequal alliances. There is no radical break between the patrilineage and the alliance, for the patrilineage is the unit out of which all other units are built, and the offices of the lineage, the village, the district, and the alliance are all tied to particular plots of land. The system is not one of segmentary lineages, however, for there is a break between the minimal lineage and the village. The village is not just a larger lineage of greater depth and span; it is an association of lineages, just as the district is an association of villages.

The *tabinau* as a patrilineal lineage, then, is a shallow unit with only limited generational depth of from three to (in certain cases of very high-ranking lineages) about ten generations. But even then its span is narrow, and it does not tend to segment into the equal but opposed units said to be characteristic of systems like the Nuer or Tallensi. Moreover, except for certain politically important lineages, that is, for certain lineages which hold high rank and high office, marriage does not have significant political functions.

It follows therefore that although the lineage (*tabinau*) is a major political unit, it is not the only political unit, for the village and district and alliance are not kinship units at all, no matter how important ties of kinship (including descent) are—and they are important—in the actual operation of the political system.

Another kind of political function which the patrilineage (*tabinau*) has is that of maintaining order within its membership and representing all members in respect to all other lineages in cases of dispute. Thus if a member of a patrilineage falls out with another member, the matter is settled within the patrilineage and no outside agency or person has the right to interfere. This is true whether the difference is between husbands and wives, or between brothers. Only in the special case of patricide may the leader of the village and the chief of the village along with the *mafen* (the father's sister and her children) intercede to punish the offender. Even then the major burden falls on the father's sister and her children (the *mafen*); the elder and the chief of the village act only as backup forces to see that the culprit is evicted from the lineage land and the village. In other cases, such as when a young man from one lineage fights with another from a different lineage, the two lineages work things out between them, and do so through the heads of the lineages, each of whom represents his lineage in the matter. In the same way, the head represents his lineage in marriage negotiations with other lineages, and in the decision to build or repair the old men's house (*pabai*) or the young men's house (*faliu*), or to repave the paths or clean up the paths, or to make war against another village. For certain of these events, the two heads of the concerned lineages simply meet and work things out. In others, the whole village becomes involved, though that meeting is attended only by heads of patrilineages each representing his own lineage. By the same token the chief of the village, the elder of the village, and the chief of the young men all represent their village in dealings with other villages within the district. And since these offices are located within the lineage it is the lineage again which serves these political functions. The lineage is thus a political unit having important political functions, and relations among its members are of a political order.

The lineage is also an economic unit with significant economic functions. Not only does the lineage derive its resources from its own land (that is, it is the major unit of production, distribution, and consumption of its own vegetable food and fish), but it is also the unit which enters into relations with other lineages in the production and distribution (but not consumption, ordinarily) of certain goods and services on certain occasions. If the village undertakes a village-wide fishing expedition using one or another of a variety of methods (outside-the-reef trolling, fishing by torch light for flying fish, inside-the-reef surrounds, seining, and so forth), then the young men of the village bring the catch to the young men's house where each lineage head is given a share for his extended family. Insofar as it is possible, of course, each lineage has one or more young men who will be part of the fishing expedition. The right to load the expedition for certain kinds of fishing (seining, torch light fishing for flying fish, for example) is a hereditary status which is held by certain lineages. Similarly, when the village enters into an exchange (*mit e mit*) with another village, or becomes part of a district-wide exchange, then each patrilineage is assigned a share to contribute, which it does through the head of the lineage, and this is then pooled with all other lineage shares to make up the village's gift. The return gift of food, shell, and stone valuables is in turn given to the village, and shares are then broken down so that each lineage gets a share and receives that share through the head of the lineage.

Whether the actual genealogical knowledge extends three or ten generations back, each patrilineage has an otherwise undifferentiated pool of ancestral spirits (*thagith*). These are the spirits of people who once belonged to the lineage. It is important to note that they include the spirits of women who died while married into the lineage and exclude the spirits of the women who died while married out of the lineage. However, regardless of the less than perfect fit between the ancestral spirits and patrilineal lineage membership, the lineage is the fundamental religious unit on Yap, for it is only through the active intervention of one's own ancestral spirits that the spirits-at-large (the spirit of the clouds, the spirit of the sea, etc.) can be moved to beneficent action. Briefly, the head of the lineage prays to the ancestral spirits, divines to find one who is happy and willing to take action on behalf of the supplicant lineage, and then approaches that spirit directly with the appropriate religious ceremonial and ritual. Thus perhaps there is an illness, or a woman has not become pregnant, or there has been an unusual scarcity of fish. The head of the lineage divines to locate a happy ancestral spirit, and on finding one, beseeches that ancestral spirit to intercede on behalf of its living lineage with the generalized spirit who can effect the cure for the illness, improve the fishing, make the woman pregnant, and so on. In Durkheim's sense, the patrilineage is a church—a body of people who worship a distinct set of supernaturals, in common and apart from other bodies of worshipers. There is no way to appeal to an ancestral spirit from another patrilineage for they could not care less; it is only through one's own church that one can expect to influence the spirit world.

However, there are certain patrilineages which hold certain lands which give them the right and the special knowledge, along with the special objects, which permit them to influence the supernatural on behalf of persons other than those who are members of their lineages. These are called *tamerong*, and the place or plot which is sacred and through which they operate is called a *taliu*. But the procedure is fundamentally the same as I have described above. If there is a need for fish for the whole village, if there is a dearth of children in the village, if there is an epidemic or sickness rife, then the elder of the village tells the chief of the village to go to the *tamerong* and do something about these difficulties. The *tamerong* then divines to find one of his own ancestral spirits who is happy, and, by appealing to that ancestral spirit to intervene with the relevant spirit-at-large, rectifies the problem for the village. The same process can be undertaken on behalf of a single individual for his own benefit where that individual has had no success working through his own ancestral spirits. But this religious function is based on the lineage, it is anchored in the lineage land, and it requires the ancestral spirits of the particular lineage to work. This does not mean that individuals do not know bits of magic, spells, or rites which they may perform on their own behalf or on the behalf of a wife or husband or child. But these are minor forms compared to the major religious functions which the lineage, as a church, undertakes.

Relations between lineage members are thus not only political and economic, but they are also religious or sacred in a very important way, and the lineage is a religious unit of major significance.

There is another unit called *genung*. The *genung* can be regarded as an exogamous dispersed matrilineal clan. The different matrilineal clans on Yap (there were more than thirty of them in 1947) all have putative ancestresses— porpoise, rat, fungus, spirits in human form—who lived long ago and are only known by their origin myths, their name and description, and the fact that they were spirits.

Being dispersed, the matriclan has almost no functions connected with either the land, political organization, or any other major social structural feature. I say "almost" because it does have a few.

There is first, of course, clan exogamy and so the matriclan plays a role—however minimal—in marriage. Its role is minimal since all the clan does is prohibit marriage between members of the same clan.

Second, certain clans have shrines, and *tamerong* (magicians, priests) associated with them which can be used for the general welfare of all of Yap. Thus the porpoise clan can call porpoises. The rat clan does not undertake increase or calling of this sort. Other clan shrines can be used to halt typhoons, earthquakes, epidemics, and certain other of the seven major disasters which are ordered by a chief to punish people for failing to show proper respect and obedience. The chief orders a particular *tamerong* to call one or the other of these disasters, and he does so using one of the village shrines, but not a matriclan shrine. Other chiefs and concerned *tabinau* heads then repair to the clan shrines and through their *tamerong* try to halt the disaster. But the fundamental point is that the matriclan shrines can only be used for the general welfare of all of Yap; they cannot be used for the benefit of any particular person, lineage, village, district, or alliance.

Third, in case of war one could claim sanctuary from a clansperson if one was caught at the wrong time in the wrong place. In principle, one went to the clansperson's house and begged for sanctuary, and in principle hostile forces could not pursue their victim into the house of one of their own side. How this actually worked out in practice when warfare was prevalent was never clear to me, and informants did not seem to put much stock in such sanctuary as a reliable mode of survival.

Technically, then, Yap has a system of double descent with a dominant, localized, landholding, highly multifunctional exogamous patrilineal lineage and a dispersed, exogamous, minimally functional matrilineal clan. All units other than these, however, are tied into the patrilineal lineage in one way or another. The village, although not a kinship group in any sense, is an amalgamation of them and is modeled after the lineage in that it is made up of an association of lineages and the relationship between its officers and the members of the village are described as those of *citamangen-fak*, or father to child. Similarly, the district is an association of villages whose relationship to the villages is again that of *citamangen-fak*, and so too the alliance to the districts it is composed of. Similarly, the so-called caste relationship between villages which hold their own land, and those villages whose land is held by *tabinau* of other villages is also organized in the framework of *citamangen-fak*. And as we have seen, *citamangen* is (among other things) father, *fak* is (among other things) child, this being a relationship where authority, superiority, and independence reside with the *citamangen* while the *fak* is dependent, obedient, respectful. The failure of the person or village or district in the position of *fak* to be obedient, dependent, and respectful is sufficient to terminate the relationship and to cause the *fak* to lose all claim on the *citamangen* for land, food, protection, representation, and articulation with the other units (village, district, alliance, the ancestral ghosts and hence the spirit world, etc.).

The matriclan is in a sense the opposite of the patrilineage. Although both are exogamous, where the one is overwhelmingly important in all major social structural functions, the other has minimal functions; where the one is hierarchically structured and highly differentiated internally, the other is an egalitarian, internally undifferentiated unit without the characteristics of a group; where the lineage is oriented to the benefits of its members against the world, the clan is oriented only to the benefits of the whole—it can only protect the whole island from typhoons, not one village; it can only bring fertility to all women, not just one woman or the women of one village or one lineage. This balanced and complementary differentiation of function is by no means uncommon in double descent systems and Yap is by no means unusual. It can take its place—analyzed in this way—along the major comparative dimensions which social anthropology has developed.

But most important for our purposes is the description of the two units as kinship (or descent—I draw no distinction here although such a distinction may be drawn) units first and fundamentally. The *tabinau* is a patrilineal lineage; the relations among its members are as agnates: father to son and daughter, a man to his sister, and so on. This is a translation of what the Yapese said to me, Labby, Lingenfelter, Kirkpatrick, and Broder, and what we saw them do. It is guided by a theory which states explicitly that because these men are agnates, they hold land together as a corporation, even though they have the odd view that the eldest of them is the nominal owner (asked who owns the *tabinau*, the name of the elder is given). Because they are kinsmen, their dead ancestors are spirits and they are related to those spirits as kinsmen; they can worship those spirits and appeal to them to help with the supernatural beings who are not localized or tied to any particular lineage.

This is a kin-based society, or as close to it as one might get, precisely because all its functions—landholding, authority, politics, religion, and so on—are phrased in terms of the idiom of kinship. Why does the *citamangen* provide food for his *fak?* Because he is his father, his *citamangen,* and the food which he provides today will be returned by the child (the *fak*) when the father is old and cannot do it himself. Why do we *not* say that the *tabinau* is simply a political unit in the village, putting in its share in the decision-making processes and in the processes of keeping order in the village, and doing its share toward the well-being and maintenance of the village? It is a political unit; but it is as a patrilineage that its political functions are discharged. It is because these are agnates that they stand together, represented by the head of the lineage, and constitute a unit in the political arena. They are not merely a voluntary association of people of good will. They are a patrilineage, and it is in terms of the idiom of their agnatic kinship relationship to each other that the political functions are carried out. They do not sit and vote and discuss what they will do on universalistic grounds of rational, enlightened self-interest; they act as a bloc because they are kinsmen, father and son, brother and brother, and lineage members, and their view is expressed through the eldest of the lineage, to whose judgment they defer. Even religion is expressed in the idiom of kinship—worship is of ancestors, not just God, or spirits, or supernatural beings. That presumed fundamental human need for dealing with the complexities of the world, the inexplicables of this life, the problems of coping where the empirical means are insufficient, is expressed through the idiom of kinship between the members of the *tabinau*. Where many Americans pray directly to God, Yapese pray to their sacred dead kinsmen, now spirits, to intercede for them. It is the sacred bonds of kinship that constitute the idiom of religious belief and feeling, the idiom in terms of which the unknown and the uncontrollable are dealt with, the meaning of life is explicated, and something is done about it through magic, rituals, and ceremonies.

So goes the theory which guided and informed this description. It is internally consistent. It appears to fit the data—because it is the idiom in terms of which the data are described at the outset.

3　The Second Description

There is another way to transform the same field observations into a description which anthropologists can then use for their comparative and analytic purposes. The theory which guides this translation of field observations into the description is less familiar and so it will seem longer, less economical, less neat in certain ways, and by the same token it may bring up some new "facts" which were not mentioned in the first description. Why were they omitted from the first description? Because they were not observed as facts, or, if they were noted, they were deemed to be minor, of no structural significance. But some of the "facts" of the first description will, if they are not omitted altogether here, be treated as minor, of no structural significance, even wrong.

There is a cultural unit on Yap which is called *tabinau*. *Tabinau* has a number of meanings and can be used in different ways in different contexts. The term can be used to refer to the house or dwelling. It can be used to indicate a person or persons who are related to the speaker through ties to the land. Such ties may be of various sorts—remote, close, via different intervening land relationships or via a particular kind of land relationship. In this sense the term is similar to the Yapese phrase *gidi rog*. *Gidi* can be translated roughly as a person or people. *Rog* is the first person possessive, roughly *my* in English. The term can also be used for a group of people living together who have different ties to the same land—perhaps a man who holds the land, the woman who lives with him, and the children she bears or they (or one of them) adopt. *Tabinau* can be used to specify a *daiv,* that is, a raised rock and coral foundation on which the dwelling is built. A *daiv* is built on a special plot of land. *Tabinau* can also indicate the place where a marriage exists—for example, the dwelling, the *daiv* on which the dwelling is located, the plot on which *daiv* and dwelling are placed. But the relationship that is indicated is the marriage, which is one through land. Under certain circumstances two different *daiv* are considered two different *tabinau*. If there are no people, land alone does not constitute a *tabinau*. And people without a relationship through land cannot constitute a *tabinau*.

Each *tabinau* is a distinct unit with its own name made up of a collection of plots of land that holds a more or less distinctive set of personal names for both men and women. These names are given to the children of women who marry men of the *tabinau*. And of course those who are now dead but were living members of the *tabinau* (called *thagith*) used to have these names too. Indeed, the name of a child ideally should be the same as that of his *cit-*

amangen's citamangen, so that over the years a man and his successor would alternate names: 1,2,1,2,1,2, etc. The successor would ideally be the firstborn male but this is not always the case. Names are bestowed by *tabinau* elders including and especially the *mafen.* The name is selected by a conference of elders. It will normally be chosen on the suggestion of an elder, the agreement of the others, and following divination to see if the predecessor whose name it was concurs in that selection. A child can be named after a living person, though this is not usual. The name comes from the store of the *tabinau* of the mother's husband, the *citamangen,* or from someone to whom he defers (mother's husband's mother's husband, for example). However, for various reasons, a name may be bestowed from the store of another *tabinau* by an elder who has a right to the names of that *tabinau,* for the name is inextricably associated with a particular *tabinau,* or more precisely, a particular *daiv* (the stone house platform). Thus an elder may use a name from a *tabinau* different from that of which the *citamangen* is part. However, this does not alter the rights of the person with respect to the *citamangen,* though it gives the person rights in the *tabinau* from which his name was taken. A name may be taken away by the head of the *tabinau* holding that name, or by *mafen* as part of the process of dispossessing a person. On adoption the child is given a name from the store of the *tabinau* of the person who adopts him. A particular name may be removed on the occasion of a serious illness. For example, if a person has a serious illness and the divining instrument (the *wei*) says that he (i.e., his name) will die, that name is removed and a new one from the *tabinau* store is given. In such a case, of course it is clear that that name died, as the divining instrument predicted. There are both men's names and women's names, and if a married woman is especially highly regarded, a girl child may be given that married woman's name, thus strengthening the married woman's tie to the *tabinau* into which she has married. But if the married woman later leaves in divorce the child may be renamed. (When a woman dies she becomes one of the spirits of the *tabinau* [*thagith*] of her husband and her name becomes part of the store of names of that *tabinau,* unless she has divorced, for on divorce she is no longer affiliated with her husband's *tabinau.* If she dies unmarried, she becomes a *thagith* of her natal *tabinau* and her name remains with that *tabinau.*)

The child is not normally named until about five or more days after birth. But birth into a *tabinau* is not taken as a precondition for membership in that *tabinau.* Rather, people say that a child "is formed on the *tabinau,*" stressing residence and activity and the relationship of child to *citamangen* over any simple rule of recruitment by birth. Yapese names stress that a person is linked to specific lands, *tabinau* lands, the land of the estate.

So the distinction between birth and adoption is in certain respects simply not significant for the Yapese. They are different, but the difference does not make adoption understandable as being modeled on birth. The establishment of the child as a person is achieved in the first instance by his birth from his mother and his relationship to her, but this is merely the beginning. Indeed, a child merely born of a mother and without a name from a *tabinau* different from her mother's is a *fak e macugubil*, a state considerably worse than the Western notion of an illegitimate child. It is not that the child is "fatherless"; it is that the child's mother has earned no tie in land for the child. Thus the establishment of the child as a person is achieved by the naming, which formally affiliates the child to a *tabinau* and with the persons in it. Indeed, it is the right of *mafen* to announce the name on the occasion of the naming ceremony, and it is this which makes the child *fak* to its *citamangen* and to its *citiningen*, which includes the woman who bore him and his *citamangen's* sister and her daughter, among others.

Some of the land of the *tabinau* is in the high grassy region where the pandanus grow, some made into terraced gardens devoted to yams, sweet potatoes, and other edible plants. Other plots are in the low-lying coastal part of the island and these are made up of taro pits, or parts of large taro pits, plots on which coconut, banana, mangrove, and other vegetation stands. Yet other plots are under the water within the reef and are part of the *tabinau* too. These may or may not contain permanent fish traps, but fish are taken from any of this land by those who are of the *tabinau*, just as they may take taro from the *tabinau* taro pits. In the low coastal areas some of the plots have carefully built elevated stone and coral rubble house platforms (*daiv*) on which a house is normally built set in the midst of an area carefully paved with flat stones. The spirits of all the dead members of the *tabinau*, the *thagith*, live in the house platform. Each plot of land has a name and a rank. The house platform and house are normally built on the highest-ranking plot of land, but where there are two or more houses and house platforms within the same *tabinau* the others are built on plots of lesser rank. Certain plots contain the offices of elder of the *binau*, chief of the *binau*, chief of the young men of the *binau*, or leader of various kinds of communal fishing and so on. Other plots have the office of those who deal with the spirits (*tamerong*) inherent in them.

As the Yapese say, repeat, and clearly affirm, all rank and all offices inhere in the land. No ethnographer has been able to miss this point, although some ignore it after they note it and do not dwell on its significance. The person who acts in the office is merely (and I use the word *merely* in its pejorative sense, following the Yapese usage) the voice (*lungun*) of the land. It is the land which holds the office, it is the land which has rank, and it is the land which speaks through some person who has the right to speak for it.

A number of *tabinau* all within a particular area are associated into a unit called a *binau*, and it is with respect to the *binau* that offices like elder of the *binau*, chief of the *binau*, chief of the young men of the *binau*, leaders of various kinds of fishing, *tamerong* (those who deal with the spirits), and so on, act. This association of contiguous *tabinau,* the *binau,* has a name and it too has a rank in an association of such contiguous *binau* which in turn make up a *bayang e nug.* Of the twelve *bayang e nug* on Yap, three are coequally of the highest rank, the others ranking below them. And again the rank of each *binau* and the rank of each *bayang e nug* is inherent in particular plots of land in particular *tabinau.* Thus the rank of the *bayang e nug* derives from the highest-ranking *tabinau* which in turn derives from the highest-ranking plot of land in the *tabinau.* This is not to say that rank may never change: it can under certain conditions, though these are not common. Rather, it is to affirm once again that the land holds rank and office, just as a group of people belong to each named *tabinau;* the people belong to the land, the land does not belong to the people. This is the way in which the Yapese formulate this relationship; this is the way they say it and think it.

Genung is used in various ways. It can be glossed initially as a kind of relationship, specifically, relationship through a common "belly." That is, relationship through the belly of the same woman from whom two persons came, or through the mythical ancestress. Mythical *genung* ancestresses (*nik*) were spirits, often in the form of common objects such as the porpoise, a kind of fungus, the rat, and some spirits who took the form of human beings. All persons who share this relationship are also related to each other as *wolagen,* that is, persons of equivalence, and in this case the equivalence is both one of common descent and of equal rank with all others of the same *genung,* for *genung* is almost the only unit in Yapese culture that is not internally ranked. Used with reference to a mythical ancestress, people of some *genung* are especially numerous in some parts of Yap. Thus it is said that people who are *gucig,* or whose *genung* is *gucig,* are more frequently encountered in the northern part of Yap. But *genung* has no special relationship with any place except its own sacred plot of land where its particular shrine is located. People of any particular *genung* are found in many different *tabinau, binau,* and *bayang e nug.*

Those of the same *genung,* relationship, or those who have the same *nik,* should not have sexual intercourse.

One keeps one's *nik* a secret, and the names of those who may be of the *genung* relationship are also held secret, and in fact people do not often know who, other than those most immediately associated with them, are or are not related by *genung.* Obviously a mother and her children are *genung;* equally obviously knowing who the mother's mother was will reveal *genung* relationship. But this is a subject which is simply not discussed openly and about which people profess ignorance.

Genung can form a set or subset marked or restricted by some point of reference. As I have already indicated, one such point of reference is the ancestress, and this marks the set of widest scope. Another point of reference restricting a set also called *genung* is *tabinau*. But *tabinau* can be used to mark different sets in different relations to each other. One is where *genung* is marked with reference to one or more *tabinau* with which it is affiliated. The other is where one such *genung* is marked by its special relation to the successively different *genung* from which its holding of its estate has derived. Here the land giving *genung* is called *mafen* by the land receivers. I will make these distinctions clear in what follows.

The members of a *tabinau* are of as many different *genung* as there are women who have married into the *tabinau* (unless, of course, two women of the same *genung* marry in). As each woman marries into the *tabinau* and becomes affiliated with it, she and her children are of one *genung*. Her sons will bring women of different *genung* than their mother into the *tabinau*. If the women divorce before having children they lose membership in the *tabinau*. If they bear children, the children will remain members of the *tabinau* and be of their mother's *genung*. The sons' wives' sons will in their turn bring wives of different *genung* into the *tabinau*. A *tabinau* is thus stratified across at least two generations (mothers and their children and the son's wives and their children) by different *genung*.

By the same token, of course, a man and his sisters and the sisters' children spread across two *tabinau* but make one *genung*. In a unit of this sort, the man (mother's brother to the sisters' children) is referred to as *matam ko genung*. *Matam* is a form of *citamangen;* the stem is *tam*, just as the feminine form, *tin*, is the stem of the form *citiningen*.

In these contexts, where the scope of *genung* is marked by its reference to the particular *tabinau* it cuts across, the point of reference for the definition of *genung* is the *tabinau* to which it is related.

There is yet another context which is marked by the relationship between two different *genung* with respect to a particular *tabinau;* where the one *genung* is in the position of land giver to the other *genung*, which is in the position of land receiver. The *genung* which gives land is *mafen* to the *genung* which receives land. From the point of view of the *genung* which now holds the estate the *mafen* are the *genung* of the mother's husband's sister and her children. The *mafen* will also include the children of the daughters and daughters' daughters, and so on. Putting it now from the opposite perspective, any given landholder has a series of *mafen* starting with mother's husband's sister in each ascending generation. In different parts of Yap there may be as few as three *mafen* (mother's husband's sister and her children, mother's husband's mother's husband's sister and her children and daughter's children, and daughter's daughter's children and mother's husband's mother's husband's mother's husband's sister and her children and daughter's children, and daughter's daughter's daughter's children) and as many as seven *mafen*.

My informants said that *mafen* has nothing to do with *genung*. But in going back over my materials I believe that this statement was made in the context of my inquiries which centered on the membership, makeup, and functions of the *genung* exclusively in the sense of an ancestress-defined unit. In the sense that *mafen* is a relationship limited to the mother's husband's sister and her children over those of the landholding *genung* of the *tabinau* from which the mother's husband's sister derived, *mafen* indeed has nothing to do with the functions of the *genung* as a whole, dispersed, ancestress-oriented category.

Mafen cannot be regarded as an ego-oriented unit or relationship. Where but a single person survives in a *tabinau*, then that person's relationship to the *genung* from which his rights in the *tabinau* were transferred are indeed his *mafen*. But even in such an instance, the relationship is between those who gave the estate and those (of whom there may be but one left) who hold various rights in the estate. The instance of the single surviving member of a *tabinau* is simply a special case of this relationship. The relationship, then, is conceived of in Yapese culture as one between the land-giving *genung* and the land-receiving *genung* and should not be confused with a relationship between persons by virtue of their genealogical connection as (for example) "father's sister" and her "children"—"mother's brother's" "children."

In this connection a tangential but relevant point should be made before the discussion of the *mafen* is continued. The mother's brother(s) may be referred to as *wa'engen*, as are the sister's children, by way of explanation, when informants are asked how the relation of such persons is named in Yapese. Or if one asks why the mother's brother(s) have a certain role the answer may be given that "he is *wa'engen*." But the mother's brother(s) is also, in a different context, *matam* of his *genung*. And when asked how the mother's brother(s) and sisters' children should act toward each other the answer may be given that "they are like *wolagen*" (glossed crudely as "siblings"). In rough translation, then, the relationship between mother's brother(s) and sisters' children can in certain contexts be stated as (1) *wa'engen*, (2) *matam ko genung*, and (3) *wolagen*.

The first term, *wa'engen*, marks a special, distinctive relationship of unique character. It is significant that the term is self-reciprocal, that is, it is used by mother's brother(s) for sisters' children and by sisters' children for their mother's brother(s). The second term, *matam ko genung*, signals the responsibility which a man has for his sister and her children and daughters' children, etc. Like the term for which it is the stem, *citamangen*, it marks responsibility, authority, and the dependence of the others. The third, *wolagen*, defines the context as one of sharing, equality, of common connection through the belly of the same woman, however remote.

Mafen retain certain rights in the *tabinau* from which their *genung* came, that is, in the *tabinau* of the woman's brother, or in the case of her children, their mother's brother. The *mafen* are accorded great respect and have the right to dispossess the wife and children of their brother and mother's brother for any reason they may wish to give, no matter how trivial. For instance, if any one of these should fail to accord the *mafen* the respect they are due by failing in any of the formal tokens of that respect they may be dispossessed. For the *mafen* are the *genung* from which the brother's wife and her children are earning their rights in *tabinau* (see below), and the relationship between those two *genung* is, as we have seen, one of superior to inferior, of dependency and obedience on the authority and bounty of the *genung* giving the *tabinau*. For example, no food may be taken from those plots which are reserved for the senior man of the *tabinau* while he is holder (*tafen*) of the *tabinau* and for six months to a year after his death. On the anniversary of his death, the *mafen* come to the *tabinau* and are ceremonially given food from those special plots reserved for his food and from which no one else took food during his tenure as holder of the *tabinau*. If members of the *tabinau*, one or collectively, break some serious rule or behave so as to bring grave disrepute on the *tabinau*, the *mafen* may dispossess them and terminate their relationship to the *tabinau*. By their delict, then, the woman and her children may lose all rights in the *tabinau* and these revert to the *mafen*, who are the *genung* of the woman's husband. By the same token a man may "discard" or "throw away" one or all of his wife's children for failing to show proper respect and obedience, or for committing some serious crime in the *binau* which casts a shadow on its honor and position. If he does this he will also take back that person's name, for the name belongs to the *tabinau* and when the person is "thrown away" he loses his relationship to the *tabinau*.

The concept of *magar* is indispensible to an understanding of the *tabinau* and *genung*. If one does something for another the recipient may say to the donor "*kum magar*" which means "you are tired" or "you have worked." *Magar* in a variety of other contexts means work, labor, creative effort—which does indeed bring on fatigue—and hence one acknowledges another's effort on one's behalf by noting his fatigue.

The land of the *tabinau* was made, and it took work, *magar*, to make it what it is. People who lived before built taro pits, planted them, terraced the inland gardens as was necessary, planted yams and sweet potatoes, built the house platforms and their surrounding paved areas, paved the paths, and so on, and those who hold the land today say they are indebted to those who came before for the work they did to make the *tabinau* what it is. However inherent its rank may be, it is work that makes and maintains a *tabinau* and people exchange their work for their rights in the *tabinau*. They must work gardens, cultivate the taro, fish the land within the reef, collect the coconuts, plant coconut seedlings, and so on. Indeed, the amount of man-made land on Yap is an awesome sight. Paved paths, fitted stone house platforms and houses, terraced gardens, landfill out from the shoreline, the great stone platforms built out into the water from the shoreline on which the *faliu* (the young men's house) stand are all man-made. Yap is no simple tropical isle in a pure state of nature; it is land which has been and is continually being transformed by work, whether it be gardening, building a house, or the repair of large stone fish traps.

When a man of the *tabinau* marries, the eldest man of his *tabinau* goes to the eldest man of the woman's *tabinau* bearing appropriate valuables. Among other things he makes a more or less formal statement that the man of his *tabinau* wants to make a mother of the woman. He does not say that he wants to marry the woman. He does not say that he wants or needs a wife. He offers to make a mother of her. In part "a mother" means a woman who has borne children. But it means more than that and these meanings will become clear.

In 1947–48 when I worked on Yap I was assured by those who were knowledgeable, and who trusted me to understand them and not mock them, that coitus had nothing to do with the conception of children. If the ancestral spirits of a man's *tabinau* were happy and looked with favor on a woman because she worked hard, took care of her husband's old parents, and acted with propriety, they rewarded her by having her become pregnant. Coitus was regarded as a pleasurable activity, a right of a husband in a wife, and she in him. But it was not regarded as necessary to conception. The decisive element was that the *tabinau* spirits (*thagith*) of the husband's *tabinau* interceded with a spirit, *marialang,* and this spirit accomplished the pregnancy by assigning a spirit to form the child in the mother's "stomach." When Dr. Labby worked on Yap about twenty years later, his information was somewhat different. Coitus was regarded as necessary to conception, though the spirit *marialang* remained important as did the intercession of the *tabinau* spirits (*thagith*). Now the view was that the man planted the seed, the woman being like a garden; the seed had to be nurtured and tended and this took place in the woman, the garden. And because the man "worked" on that garden, he had rights to the product of that garden, though that product did not belong to him; the child belonged to the mother and to her *genung*. Both in 1947–48 and about twenty years later the sense was clear that the child "belonged" to the woman, not to the man. But this did not mean that she could take her child with her on divorce. The child had to stay at the *tabinau* of the woman's husband. I have used the word "belonged" in quotes to indicate that Yapese usage invoked the personal possessive form. However, the notion of "belonging" and "possession" are not isomorphic in Yapese and English and certainly the Yapese does not imply the English conception of "ownership" as of property. Perhaps "to be of," "associated with," "under the care of," are closer to the Yapese "belong" than is "ownership."

A woman marries and goes to live with her husband on his *tabinau*. She tends the gardens, works the taro, cooks the meals, takes care of the vegetable food generally, and helps care for his aging parents as well as her children. The relationship between the wife and husband is phrased as the exchange of vegetable food for raw fish and betel nuts, and these appear frequently in ceremonial exchanges not only between men and women, but men's sides and women's sides, superior and inferior, and so on. All of this is *magar*, work. In return for the work she invests in the *tabinau*, her children gain the right to hold that *tabinau* when their mother's husband is no longer capable of doing so—when he is too old to be effective or when he dies. But the children are obliged to do their share. When they are young and weak, the mother's husband (*citamangen*) cares for them. As they get older, they are also required to work for the *tabinau* to secure their rights in it. The wife's son will fish, help with heavy garden clearing, and house building, obey his *citamangen*, and follow his directions doing what he is asked. Later on he will provide the old people with the care and help they require by providing fish, tending them when they are ill, and continuing to be an obedient and supportive *fak*, for only by doing their share of the work do they secure the rights which their mother's work gained them at the outset. If at any point along the line the wife or her children fail to do the work which custom stipulates can be expected of them they can be summarily "thrown away" or sent from the *tabinau* and lose all rights in it. The wife may leave in divorce if she wishes but her leaving does not terminate the children's rights that she has gained, and the fact that they have *tabinau* names and do their work maintains their rights. Such "throwing away" of children (regardless of their age) is not done lightly for there is a great loss on both sides, but it is clearly the right of the seniors, the mother's husband, to do so if in his judgment the dereliction of duty has been too great.

This, then, is the crucial point. The right to succeed to the position of head of the *tabinau*, the right to the products and resources of the land, the right to use the land, are established by work which the child's mother first does and continues to do for the *tabinau*, and which her children take an increasingly greater role in doing. It is described by the Yapese as a simple exchange: the woman and her children (one *genung*) work for husband and mother's husband on his land, and this establishes the right for her children (another *genung*) to hold that *tabinau* when their mother's husband is dead, provided that they too do the work required of them, and the right to its products and its protection while the mother's husband is alive. For this work, the husband owes his wife's children food, care, protection, instruction and guidance, and training in the special traditions and perquisites of that *tabinau*, as well as representation in the affairs and activities of the *binau* and in inter-*tabinau* affairs (disputes, marriage arrangements, etc.).

The Yapese formulate the relationship between *citamangen* and *fak* in terms of authority and dependency which is either exchanged over time in certain instances, or for which a steady state of exchange is maintained. *Citamangen* provides for his *fak* when they are young and weak and without knowledge, but when the *fak* grow to near-adulthood the child returns the care and the provisions which the old person needs. A mother's husband and her child (among many others) are *citamangen* and *fak* respectively to each other. But this terminology may be reversed when the mother's husband is old, relatively helpless and dependent on his wife's son. Then the mother's husband may call the wife's son *citamangen* or *tam* (the stem of the longer word). And so too he will call his wife's daughter *citiningen* or *tin* (the stem), for these terms express the asymetrical dependency relationship. Forms of dress reiterate these signs. A small boy at first wears no covering. Then he wears a single bit of loincloth. Later he adds two different colored pieces, still later he adds a long swath of hibiscus fiber tucked in fore and aft, with a long loop hanging between his knees, sometimes dyed red or left in its natural yellowish-white color. But as a man gets old and no longer fishes, his loincloth changes accordingly so that an old man wears but a single meager cloth, if that, and the Yapese say, "You see, he is like a child." He is, for he is weak and dependent and needs care just as a child does: he has become *fak* to the child who was *fak* to him. Moreover, if an old man is neglected by his wife's son, another man may take care of him, bring him food and tend to his wants. He thereby becomes *fak* to the old man, the old man *citamangen* to him. The wife's son loses his claim to the *tabinau* while the new *fak* succeeds the old man on his death and holds the *tabinau*. During the war between Japan and the United States food was very scarce and some men who were required by circumstances to live in the colonial center, Colonia, made arrangements with others to take food from the land of the others—who lived outside Colonia. Such an arrangement made the food-giver *citamangen* to the food-taker, who was *fak,* and the relationship was such that the *citamangen* were able—and had the proper right—to exact various political and practical favors from their *fak,* who were usually "in" with the Japanese.

Consistent with the *citamangen-fak* relationship is the fact that a woman who is married and bears a child is the *citiningen* of that child. But she is no longer the *citiningen* when she leaves her husband in divorce, leaves his *tabinau* and returns to the *tabinau* of her *citamangen* and *citiningen*. The *citiningen* of the child will then be the next wife, or if the *citamangen* does not marry again, the *citamangen*'s sister. The term *citiningen,* like *citamangen,* "names" a role that is performed, not a state of being or a set of attributes.

The term *fak* in Yapese is an animate possessive (recalling once again that the English word *possessive* should not be confused with the English concept of ownership). One may say *"fakag"* (*-ag* being the first person suffix, *my, me*) of one's chicken or one's pig or one's dog. The inanimate possessive is *fon,* thus "my" (canoe; knife) would be *fonag* (i.e., "mine inanimate"). But the formal grammatical statement distorts the meaning of *fak* as I have suggested all along, for there again the problem of translation is such that to understand what a Yapese personal animate possessive is is to understand in the first place that it is *not* the same as the English possessive. So too *citamangog* might be taken as the first person possessive form of *citamangen.* Three terms are useful to note here. In some contexts they are combined, in some distinguished; *citamangen, suwon,* and *tafen. Tafen* is used to mean "container" sometimes, "the place of" at other times, "to belong to" in other contexts. These forms are all closely associated since they center on aspects of land. *Tafen* as the place of, belonging to, and container minimizes the relational. *Suwon* maximizes the right to direct, instruct, decide, give instruction, and superiority over in authority terms. *Citamangen* stresses the exchange of care and protection although it entails guidance, authority, and superiority, and also the relationship.

The description of the *citamangen-fak* relationship thus far immediately raises the question of whether the statement that the *tabinau* is a corporate landholding unit is correct or not. It will be recalled that the head of the *tabinau* was described as its "nominal owner" or as the landholder.

First, it is clear that the *tabinau* is not a corporate landholding unit. Second, the whole concept of ownership and of various kinds of rights in land is extremely complex, and to say simply that the *tabinau* head is the nominal owner or the real owner is to fail to describe the Yapese situation even remotely accurately. The whole Western notion of ownership of a free good is simply not applicable to Yap. What would be appropriate would be a carefully detailed account of the different characteristics of land. Unfortunately that is not possible here. Without going into the extensive detail that would be desirable, it is clear that the head of the *tabinau* has the right to allocate different plots to different people and that those people in turn assume various obligations both to the land itself and to the head of the *tabinau.* To avoid the misleading term *owner* I will simply use the term *landholder,* implying by this only that ownership in the Western or American sense of this term is almost entirely inappropriate. The landholder can dispose of the land to those who earn the right to it, and those who fail to perform the role of *fak* according to the standards customarily set for it may lose all rights even after many years of work. That these rights do not depend on so-called kinship ties is evident from the above description. Persons who cohold land are *wolagen,* persons who share the same rights in the same land are *wolagen.* If the person who was *fak* fails in his duties and a person who pleases the *citamangen* or landholder comes along and assumes that role, the former *fak* loses all rights and the new person becomes *fak* even where no "kinship" relationship existed or exists. The new *fak* becomes the landholder when the landholder becomes incompetent or dies. Similarly, the wartime dependents in Colonia, living off the land held by others, became *fak* to the landholders, their *citamangen*.

The *citamangen-fak* relationship applies also to the *tabinau* which owns land in a *pimilingai* (low-caste) *binau*. The high-caste *tabinau* and those belonging to it are *citamangen* to the low-caste *tabinau* which is *fak* to the high-caste *tabinau*. Unlike the relationship between wife's son and mother's husband, however, the low-caste persons never succeed to the position of the high caste but instead remain in a permanently dependent position. In exchange for living on that land and using it, they must perform work of various sorts for the high-caste *tabinau* which is *citamangen* to them. Here too, then, *tabinau* rights are secured by labor.

The *citamangen-fak* relationship includes the relation between the *pilibithir ko binau* (the elder of the *binau*) and the rest of the *binau*, as well as that between the elder and the *pilung ko binau* (the chief of the *binau*). The *pilung ko binau* is in turn *citamangen* to the *pilung ko pagel* (the chief of the young men) and of course the *pilung ko pagel* is *fak* to the two senior offices. These various officers of the *binau* have special roles in the activities of the whole *binau*. They meet with the heads of all the *tabinau* and decide when communal fishing is to take place, the ceremonial cycle, when to undertake wars or skirmishes with neighboring *binau*, what to do about various problems within the *binau* such as (in the period until around 1950) the dearth of children and the falling population, problems of drunkenness and unruly youth, relations with other *binau*, the arrangement of large exchanges between *binau*, and so forth.

Every *tabinau* has its predecessors who are now spirits (*thagith*) and has living people, and it will see those living people become predecessors. Respect for the *thagith* and their power to intercede with spirits on behalf of the *tabinau* is quite important, so the *tabinau* not only has roots in the past and, through its predecessors' spirits (*thagith*), links to the spiritual world, but it also has a present, and along with that, a future.

The Yapese say, "Our land belongs to someone else; someone else's land belongs to us." It should not be hard to see what they mean. Each man who marries brings a woman of a different *genung* into the *tabinau*, and so the *tabinau* normally passes from the people of one *genung* (in the restricted sense of a small part of a matriline) to the people of another *genung*. Yet it is not a simple matter of one *genung* wholly succeeding another, for the *mafen* are the guardians of the land and retain the right to evict the succeeding *genung* from the land for just cause. They jealously guard the respect in which they must be held and their right to protect the rights of the landholder, who is the *matam* of their *genung*. Thus each person is part of a *genung* which is *mafen* to some other *genung* ("our land belongs to someone else") and part of a *genung* which holds land at this moment ("someone else's land belongs to us").

But all of this is not a state of being, a simple matter of the attributes of common descent or consanguinity. It is instead a continuous process of doing; for it depends on *magar*, on the work of building the land, of being respectful, of doing one's duty, of being obedient, of caring for the elders. One cannot just sit and say, "This is my due because of what I am"; one must constantly do, work, pay respect, exact the obedience, and so on.

Although *genung* (including *citiningen-fak*) and *wolagen* are egalitarian relations of sharing and cooperation, all other relations in Yapese culture are hierarchical and are relations of contingent exchange. That is, the maintenance of the relationship is contingent on the continuity of the exchange. Two other qualities pervade all relationships except those of *genung*, particularly in its narrower sense of a man, his sister, and her children, and of a woman and her children, and in the narrower sense of *wolagen* of the same *citiningen*.

The first of these is the quality of *tabagul* and *taay*. Labby translates these as "pure" and "impure," and sometimes also as "sacred" and "profane." Rather than offer yet another gloss, suffice it to say that this hierarchical opposition defines every relationship—be it between persons or objects such as food from certain plots of land or plots of land themselves—other than that of *genung*, *citiningen-fak*, and *wolagen* of the same *citiningen*. In the broadest sense *tabagul* and *taay* are the two poles of a hierarchical relationship. In some contexts bringing these together pollutes by bringing the impure in conjunction with the pure. In some contexts it simply breaks down the polarity. In other contexts it states the privilege and prestige against the subservience and deprivation. The comb is the special perogative of the landholding *pilung* and hence the *pimilingai* should not wear it, for to do so defiles it or at least threatens the polarity or hierarchy for which it stands. A host of signs, acts, modes of speech, restrictions on eating, places, and so on mark the distinction between *tabagul* and *taay*. Yet these are not really absolute qualities inherent in objects, although often they appear to be. The old man is *tabagul* to the young man, but the young man is *tabagul* to the young woman or child. On the other hand, *pilung* are *tabagul* to all *pimilingai* and *pimilingai* are *taay* to almost everyone and everything else. This means that those people who are given the privilege of living on land that is held by someone else are the lowest of the low.

The second quality is that of *runguy*. Kirkpatrick (personal communication) glosses it as "compassion" and is very clear that it is not to be confused with amity. It is *runguy* that makes a citamangen care for his *fak*, that holds together those who are hierarchically related. It is the quality that infuses exchange in that it is the motivating feature of the gift. *Genung, citiningen-*

fak, wolagen of the same *citiningen* do not have *runguy*. If one comes to another and begs, saying "*Ah gafago*" ("I am destitute") then the other should have *runguy*, and help the destitute person, who will then be subordinated and owe an eventual return. But it is not *runguy*, and not because a child is *gafago*, that a *citiningen* nurses it or mops its bottom; it is because they are one.

4 Is Theory Alone Responsible for the Weakness of the First Description?

Is theory alone responsible for the defects of the first description? Obviously not. Many of the defects of the first description are clearly the consequence of the fact that the received wisdom, the theory available to me was not used with skill. Certainly some of the difficulties of the first description derive from my failure to use the theory in the best way possible. What was wrong with the tool is one question; how well I used the tool quite another.

For example, I described the *tabinau* as composed of two kin groups; a patrilineal lineage and a patrilocal extended family. This view of the *tabinau* makes it what Murdock (1949:66ff) calls a "compromise kingroup," that is, the association of persons related by bonds of descent (or kinship) as well as coresidence or propinquity. I could well have followed this useful suggestion to see how the principles of descent (or kinship) were related to those of residence, which bonds were invoked where, whether one or the other principle was consistently dominant or not, and so on.

Another example: patrilineal descent is affirmed. It is affirmed on the basis of the rule of recruitment essentially since the "son" and "daughter" belong to the "father's" *tabinau*. This treatment follows from the older theoretical view that descent units are created by a rule of affiliation. It neglects the more recent but well-established (by now) view that descent units need not necessarily have a single rigid rule of recruitment but are constituted by persons who claim descent from a common ancestor or ancestress. The material is there, in the first description, to support such a view. But I did not use it. The *thagith* are glossed as "ancestral ghosts." These live in the house platform and are the ghosts of all previous members of the *tabinau*. Since according to the first description members of the *tabinau* are a man and his sister, his son and daughter, his son's son and son's daughter, and so on up and down a patriline, then the fact that the *tabinau* is defined by its orientation to ancestors makes it a descent group. That members may be recruited by marriage (in-marrying wives) is irrelevant, for their membership is confirmed by the fact that when they die (if they are still married to a member of the *tabinau*) they become *thagith* of the *tabinau* into which they married, and not of the *tabinau* into which they were born. This would be by no means the first culture described where membership in a descent group was only certain after the death of a person, but always ambiguous before.

A further example of what might fairly be described as my poor use of existing theory is the failure to clearly describe the cultural value or signifi-

35

cance of agnation. Do the members of a *tabinau* formally and forcefully conceive of themselves as being agnatically related? That is, how do they formulate their bonds to each other? Do they say, perhaps, "I am a member of this *tabinau* because my father was a member and his father and his father before him, back to the founding ancestor"? This would affirm that agnation was indeed culturally significant. I offered no such information, yet good use of kinship theory called for it. From the second description it seems that agnation in the sense indicated in the preceding sentence is not culturally significant, but the question should certainly have been raised and discussed.

Continuing with the question of descent, the discussion of *genung* in the first description is clearly much less than exhaustive. Not only is material left out which appears in the second description, but the analysis itself seems inadequate even by the standards of the theory which the first description is supposed to exemplify. In particular the account of *mafen* is quite inadequate. In the first description it is not clear that every predecessor of every *cit-amangen* (or, in terms of the first description, every father's sister's line going back five to seven generations) represents an intersection of a matriline brought in by the wife. Even if one were to accept the notion of double descent and the ascendant patriline was seen as crosscut at each generation by a matriline, this implicates the cross-sibling relationship in some significant ways. The cross-sibling relationship, then, is radically different from the same-sibling relationship. Here Radcliffe-Brown's old views ([1924] 1952) could form the basis for understanding the "solidarity of brothers" as necessary to the solidarity and unity of the patrilineal lineage, but a further step could be taken. The further step would be to show the contrast between same-sex siblings and cross-sex siblings. Cross-sex siblings are at every point the continuation of matrilines and patrilines which insure their divergence. This in turn suggests the possibility of some kind of marriage rule, or at least some sort of systematic relation between sister-giving *tabinau* and sister-receiving *tabinau*. None of this is touched in the first description.

The reservoir system is raised but confuses many readers. I could well have been much more clear on that. Nevertheless I am on firmer ground on this problem, for it was a problem from the moment I first worked on kinship terminology in the field. When I first described the system in my doctoral dissertation, one of America's most eminent experts on kinship terminology expressed withering incredulity until he himself (to my good fortune) had the chance of working closely with a Yapese informant while he checked my manuscript at the same time and confirmed my report. To oversimplify, there is essentially no vocative system, all persons being addressed by their names except in certain very restricted ritual and formal occasions. Further, if we accept the untenable assumption that vocative/referential exhausts the data, there are certain restrictions on the referential use of certain of the terms. For example, the term for spouse is never used by a speaker for his or her spouse's sibling of the same sex as the spouse if the spouse if alive. But spouse's sibling is classed as "spouse"—again if one wishes to accept the untenable premise that referential meaning is all we are seriously concerned with, then here is a term that is never used in address or reference. It was rules like this that disturbed my eminent critic, for how could there be a term that was never used in address or reference? Similarly, father's brother is never addressed as or referred to as *citamangen* ("father") so long as "father" is alive. However, when "father" dies, father's oldest surviving brother becomes *citamangen* and can be referred to by that term. I saw and described this as a system in which one person occupied a status and played a socially prescribed role and was, therefore, referred to by the kinship term. When the person in that status died or left it, someone always replaced him or her. Thus there was a reservoir of "fathers" lined up ready to fill the father role; a reservoir of "mothers" lined up to replace "mother" if she died or left in divorce; and so too, of course, given the levirate, a reservoir of husbands so that if a husband died, he could be replaced by a husband's brother.

Perhaps, indeed, *the reservoir system* is not a good name for this because it assumes that status and role are all that an ethnographic statement need make. That assumption is certainly questionable. The phrase "rules of (or for) reference" which I have also used is probably better, for it allows for the rules of actual use and different contexts of use can be clearly stated instead of assuming stagnant statuses. But I had never heard of "pragmatics" (in this connection) and did not know the Prague school existed; if anyone at Cornell, Yale, or Harvard ever mentioned C. S. Pierce it was not mentioned in my presence when I was first trained and went into the field. In any case, the interested reader can refer to the original paper for a fuller description (Schneider 1953). I only raise it here because, although I have tried to avoid bringing problems of kinship terminology into this book, some of this material is germane to both descriptions.

One of the gravest defects in the first description is largely my fault. I simply used glosses for Yapese words which seemed to me appropriate and which stood up as best they could by the time the fieldwork was over. Here poor fieldwork might also account for some of the deficiencies in the first description, though I am not convinced that any of my fieldwork was poor. I think that my fieldwork was really pretty good and that it has not been seriously contradicted by any of the field-workers who followed me. What was poor was the way I used the available instruments of analysis.

One of the most important instruments of analysis is the correct translation of Yapese words and sentences and utterances. Here again kinship terms rear their head, but not only kinship terms. Take the word *tabinau*, which is so central to both descriptions. If *binau* means land, village, what does the *ta-,* which seems to modify it, mean? If *citamangen* and *citiningen* can be reduced to the stems *tam-* and *tin-,* and these are the proto-Austronesian terms for either father and mother, or male and female (depending on which historical linguist you read), does this not give us an important way of reaching an accurate translation of such words as *tabinau, citamangen,* and *citiningen?*

Alas, no! This is the problem that this book is about. How does one properly translate not just the single words, but the sentences, acts, the states of affairs? To shortcut the whole process by assuming somehow that a linguist or grammarian really knows what *ta-, tam-,* and *tin-* mean and that the gloss such an "expert" provides is necessarily correct begs the question of how to determine the proper translation. Over and above that there is the question of the utility of such glosses of specific terms or grammatical forms without taking into account the culturally distinct kinds of uses in discourse. Whatever *ta-* "means" to a historical linguist, I doubt that it means that and only that every time and everywhere it occurs. Glosses and historical linguistics are part of the problem; they are neither the solution nor even good evidence.

By the same token, my translations of Yapese terms, concepts, and ideas in the first description are open to serious question, which an anthropologist with a better facility with the conventional wisdom of kinship studies could well have avoided by providing detailed documentation on how these translations were arrived at and others rejected. Instead I merely asserted that *citamangen* meant "father," that *thagith* meant "ancestral ghost." I might, in my own defense, claim that limitations of space precluded such documentation, but even I would reject that argument as specious. In my earlier publications there was lots of space and lots of time to explain on what evidence I had reached those and not other translations.

What difference would it have made if the first description were the very best possible? More could have been done with the data. The analysis would have been more elegant, more of the data would have been engaged and apparently accounted for. But in the end the analysis would have been of the same kind. Kinship would still have been assumed. The native conceptions would still have been translated into the conceptions and formulations of the received wisdom of kinship theory such as it is. Even if a more skillful analysis had shown that the transmission of land is from *genung* to *genung,* the *citamangen-fak* relationship would still have been treated as a father-son bond and thus the essential element of an agnatic relationship of some kind, and the *thagith* would still have been ancestral ghosts, implying descent from a known or putative ancestor rather than just a founder or predecessor, which implies no descent bond.

What I am trying to make clear here is that even if it is granted that many of the defects of the first description can be traced to my crude use of the available theory of kinship, and not to defects of the kinship theory itself, the questions I am raising in this book are about kinship theory, not about how best to use it. Even if we imagine the most skillful and efficient use of the ideas of kinship, the kin-based society, kinship as an idiom, the question which this book poses is this: *Are those ideas tenable?* The purpose of the first description, then, is to provide a body of material that is built on the traditional and generally accepted tenets of kinship theory in order to bring out, to make explicit, that theory and its presuppositions so that they can be examined with care. The fact that the first description is far from the most elegant or the best that might have been developed from the received wisdom of the study of kinship is quite beside the point of this book. The point of this book is to make explicit and examine carefully the implicit and explicit assumptions and presuppositions about kinship, and to evaluate them equally carefully.

PART II

Some Questions Raised by the Yapese Materials and a Critical Look at Some Answers

Introduction to Part II

This part of the book has two aims. The first is to state some of the major assumptions made in the study of kinship which inform the first description. Among these are the notions of the kin-based society, the idiom of kinship, and the content of kinship, but there are many more. Much of this is done in the chapter which follows this introduction. The second aim is to then examine the Yapese material carefully in order to raise questions about the assumptions and presuppositions of the usual modes of describing kinship. The point here is to bring out problems in part through showing how well or how badly these assumptions fit the Yapese materials. Other problems are brought out directly, without reference to the Yapese materials.

I have used, and will continue to use, such phrases as "the theory" and "the received wisdom" of the study of kinship, despite the shortcomings of such usages. One shortcoming is that these phrases imply that there is a single body of integrated, universally accepted theory of kinship. Even the most casual student of the subject knows that this is not true. Functionalists differ with each other and with structuralists, who are not at one with evolutionists or Boasians or anyone else. But there are some points on which there is more or less general agreement. There is general agreement that there is such a thing as kinship (with only a rare exception or two). There is general agreement that there is such a thing as a "kin-based society," though just exactly how this is defined may vary from scholar to scholar. With a few exceptions there seems to be general agreement that an important aspect of the definition of kinship is its entailment in biological and/or social reproduction. With a few exceptions there is a general commitment to the notion that kinship provides a network of ties of a distinctive, additive sort, a system of ties built on the relative products of the primary relations.

When I say, therefore, "the conventional wisdom" or "the theory" it must be understood in the context of the specific point which is being made and understood as applying only to those scholars who take that position. Where possible I will try to indicate at least some scholar who takes a position I discuss, for I do not want to erect straw men or attack positions that no one holds. The ultimate test is "if the shoe fits." But the burden is on me not to force the shoe on where it obviously does not fit.

Although ostensibly aimed at raising questions, this part of the book makes no pretense of avoiding criticism. My pose is not one of neutrality. My position is clearly to raise questions critical of the various theories of the study of kinship which are in common use today.

43

5   Some Assumptions behind the First Description

I will try to present in as faithful and careful detail as possible the theory which underlies the first description. I will start with some quotations from some of the leading exponents of this theory and then proceed to state point by point the general outlines of that theory. Thereafter the exposition will be such that at certain points it is not at all clear what theoretical assumptions or presuppositions underlie a particular point. At such places I will do my best to review as faithfully and realistically as possible the different possible premises. At one or two points I will have to confess that I cannot imagine what theoretical premises are involved, and in one or two other places there seem to me to be grounds for suggesting that a usage is based more on a very complex historical tradition than on any clear, simple premises. Soon thereafter I will make my criticisms point by point.

It is not really possible to present any one of the ideas of "kinship", the "kin-based" society, the "idiom of kinship," and the "content of kinship" without invoking the others. Moreover, different anthropologists seem concerned with more or less different formulations and aspects of these ideas. Radcliffe-Brown is concerned with social cohesion and stability and the role which kinship plays in promoting those states, while Beattie is more concerned with kinship as a code or idiom in terms of which social relations are formulated. Yet both concur with J. W. Powell 1884 (who followed Morgan 1877, who was followed by Sahlins 1968, and by Makarius 1978, for example) in the premise that the "tribal," "primitive," or "small-scaled" societies are generally "kin-based."

The following quotation from J. W. Powell is not the earliest that can be found, but it is sufficient to suggest that the idea is by no means new. "So far as is now known, tribal society is everywhere based on kinship" (1884: xxxviii). He then goes on to identify the kinship group with the tribal group, as did Maine (1861), thus treating the kinship group and the polity as a single body.

A. R. Radcliffe-Brown was of the opinion that "in most primitive societies the social relations of individuals are very largely regulated on the basis of kinship" ([1924] 1952:18). He had not significantly changed his mind twenty-six years later when, in the introduction to *African Systems of Kinship and Marriage*, he said, "in so many non-literate societies, the chief source of social cohesion is the recognition of kinship. . . . there are innumerable social activities that can only be efficiently carried out by means of corporate groups, so that where, as in many non-literate societies, the chief source of social cohesion is the recognition of kinship, corporate groups tend to become the most important feature of social structures" (1950:42–43). In 1964, in a textbook written by John Beattie, a slightly different view is advanced.

> Why is kinship so important in small-scale societies? The short answer is that in all human communities, even the most technologically simple ones, the basic categories of biological relationship are available as means of identifying and ordering social relations . . . of course biologically not only human beings but all animals have "kinship." But the vital point is that unlike other animals, human beings consciously and explicitly use the categories of kinship to define social relationships. . . . a consequence of the biological reference of kinship terminology is that to say that a relationship is one of kinship may convey no information about its content. (1964b:94)

Or, in 1949 Fortes says, "The idiom of kinship has such a dominant place in Tale thought that all social relations implying mutual or common interests tend to be assimilated to those of kinship" (p. 19). In the same vein and almost the same words he says, "The extent to which the idiom of kinship dominates Tale thought about human affairs is shown by the tendency of the people to explain conduct that conforms to the norms by appealing to kinship" (p. 13). These phrases merely echo those he wrote earlier, in 1945: "Owing to the dominance of genealogical relationships and the ideology of kinship in Tale social organization, most of the formulas accounting for the clanship ties of maximal lineages are couched in the idiom of kinship" (p. 97; see Fortes 1969:101–37, for his most recent, fullest discussion of this view).

Evans-Pritchard makes a similar point in 1940. "The assimilation of community ties to lineage structure, the expression of territorial affiliation in a lineage idiom, and the expression of lineage affiliation in terms of territorial attachments, is what makes the lineage system so significant for a study of political organization" (p. 205). Or again, "The system of lineages of the dominant clan is a conceptual skeleton on which the local communities are built up into an organization of related parts, or, as we would prefer to state it, a system of values linking tribal segments and providing the idiom in which their relations can be expressed and directed" (p. 212). The point is reiterated as follows: "In the absence of a chief or king, who might symbolize a tribe, its unity is expressed in the idiom of lineage and clan affiliation" (p. 236).

This view is not confined to the British or the followers of Radcliffe-Brown. Marshall Sahlins writes,

> The tribe is also uncomplicated in another way. Its economics, its

politics, its religion are not conducted by different institutions specially designed for the purpose but coincidentally by the same kinship and local groups: the lineage and clan segments of the tribe, the households and villages, which thus appear as versatile organizations in charge of the entire social life. (1968:viii)

And again, "The bias is that of an economy in which food holds a commanding position. . . . It is the bias, finally, of societies ordered in the main by kinship" (1972:187), and "Kinship is more significant in primitive society. It is, for one thing, the organizing principle or idiom of most groups and most social relations (1972:196).

So much for tribesmen. Of hunters, presumably a different level of evolutionary development than tribesmen, Elman Service says:

The loose integration of families in band society is achieved only by conceptions of kinship extended by marriage alliances. . . . the domestic family is often the only consistent face-to-face group. . . . The groups, the subdivisions of the society, are thus all *familistic* in nature, however extended the kinship ties may become. . . . The family itself is the organization that undertakes all roles. . . . the band level of society is a familistic order in terms of both social and cultural organization. (1966:7–8)

Sahlins and Service imply a position far more widely held than by these two scholars alone. In the most general terms, it is the position that the kin-based society takes a certain place in either the evolution or the development of societies, or at least, that there are different types of society, and the kin-based or tribal is one of these, while hunters-and-gatherers is another, the modern nation-state yet another. That is, the notion of kin-based may be part of some evolutionary, developmental, or typological scheme. Sahlins, in his book *Tribesmen,* suggests that the dimension in terms of which he distinguishes the kin-based, tribal kind of society from others is that they do not differentiate distinctive political or economic institutions. That is, the tribal kind of society is one where kinship is the only structure available, and therefore it is in terms of kinship that political and economic functions are carried out.

The view that most, if not all, primitive societies are kin-based or ordered by kinship may not be unanimous, but it is certainly ubiquitous. And it is obvious that it has somewhat different meanings in different wider theoretical contexts.

Explicit in the idea of the kin-based society is the conception of the kinship unit or group as multifunctional, or functionally minimally differentiated. That is, the kin group or unit is at the same time the economic, political, religious unit, and may assume other functions as well. The point has been made repeatedly in the quotations above from Beattie, Evans-Pritchard, and Sahlins among others. From one point of view, primitive society is characterized by the fact that it is not highly differentiated along institutional lines defined by a specialization of function. There are often no or only rudimentary politically specialized institutions; no or only rudimentary economic institutions; no or only rudimentary religious institutions. The kinship unit is the unit which undertakes all of these, as well as other functions. It is true that kin units may be multifunctional, or versatile in Sahlins's terms, yet the society may not be kin-based (but land-based perhaps—we will come to this point again later). The point that kin groups can be, and often are, highly multifunctional units is not in itself dependent on the idea of the kin-based society, despite the obvious and often close association between these ideas.

The multifunctional or versatile quality of the kin group may depend on its corporate character which in turn may depend on its being a unilineal descent unit, but this point carries us farther than is necessary to the present discussion. What is necessary to point out here is the multifunctional character of the kinship unit and the fact that it is often but not necessarily associated with the idea of the kin-based society.

Inextricably embedded in some of the views I have offered is the idea that kinship is an "idiom" in terms of which other kinds of social relations and functions are expressed. Fortes uses the term *idiom* explicitly as does Sahlins, who also uses the phrase *versatile organizations,* which means that the kinship units are the medium through which economic, religious, and political functions are expressed. Elsewhere Sahlins explains that in primitive societies economics is not something like an institution, a group acting in a particular way, but is rather something which kinship and family groups *do* (1972:76). Leach affirms that "what the social anthropologist calls kinship structure is just a way of talking about property relations" (1961:305), and that "the kinship system is not a 'thing in itself' but rather a way of thinking about rights and usages with respect to land" (1961:146). His position seems much the same as Beattie's.

> To say . . . that a social relationship is a kinship one is to tell us nothing at all of its content. The whole point about kinship relations for the social anthropologist is that they *must* be something else, for example, political, jural, economic, or ritual. Kinship is the idiom in which certain kinds of political, jural, economic, etc., relations are talked and thought about in certain societies. It is not a *further* category of social relationships, which can be set beside political relationships, economic relationships, and so on, as though it were commensurate with them. (Beattie 1964a:102)

The relationship between the ideas of the kin-based society, the idiom of kinship, and the content of kinship take somewhat different forms with different anthropologists. It will be helpful to sort out some of these different forms.

One relationship between the idea of the kin-based society, the idiom of kinship, and the content of kinship turns on the question of whether the "base" of the society is kinship or something else. For Radcliffe-Brown, as for Maine and Morgan before him, "the chief source of social cohesion is the recognition of kinship" (Radcliffe-Brown 1950:43). This is especially so in primitive societies (for Radcliffe-Brown) and for societies at the very early stages of development (for Maine, McLennan, and Morgan). For such societies it is kinship that is the organizing principle. It is kinship that is valued as fundamental and unbreachable. It is kinship that is held to be the basic referent and touchstone for everything else. It is the bonds of kinship which either alone or above all else hold the society together. There may be a further corollary here in some views that is lacking in others—that there is a quality, which is both social and biological, to kinship which gives it its special power as a cohesive force. Certainly for Morgan (1870:10) the actual bonds of blood relationship had a force and vitality of their own quite apart from any social overlay which they may also have acquired, and it is this biological relationship itself which accounts for what Radcliffe-Brown called "the source of social cohesion."

The assumption of a psychobiological base may not be entirely necessary. It can be argued simply as an empirical generalization that in primitive and small-scale societies kinship, for whatever reason, forms the major if not the only base in terms of which groups are formed and relations are defined. In this view the "base" of the kin-based society is kinship as a sociocultural system, and kinship is thus the idiom in terms of which relations are codified. In this view, then, kinship is both the base and the idiom, while the content of kinship is essentially that cohesion which arises out of the establishment of a form of social order. In Radcliffe-Brown's words, "the chief source of social cohesion is the recognition of kinship" (1950:43).

Where the base of the kin-based society is thus conceived of as kinship itself, where kinship is the organizing principle as well as the language of social relations, there is a set of related ideas which should not be confused with them. These are the ideas of ascribed versus achieved status (in Linton's 1936 terms) or particularistic versus universalistic grounds for status ascription or quality versus performance (in Parsons's [1937] 1949 terms). Kinship is made up largely or wholly of ascribed or particularistically based statuses. But the condition of status occupancy is not the main point. A society could be built on ascribed or particularistic statuses which were those of rank, race, and sex, and not on kinship. Hence these ideas should not be confused, although they are obviously related. My concern here is with kinship, not with ascribed or particularistic status systems. That kinship happens also to be largely ascribed or particularistic is tangential to the discussion here.

Another view treats "base" not in terms of an idiom in which relations are ordered or expressed, or as organizing principles, but rather more directly as the very ground on which the society itself is built, the crucial set of conditions which determine the kinds of social relations which may then be codified in the language of kinship. For Leach (1961), Pul Eliya is a society which is based on land, and relations of land are spoken of or formulated in the idiom of kinship. Thus kinship is not the "base" of Pul Eliya—land is, and kinship is merely the idiom. Similarly, Worsley's interpretation of Tall-ensi agrees with Fortes that relations are codified and expressed in the idiom of kinship, but for Worsley they are based on the mode of production (Worsley 1956). In this sense the idea of a kin-based society refers to the code or the idiom in terms of which its relations are cast, but quite clearly not to the fundamental or underlying "base" on which those social relations are built. In such views the content of kinship may either be nil or perhaps, as in Fortes's view (1969), consist in the axiom of prescriptive altruism. With this conception of "base" there seems to be no necessary correlation with any particular idea of the content of kinship.

I turn to the question of kinship as idiom or code in terms of which social relations are expressed, formulated, talked, and thought about. For the anthropologists who use the idea of kinship as code or idiom this does not necessarily exhaust the functions or the uses or the relevance of kinship.

A kin-based society is one in which kinship forms the major if not the only language, idiom, code, etc., in terms of which groups are formed and relations are defined. Such kin groups and such kinship relations are multi-functional or, as Sahlins (1968:viii) puts it, "versatile," that is, they serve many different functions. For example, lineage functions not merely as a kinship group for the Tallensi and other so-called segmentary societies, but also constitutes a multifunctional unit having economic, political, religious, and ideological as well as other functions.

Now if the lineage is the landholding unit, or the political unit, then, as Leach and Beattie say, kinship is but the idiom in terms of which property relations are both thought of and talked about. The same applies to politics for Evans-Pritchard, the lineage being the idiom in terms of which politics proceeds or the political order is formulated. The fact that all of these functions are carried out in the vocabulary of kinship—of agnatic, uterine, or cognatic descent (ignoring the distinction between kinship and descent for the moment), of marriage, of domestic units, of the relations between father and son, mother's brother and sister's child and so on—makes it quite clear that these are kin-based societies. They are quite unlike modern states, Asian or Western, where material is held by individuals and conveyed by them with little or no normative regard for kinship relations but with a primary regard for profit. Surely kinship is not an idiom for property relations in modern America.

By saying that kinship is the idiom in terms of which "versatile" or "multifunctional" units are formed, we raise a problem with regard to function. In such a formulation *function* may have different meanings. One meaning is simply "a kind of activity." Thus if it is said that the lineage has economic functions, this may mean no more than the fact that this unit, formulated in terms of the principles of unilineal descent, undertakes some economic activity. A multifunctional unit would be one which undertakes many different kinds of activities. It may be at once a religious, economic, and political unit. In this formulation the different functions seem to be modeled on those institutionally differentiated activities of modern European society. Where economic institutions, religious institutions, and educational institutions are all structurally differentiated in European society, and appear to constitute distinct domains, each oriented to specific ends, they are undifferentiated in primitive or small-scale societies. But they do not take the form of an undifferentiated blob; they take the form of a kinship or descent unit or a pattern of kinship relations, and it is these kinship forms which carry out these different kinds of activities. In another formulation, they all fall within the domain of kinship and/or descent.

Yet another meaning of *function* is simply "connection" or "relations" such as that of contiguity. This is perhaps the simplest view of function that can be taken—that every part of the whole is related or connected to every other part.

A closely related meaning of the term *function* is that of "effect," perhaps "consequence," or "implication." This is not quite the same as simply saying "a form of activity." So where kinship is considered to be an idiom it has a function in this latter sense; it constitutes the code or the model in terms of which other activities and other relations are formulated or conceptualized. This is a function which, for example, economic activity may not be able to fulfill. In this sense, then, kinship as an idiom functions as, or has the effect of, a model or metaphor.

The notion of kinship as an "ordering principle" implies a somewhat different emphasis than kinship as an idiom. Here the implication seems to be that there must be some form in terms of which groups, categories, or social units are constituted. Kinship relations, or even the genealogical grid, can provide certain features in terms of which different groups, categories, or social units can be constituted. Bilateral principles can be used for certain purposes, unilineal principles for certain others, genealogical distance for yet other ways of bonding social units. Since the domain of kinship is made up of different constituent parts (age, sex, lineality, collaterality, generation, and so forth), different permutations and combinations of these elements can provide for the necessary social or cultural differentiation. At the same time, since these are all aspects of a single domain, they can remain integrated into a single social system, or a single part of a larger social system. Where the whole of the system is defined in terms of different aspects of kinship, the resultant social order is, of course, a kin-based system. When only a part of the total social system is ordered by the principles of kinship then the question may arise as to whether it is a kin-based system or not. However, this question requires further consideration before it can be answered. Is there, for example, a priority to that part of the system ordered in terms of kinship?

It is possible to see a connection between the idea of kinship as an idiom and kinship as an ordering principle, though they can also be regarded as quite distinct. Insofar as the notion of idiom suggests ways of talking, thinking, or symbolizing other things, then *idiom* and *ordering principle* are not the same, for one would seem to have to do with a mode of representation, the other with the mode of constitution. In this view, representation and constitution are quite distinct. However, where the mode of representation is at the same time the mode of constitution, then the idiom is indistinguishable from the organizing principle. So too, of course, the idea of kinship as idiom which functions as a model need not necessarily be the same as kinship as metaphor except in the limiting case where the metaphor is the model. But I am perhaps drawing finer distinctions here than are usually encountered in the study of kinship. Nevertheless, these distinctions could be important for certain scholars (see, for example, La Fontaine 1974).

The notion of the "relative product," "network," or "web of kinship" (see, e.g., Barnes 1974b:477) is related but not identical to the notions of kinship as idiom and kinship as organizing principle. The point is that kinship can provide a way of relating a large or small number of persons through formal culturally defined categories of the same kind. It does this by simply taking the primary relations of mother, father, brother, sister, son, daughter, husband, and wife, using these in the possessive form, and adding one or more other primary terms in the possessive form except the terminal term. Thus there may be father's brother, father's brother's son, father's brother's son's daughter, mother's mother, mother's mother's father, mother's mother's father's sister, and so on. A web of kinship relations is thus established which can relate a group of almost any size, in principle, especially if the kin are classed or categorized. The primary relatives can be included in classes so that, for example, all women of the generation senior to ego are classed as "mother." This network or web can then be differentiated according to certain other kinship principles—mother's side versus father's side, agnates, uterines, ascendants, descendants, and so on. The basic point is that the web of kinship relations that can be constituted by the relative products of the primary terms is a way of relating into a single body (kinsmen, or kinsmen versus affines) a large number of persons.

Here again, it is possible either to see the relative product or network as a variant of the ordering principle, or to see them rather differently. Kinship as an ordering principle is oriented to the problem of establishing a form of social order; kinship as a web of kinsmen is oriented to the problem of relating a number of persons through the establishment of a network of related social categories, all of the same kind, that is, of kinship. Moreover, the notion of the relative product implies the ability to use the system flexibly, to include more or fewer persons or categories by multiplying the relative products or restricting their extension. This point is not so clearly implied in the notion of kinship as an ordering principle, though it could be accommodated without straining the point. Another possible difference between the two points is that the relative product seems to be most readily understandable and workable as an ego-oriented system, while an ordering principle is more readily imagined as a sociocentric or a system seen as a whole from the outside and without reference to any particular ego.

Do these last points relate to the question of "the content of kinship"? Fortes (1969) has taken a clear stand on this question by arguing that although kinship is indeed an idiom, it also has its distinctive content, the "axiom of prescriptive altruism." Beattie (1964) has taken the opposite position, arguing that kinship as an idiom lacks any content. Schneider ([1968] 1980) only affirmed that American kinship (not kinship in general) has the special content of shared biogenetic substance and a code for conduct enjoining diffuse, enduring solidarity. Otherwise I do not know of other anthropologists who have addressed this question directly, though others have done so indirectly.

The idiom of kinship, the content of kinship, the web of kinship, the kin-based society all depend in large part on the idea of kinship itself. From the beginnings of modern anthropology, around the middle of the nineteenth century, the prevailing conception of kinship has been fairly stable and only underwent one significant modification. At first kinship was taken to be a purely biological relationship deriving from the facts of human sexual reproduction. The social or cultural component of kinship consisted in the knowledge of the existence of some or all of these relations between persons. Where the role of paternity was understood, then of course kinship could be reckoned through the father as well as the mother. Where the procreative role of the father was not acknowledged, or not recognized, then kinship could only be traced through the mother, for the maternal relationship was deemed too obvious to mistake. Marriage was defined essentially as a sexual and reproductive relationship. Given marriage, and given sexual intercourse as its central feature, the birth of offspring created parenthood. Or, to put it the other way, if there was parenthood this implied sexual intercourse and the birth of offspring, so that in a sense parenthood could be seen as the fundamental fact out of which all kinship relationships arose. However it was figured, the reproductive relationship was taken as the central feature of kinship. Kinsmen, then, were those who were related through "real" biological ties. Insofar as kinship was a sociocultural phenomenon it consisted in the social acknowledgment, consistently called "recognition," by Radcliffe-Brown among others, of these actual biological ties.

Morgan's position is a good example. For Morgan kinship consisted in the knowledge of the existence of relationships of human reproduction. Before the facts of human reproduction were known there could be no kinship. When the facts of human reproduction were not possible to establish, as in a situation of group marriage where many men had sexual access to one woman, then all such men were the "father(s)" of the offspring of that woman since it was not possible to establish who the particular father was. Thus what Morgan called the "descriptive system" of kinship terminology was, in his view, a "natural system" precisely "because it is founded upon a correct appreciation of the distinction between the lineal and several collateral lines and the perpetual divergence of the latter from the former. Each relationship is thus specialized and separated from every other in such a manner as to decrease its nearness and diminish its value according to the degree of distance of each person from the central Ego" (Morgan 1870:142–43). Indeed, Morgan stresses the fact that a high level of intelligence was necessary to the recognition of the existence of divergent collateral lines, classes of relatives such as "cousins," thereby implying that it was the discovery of the biological facts, and thus the facts of such relationship, that were, for him, the essence of kinship (Morgan 1870: chap. 6).

The major modification was in the shift of emphasis from the social recognition of biological bonds arising out of procreation to the sociocultural aspects themselves, ostensibly giving the real or putative existence of the ties lesser, if any, importance. Certain facts of biology might be well known but not accorded cultural value, or conversely, as in the case of adoption, sociocultural relations could be patterned on biological relationships even when no actual biological relationships existed.

But the concept of adoption demonstrates that the ultimate reference remained biological. That is, it is the sociocultural attribution of meaning to the biological relationship (real or putative) which is the central conception of kinship. Without the biological relationship there is nothing. Indeed, without the biological relation it is called "fictive kinship," presumably following Maine (1861:27), who argued that where no actual biological relationship exists it can be treated as if it does by a legal fiction, as in adoption. This is only another way of bringing in the biological facts, for even in such instances as ritual kinship, adoption, and the like, the premise is that the social relationship is modeled on the biological; that adoption is only understandable as a way of creating the social fiction that an actual link of kinship exists. Without biological kinship as a model, adoption would be meaningless.

Another way in which this is sometimes stated is in terms of the difference between pedigree and genealogy. Pedigree is the statement of the actual biological relations between humans or animals. A racehorse has a pedigree, which lists its dam, its sire, and their progenitors. But racehorses do not have a genealogy. A genealogy is a statement of social relationships, not biological ones. It is the social mother and father, the social brothers and sisters, that are listed on a genealogy. But here once again, it is simply not possible to conceive of a genealogy without the model of the pedigree. What exactly is a social mother or a social father, if it is not the social value and meaning which is attached to, and takes its reference from, the presumption of relations arising directly or indirectly out of human reproduction, of conception, creation, gestation, and parturition? (This point was made by Gellner 1957 and in 1960 contra Needham 1960. Needham 1960 was quite inadequate on this point. The problem will be addressed at greater length below.)

Fatherhood has been a vexing problem in this regard. Because in some societies physiological paternity may either be denied or ignored, some anthropologists (Malinowski 1913; Goodenough 1970; Barnes 1974a, 1974b) define the father as the mother's husband. The status of father as mother's husband may invoke a biological reference in different ways or some combination of them. The husband's legitimate sexual access to the wife-mother may be one ground. Given such access, the biological tie to the child may be presumed by some anthropologists (Scheffler and Lounsbury 1971). For others the stress may be on the tie to the child generated by the husband's special bond to his wife and the mother's special bond to her child, the tie conceived in psychobiological terms (Goodenough 1970; this position will be discussed in detail below). But even with fatherhood, the ultimate biological reference of the definition of kinship seems clear.

Given, then, the array of biological relationships, kinship constitutes a selection from them which are given sociocultural value; sociocultural relationships are added to the biological relationships which are recognized and valued (and which are, therefore, themselves sociocultural). Since these relations all start with those of reproduction, and assume an incest prohibition, two kinds of relationships emerge as fundamental: relations of consanguinity and relations of affinity. These in turn provide a genealogical grid in terms of which different sociocultural systems can group and classify, make distinctions, and create a relational system of both kinds or of categories of persons. The categories of persons can in turn be organized as groups or they may remain as categories defined in terms of some kind of relationship. But however the genealogical space is partitioned, the ultimate reference must be to some real or putative set of biological, reproductive relationships. As Lévi-Strauss says, "the limit of elementary structures lies in the biological possibilities which always provide many solutions to a given problem, in the form of brothers, sisters, or cousins" (1969:xxiii). Similarly Fortes says, "the facts of sex, procreation, and the rearing of offspring constitute only the universal raw material of kinship systems" (1949:345).

The facts of sex, procreation, and the rearing of offspring constitute the raw material out of which kinship systems, as sociocultural systems, are built; the limit of [elementary] structures lies in the biological possibilities—in the form of brothers, sisters, or cousins—the degrees of *real* (i.e., biological) kinship then provide a "natural" or biological model for a network of relations which we call "genealogical." That is to say, for any ego there is a real biological father, mother, brother, sister, son, and daughter. He or she may have a husband or wife and through each of them there will be mothers, fathers, brothers, sisters, sons, and daughters such that a complex set of interrelationships obtains. It is the social segmentation or the sociocultural partition of this network and the roles, values, and relationships which then become the kinship system of the particular culture. Some relations may be recognized, others suppressed or ignored; some may be summarized so that all agnatic relations are grouped or all uterine relations may be grouped; relations may be counted through males but not females or vice versa. But always it is the genealogical grid, a construct modeled on the presumption of actual biological relations, that underlies the sociocultural product called kinship.

The ideas of the kin-based society, the idiom and content of kinship, and kinship per se form a closely intermeshed set so that it is not always possible to isolate each one and treat it systematically. This will complicate the exposition which follows somewhat, but I do not think that it will cause undue confusion. In the end, of course, all of these ideas depend on the notion of kinship. If kinship falls, all of the others fall too, but life need not be made so rigorously logical. Even if we accept, for the sake of the discussion, the notion of kinship, the idea of the kin-based society and the conception of kinship as an idiom may well be worth close critical scrutiny.

6   Is Kinship a Privileged System?

According to the first description the *tabinau* is made up of a patrilineage and a patrilocal extended family. The second description does not speak of *tabinau* as a kin group; in fact it does not speak of *tabinau* as anything but *tabinau*. There is at least this discrepancy to account for.

The first problem which the first description raises is the problem of kinship as an idiom in terms of which other kinds of relations are formulated. I have already outlined the key features of this view and it will suffice to merely restate them here in terms of the Yap *tabinau*. The *tabinau* is a kinship group. As a patrilineage it holds land, undertaking all those activities which are associated with land such as succession to landholder, to spokesman for the offices inherent in the land, and allocation of rights to the use of different plots. The *tabinau* as a patrilineage undertakes economic relations both within and between *tabinau*. It produces and consumes goods for its own use as well as for exchange. It undertakes ritual and religious relations within the unit, between *tabinau,* and within the village, and it constitutes the basic political unit out of which all other, larger political units are built as well as holding within the land those differentiated political offices such as village chief, chief of the old men, chief of the young men, and so on.

Parenthetically, if we stay within the confines of the conventional wisdom about kinship, as I have thus far, this much can be said. If Yap is a kin-based society, it is kin-based only in the sense that kinship is the idiom in terms of which the system is phrased. In that other sense of "based," Yap seems to be "based" on land, as is said to be the case for Pul Eliya, for it is land that is fundamental, holding as it does not only the very foundation of the subsistence but also the political offices, the place of the ancestral spirits, rank, and so on. Land holds almost all resources considered valuable by the Yapese, from food to rank. But this, of course, only begs the question of what the terms *based* or *fundamental* are supposed to mean.

No matter how the Yapese themselves phrase the relationship between land and people, the first description follows the theory that we can cut through their cultural rhetoric and see immediately that the *tabinau* can be analyzed as two kinds of kin groups: the core patrilineage and the domestic unit, the patrilocal extended family. The patrilineage includes the out-marrying sisters and daughters who in turn form distinct matrilines (*mafen*). *Mafen* hold rights over *tabinau* land and have authority over the members of the succeeding generation of the patrilineage, and they must be respected and obeyed.

Such is the first description. Let us for the moment accept the assumption that the *tabinau* is (among other things) a kinship group and that it contains a patrilineage at its core (although what "at its core" means is left unclear). The central question concerns the nature of the relationship among its members and between that kinship group and other kinship groups. The theory of Fortes, Leach, and Sahlins says that it is within the framework of kinship and descent that the economic, political, religious, and other such relations are to be found, and they are not found to be clearly differentiated as such, but only as functions of kinship or descent. That is, the Yapese do not differentiate economic from kinship relations. Examined with care, and with a clear idea in mind of the distinction between kinship and economic relationships, it can be seen that the kinship relationship embodies an economic one and not vice versa. The Yapese do not seem to differentiate a set of land relationships and speak about them as such or conceive of them as distinct; only on analysis can it be seen that it is as kinship relationships that the land relationships are in fact defined, discussed, described, and conducted. Recall: a man succeeds to the office of the head of the *tabinau* (the patrilineage) and thereby to the position of nominal landholder and it is as head of his *tabinau* that he holds the land. A man must be dependent, obedient, respectful to his father in order to succeed to the headship of the patrilineage. And so on. Such is the conventional wisdom.

If we ask why we translate the *tabinau* as a kin group and the *citamangen-fak* relationship as a kinship relationship in the first description, the most readily apparent answer is that this is in fact an accurate translation of what the Yapese say and do. *They* call it a kin group; *they* speak of the relationship as a kinship relationship. *They* make it plain that that is what they are talking about and the way in which they talk about it. If the Yapese say that the *tabinau* is a kin group, on what ground can we challenge them?

But in the matter of translation we must proceed with the utmost care. In 1947–48 there were no English-speaking Yapese on the island. Most spoke Japanese, but I did not, so I learned Yapese and commanded a moderate fluency in the language. Twenty years later American schools were operating in full force, and most young Yapese spoke English with more or less fluency. In 1947–48 what the Yapese spoke about was *tabinau, citamangen, fak,* and so on. I had to translate these terms into English and I did so, producing the first description. But my field notes are clear. The Yapese spoke of *tabinau.* Having learned anthropology at Cornell, Yale, and Harvard, I examined these terms, learned about how the *tabinau* was structured, its membership, and the rules relating to it, and came up with the translations "patrilineage" and "patrilocal extended family." What the Yapese actually said and did went through my translation machine, and my translation machine was wired by a course on kinship taken from G. P. Murdock at Yale, by lectures on kinship by R. L. Sharp at Cornell, by the writings of Morgan, Rivers, Malinowski, and Radcliffe-Brown, and by a host of monographs and texts about anthropology and how primitive societies are put together. What the Yapese said and did was filtered through a well-organized, well-structured set of assumptions and presuppositions. I was a diligent, fairly well trained graduate student; I could even tell the difference between a patrilineage and a patrilocal extended family.

Twenty years later when David Labby, John Kirkpatrick, Charles Broder, and Sherwood Lingenfelter were there, Americans had long since provided the Yapese with the "correct" English translations for such terms as *tabinau* (family), *citamangen* (father), *citiningen* (mother), *fak* (child), and so on. But such translations as were provided by American school teachers and others can only be taken as naive and not necessarily up to the highest technical, anthropological standards. Nor can they be considered valid without extensive, carefully collected supplementary evidence.

What the Yapese actually talk about and what they actually do is *tabinau*. Even if we grant for the moment that *tabinau* is a kin group, we must also grant that *tabinau* is a landholding group, plays economic roles, conducts religious activities, and undertakes important political actions. It does so as *tabinau*. We might say that if we are to give kinship the number 1, economics the number 2, politics the number 3, and religion the number 4, and whatever else it does the number 5, then *tabinau* can be understood as a unit which has functions 1,2,3,4, and 5. It undertakes activities 1 through 5, and it does not differentiate these into separately conceived or differently named activities or functions as we have done here by giving them distinct names and numbers.

Who are actually engaged in these activities? There are, as the Yapese see it and say it and do it, the *citamangen,* the *fak,* the *wolagen,* etc. We can ask two things about these Yapese words: who are they and what is their relationship to each other? In the first description we can identify *citamangen* (*among others*) as "mother's husband," "father," "father's brothers," "father's male patriparallel cousins," and "father's sister's son" *if we choose to identify them in genealogical terms.* But as we have already seen *citamangen* can also be the person who provides another with food so that such a person must also be included "among others." In the terms of the first description, we can identify *citiningen* (*among others*) as the wives of *citamangen,* "mother," "mother's sister," as well as "father's sister" and her "daughter"; and *fak* (*among others*) is identified as the children of any of these. *Wolagen* are persons who are *fak* to the same *citamangen* of the same *citiningen* or both.

What is the relationship between *citamangen* and *fak?* It is a relationship of dependence, obedience, respect on the part of the *fak* for the *cit-*

amangen or the *citiningen*. The *citamangen* is superior, has authority, provides care and protection for the *fak,* and demands and expects respect and obedience from the *fak.*

I have put the phrase "among others" in italics to call attention to the fact that these terms include some whom anthropologists may or may not consider to be kinsmen. But by the translation of the first description I have offered, *citamangen* and *fak* are primarily "father" and "child," and by that translation these are kinship terms as well as terms for kinsmen. Therefore *we* have defined these as kinship relationships. So too, all members of the *tabinau* are related either as agnates or as wives; they are all relatives by consanguinity or affinity and therefore they are all kinsmen *by our anthropological definition.* This is the way in which the first description translates what the Yapese say and do.

According to the theory behind the first translation, it is not enough to simply say that the Yapese consolidate a collection of analytically differentiable functions into one unit called *tabinau:* these different functions bear a special relationship to each other. Function 1, kinship, is the idiom in terms of which all other functions are conceived, formulated, phrased, named, described, thought about, and talked about. Function 1, kinship, has a privileged place among the functions for it is the explicit "language" in terms of which the others are defined and conducted.

There is one thing about kinship which, it is said (for example, Barnes 1974b:477), distinguishes it and makes it ideal as a language in terms of which all sorts of functions and activities can be described. The simple presumptive biological relations of kinship as a system of relationships constitutes a kind of model, as well as a grammar and syntax, and provides an extraordinarily flexible yet standardized system of signs for other meanings. First, of course, there are the simple primitives themselves. There is parent-child, which can be broken down into father-son, father-daughter, mother-son, mother-daughter, and given sexual reproduction, father-mother are related as husband-wife. Thus the system is immediately given as two kinds of relationships, one of consanguinity and one of affinity. A son's wife's relationship to her husband's father might be counted as affinal where the son's wife's relationship to her own mother is consanguineal. Then, the relative products can be multiplied ad infinitum. This is hardly practical, so they are only multiplied as primary, secondary, tertiary, and quarternary relationships though they can go further. That is, there is father, mother, brother, sister, son, daughter, husband, and wife as primary relations, father's brother as a secondary relationship, father's brother's son as a tertiary relationship, father's brother's son's daughter as a quarternary. Given any such genealogical relationship the position of any other kinsman can immediately be established with respect to ego if the genealogical links are known or presumed.

Even if the genealogical grid is extended only to tertiary kin, the number of different relatives so distinguished is very large and cumbersome and we find that groups of them may be classed together in categories. Thus, for example, MZS, MZD, MBS, MBD, FZS, FZD, FBS, FBD are all classed as "cousin" in English kinship. The genealogical grid thus also allows for different kinds of classifications of the genealogical nodes or kin types.

Just as two broad kinds of relationship, consanguineal and affinal, can be distinguished from the genealogical grid, so too other kinds can be distinguished which in turn allow for the creation of both categories and groups. There is, for example, father's side of the genealogy versus mother's side. Then, all those relations which go through males, including but not going through females (agnatic relations), can be distinguished from all others, and out of these either a category of agnates can be defined for some social function, or they can be formed into a social group. Conversely, all relations which go through women, including but not going through males, can be distinguished either as a category or as a group as uterine or matrilineal relations.

Notice that I have repeated here the idea of the "relative product" or "web of kinship," but I have done so to a quite different end than before. The point was made in the previous chapter that kinship could be used to relate a wide network of persons into a single coherent system, to bring them together in such a way that each could establish a particular kind of relationship with any other person—as ego to FZD, or MMBDS for example. But here the point is that this same "relative product" system, the same "web of kinship" can constitute a code, a system of abstract signs to which meanings can be attached.

The fundamental point is that whatever the biologically putative relationship may be, the genealogical relationship can serve as a framework onto which any other meaning—relationship, activity, or function—can then be grafted. A father-son relationship can be one of fondness or distant respect, of authority and obedience, of competition; it can involve economic considerations or it need not; it can have religious functions or it need not; succession to land may be attached to it or it may not. The genealogy, that is, serves as an independent system of signs with its own rules for construction, and to it any or almost any constellation of functions or activities or meanings can be attached. So too, the sounds of a language can be grouped into words, and any (or almost any) meanings can be attached to those words and the rules for their combination. The genealogy has rules for the combination of the kin types of the system, and in this sense the genealogy or kinship constitutes a sort of grammar and syntax, while the different, specific genealogical relationships are the vocabulary. Thus kinship operates as a kind of language or, as Fortes would have it, an idiom.

Two crucial assumptions underlie the view of genealogy as a framework onto which other meanings can be grafted. The first is that there is indeed a socially recognized or culturally explicitly formulated system of kinship relations, defined specifically in the culture as a genealogical relationship based on real or putative biological bonds or their culturally defined equivalents (as adoption). I stress that the genealogical relationship must be culturally "recognized" or culturally constituted, for it is hard to see how it could serve as a language or idiom if it were not given clear cultural formulation. We believe that all mammals have real biological relationships which can be stated in genealogical form. But where such biological relationships are given no social or cultural value whatsoever, or are treated as irrelevant or nonexistent, or are not recognized to exist, it is hard to see how they could serve as a language of any sort. To press the analogy, it would be difficult to see how a language—by definition a meaningful system—could depend on sounds if no cultural value were given to the sounds and their differences: if sounds are not distinguished and put into relationship to each other as a culturally defined phonetic system, they are meaningless.

The second crucial assumption in this view is that if there is kinship, it must be kinship itself which in fact serves as the idiom or language. The mere presence of kinship does not necessarily mean that it serves as an idiom, or even the only idiom, in terms of which other relationships are expressed. A system of signs other than kinship could conceivably serve as the idiom or language, and the relations of kinship themselves could be expressed in that other form.

It is undeniable that relations arising out of human reproduction *can* indeed serve as the material out of which a system of relative products can be constructed, and that this system *can* conceivably act as idiom or language as well as a system in terms of which large numbers of persons or social categories can be placed in systematic relationship to each other. *But does it?*

The problem, which the conventional wisdom does not address directly, is this: is kinship "a way" of doing this job? Is kinship "the only way" of doing this job? Or is it just "the way it happens to be done, perhaps universally"? Or, to put the matter in another way, is kinship a privileged system?

One might argue that kinship is not the only conceivable way in which an idiom or language can be constructed which also serves as a system of relative products. For example, numbers are used and can easily be used to form a relative product code of this sort. Given a few simple rules of arithmetic and numbers up to four, five, or six, these can serve as well. One plus one equals two (father's father is a grandfather). One plus two equals three (father's grandfather is a greatgrandfather). Indeed, what has often been called "the language of mathematics" serves far more complex and involved functions than those which kinship are said to serve. And numbers and arithmetic are as "deeply rooted" in human life as is sexual reproduction. Perhaps (it might be said) numbers are too abstract: many peoples count only up to a very small number. Substitute any set of arbitrary signs, then, for the relative products that are given. A glurp, a glimph, a gloop, a grump, and a gragh are our fundamental units. A glurp and (or plus) glimp are related as a gragh. A gloomp is the product (the outcome perhaps) of a glurp and a glimp. A glurp's glurp is by definition a grump. And on we go into the wild blue. Surely man's imagination is not so constrained that if a code constructed so as to produce relative products is required, man could not have invented one—he has many times over.

If the argument is that kinship, defined as real or putative relationship through sexual reproduction, *can* serve as a code which provides relative products and *can* serve as an idiom or language, then there can be no dissent. It is an irrefutable statement. If the argument is that it is the only such code available to man, the argument fails if one can cite one other code which is possible and would suffice equally well. I think I have done just that: numbers, as in library call numbers, can serve as a code. If the argument is that kinship is the universal code in all human cultures, that remains to be demonstrated, if, indeed, it can be demonstrated. And if the argument is that kinship does often, if not always, serve as such a code, and that as such it is comparable from culture to culture, this is also an argument which needs demonstration. I am here raising the question as to whether it can be demonstrated.

Moreover, the full argument for the last two formulations has yet to be laid out. There are still a number of possible grounds on which it could be argued that kinship is in fact a privileged system, and we will pursue them in the following chapters.

There is one more formulation which merits recognition. That is the argument that takes "kinship" and "the family" as given and then finds that, since they exist, they serve these two functions—of idiom and web. (This seems to be Goodenough's 1970 position, but see below. This position is almost identical to that taken by Malinowski [1930a, 1932].) If kinship is to be taken as given, and the only question that can be asked is what its functions are, the problem that I am raising can be rephrased in this way; what is kinship? Can it be taken as given? Is it so clearly defined, so well demonstrated as a fact of human culture that it is identical wherever it appears? Is it indeed universal? These can be considered as reformulations of the question asked in the title to this chapter: is kinship a privileged system?

I will close this chapter by returning to the first description and the Yapese material once more. I will do so in order to raise in yet another way the question of whether kinship is a privileged system in Yap.

The theory behind the first translation says that of all of the different kinds of relations encompassed by the *citamangen-fak* relationship, the kinship relationship is privileged and serves as the language or idiom in terms of which the other relationships are constituted. That is, though the relationship between *citamangen* and *fak* is made up of a bundle of kinship, politics, economics, religion, etc., it is best described as a kinship relationship within which these other functions are subsumed and in terms of which these other relationships are constituted, thought of, spoken of, and proceed.

For Yap, as both descriptions suggest, it is land which is held in highest value. The relationship between *citamangen* and *fak* is one between those who hold land and those who, if they behave themselves, can gain the fruits of that land and under certain circumstances may have the right to succeed to the position of landholder. Their kinship relationship is, in this sense, encompassed in the idiom of land. Land is the rhetoric in terms of which political affairs are conceived, discussed, described, and transacted. Indeed, as we have seen, the Yapese go so far as to say that the land holds the status, while the landholder is merely its transient spokesman; land holds the rank, while its landholders merely act in accordance with that rank; "the land is chief, not the person." The Yapese go so far as to say that those who share equal rights in land are *wolagen,* and when two persons who were previously not related by land become joint holders of a parcel of land, they become *wolagen* for that very reason. Or when a man takes pity on another man (as happened during the war) and permits him to take food from a plot of land and to use that land, that other man becomes *fak* to the landholding *citamangen.* Further, if a *citamangen* is old and feeble and his *fak* shirks his obligation to care for him, anyone may arrange to be the old man's *fak* and assume that responsibility. The previous *fak* is no longer *fak,* and on the death of the old *citamangen* the genealogically unrelated *fak* becomes the holder of the old man's land. In this arrangement the *mafen* back up the claims of the new *fak,* condemning the original *fak* for his failure to care for the old man properly, and confirming the transmission of the title of landholder to the new *fak.*

The contention that there is some reason to treat kinship as a special, privileged system of relationships and to give it some priority *because* it is able to express other kinds of relationships holds equally well if not better for land on Yap (and for many other Oceanic societies as well). But such a view would accept the validity of the idea of "based" and merely substitute one "base" for another, still without justifying the whole notion of "base." Hence the purpose of the critique presented above is not to substitute one "base" for another, but rather to dramatically point to the fact that unless the idea of "base" is given a defensible rationale, it is empty to argue that Yap and Pul Eliya are either "kin-based" or "land-based" societies.

From the point of view of the analyst, it is clear that a bundle of different kinds of relationships is contained in the *citamangen-fak* relationship, and in all relationships within and between *tabinau.* What the Yapese say and do, and what the observer can see quite clearly is *tabinau*, inter- and intra-*tabinau* relations, relations between *citamangen* and *fak*, between *wolagen*, etc.

So the problem remains, and resolves itself into this simple question: How should the Yapese concepts of *tabinau, citamangen, fak, wolagen*, and so on, be translated? As I have said from the outset, the problem is to translate the field observations into a description. But that problem in turn depends on instructions for decoding, and it is these instructions that are at issue. Should the instructions include (as they do in the conventional wisdom) the specification that kinship is a privileged system, and that therefore the primary meanings given in translation must be kinship meanings?

7   *Tabinau*, Father-Child, and Patriliny: Is This Kinship?

The first description has the *tabinau* made up of a patrilineage and a patrilocal extended family. The second description contradicts this. Is patrilineal descent really involved in the *tabinau?* Men belong to only one *tabinau*, but women belong to the *tabinau* into which they are born as well as to the one into which they marry. Is this consistent with the interpretation of the *tabinau* as a descent unit? The second description gives a very different picture of the *citamangen-fak* relationship than the first. How does this bear on the first description's assertion that there is patrilineal descent? How is the *tabinau* to be understood? Do *tabinau* and *citamangen-fak* relations really involve kinship at all? These questions are closely interwoven, and in turn raise other questions. I will start with the problem of how the Yapese ethnography fits the conventional wisdom on descent and go on from there. It must be kept in mind that the central question of this chapter has to do with how to translate *tabinau* and *citamangen-fak* and whether these relations can be regarded as kinship relations, within the framework of the conventional wisdom of kinship theory. I begin with the problem of descent as a convenient way into this problem, but do not intend to deal with all of the problems of descent theory.

The conventional wisdom is that descent can be understood in either or both of two ways, sometimes modified by one further consideration. First, descent can be understood in terms of recruitment to a social unit or category as determined by birth or adoption through the parent of one sex or the other, through both, or through either. In the first instance, unilineal descent is the rule (through the father for patriliny, through the mother for matriliny; through both for double unilineal). In the last instance, the rule is non-unilineal. Second, descent can be understood in terms of the ideology that all members claim descent from a common ancestor or set of ancestors who are themselves closely related, regardless of how the relationship is traced, or even whether it is traced at all. All that is necessary is that descent is claimed from some ancestor, so that all who make such a claim with respect to some particular ancestor constitute a distinct culturally recognized category—members of the Bear Clan, for example. The modifier which is sometimes used before true descent is recognized by the analyst is that the resultant unit must be a corporate group. This modifier will not concern us here. But in either of the first two ways of understanding descent a unit is formed in which its members claim common descent. Whether descent is "real" or putative, including adoption, is of no theoretical relevance.

67

These two ways of treating descent have long and complex histories, some of which I will discuss in the next chapter. Treating descent as recruitment through a parent was the earliest formulation. When certain difficulties were encountered with that view, the second, ancestor-oriented view became prevalent but by no means universal. One of the more important difficulties that the first mode of defining descent led to was that the resultant unit (category or group) need not necessarily hold an ancestor in common. Members of the category may only have a kinsman in common or be related to each other by ties of kinship and without an overriding common bond as would result from their affirmation of common descent above and beyond the various particular bonds of kinship. If people are related only by the network of kinship ties but do not acknowledge descent from a common ancestor, then the ideology of *descent* is absent, even if kinship can be traced back to various ascendants. If, however, the members of a category or unit do claim common descent from an ancestor, then the fact that they may also be related by ties of kinship, which they may or may not be inclined to trace, is of no consequence for the question of descent. Members of a category or unit which claims common descent may not know or care about the particular kinship relations which may obtain among them. Carried a step further, although the ideology of descent might be agnatic, some or many members of the unit might trace their descent from the ancestor through uterine bonds, but this would be of no consequence as far as descent was concerned since membership is defined by the affirmation of agnatic connection to an ancestor. By the same token, if the ideology is that it did not matter through which parent or along which line descent from the ancestor is traced, even though the predominant mode of tracing might in fact be agnatic, the unit would still be a nonunilineal descent unit or category.

Mode of recruitment (through a parent) or ancestor orientation or corporate groupness are not mutually exclusive. An analyst may use one, two, or all three criteria, or any combination of them, and even fail to be clear as to which criteria are being used. For this reason, among many others, the literature on descent is quite chaotic.

The notion of "descent" itself is crucial. Here the literature containing the conventional wisdom is sparse and what little there is is vague and often contradictory. I think that this is because the notion of descent seemed self-evident to most writers until very recently. I will therefore state as simply as I can the presupposition on which I think most of that literature is based.

An ancestor is different from a predecessor or a founder. In America it is sometimes said that George Washington was the "father of his country." This does not mean that all Americans trace descent from George Washington. Few if any believe that George Washington begot those who begot those, etc., who, today, are living Americans. Neither did he give birth to them. A commercial enterprise may claim that it was founded at a certain time by a certain person, or perhaps a father and son or a group of siblings. This does not mean that everyone now in that establishment is a descendant of those founders. Descent implies that there is some real or putative connection through the links of procreation to an ancestor. There are situations when the term *descent* may be used in other ways. For example, one may trace the "descent" of certain ideas, philosophies, musical styles, and so forth by showing how each succeeded from some preceding form and was in turn the predecessor of another. But this sense of descent is usually excluded from anthropological usage. If however the idea or philosophy *gave rise to,* or generated its successor, then *descent* may be appropriate. In dealing with social organizational forms, as culturally constituted, descent is explicitly reserved to links of procreation or physical reproduction between a particular ancestral figure or figures and the living who claim such links as culturally significant.

Descent, then, assumes a particular kind of relationship as culturally significant which is different from that with a founder or predecessor, except, of course, where the founder or predecessor was also the procreator. The link is one of procreation or reproduction. In the most general terms, this involves begetting by a person, spirit, natural object, or anything whatsoever. Such objects may at times serve as emblems of the unit, but they are only ancestors if they have descendants, and descendants are those who are born of or begotten by the ancestors, and those who engendered those who are the present living members. The existence of an emblem does not in and of itself imply descent. Members of the Democratic Party in American politics do not claim descent from a donkey, affirmations to the contrary by their Republican opponents notwithstanding.

One further point. The phrase *common descent* is often used and its use is important. Where descent is traced from a single person or object, or a group of persons who are themselves related by close ties of kinship—siblings, parent(s) and children, for example—then all of their descendants will be related to each other both by ties of kinship (even when these are not, or cannot be traced) as well as by sharing descent from the same ancestor(s). Difficulty may arise when a set of unrelated founders constitute the ancestors of a particular group. For example, the Daughters of the American Revolution constitute a set of persons who claim descent from persons who had some part in the American Revolution. But since most of those who were in America at the time of the revolution were not related to each other by ties of consanguinity, their descendants are not related to each other by such ties either. Yet admission to the group or category is by descent. That is, if one's mother or father's mother was a member, and the tie to the particular ancestor can be affirmed, then one is by virtue of descent a member. But the members of the group are related to each other in a very different way than the members of a group who are all descended, for example, from Richard the Lion-Hearted. Thus, where *unrelated* founders are ancestors, members are not tied to each other by the bonds of kinship as well as descent, as they would be if they were descended from founders or ancestors who were kin to begin with. Whether groups like the Daughters of the American Revolution can be called proper descent groups is a nice question but not one that we need decide at this point.

We can now return to the first description. The problem raised by the dual membership of women is simply this; if a lineage is by definition a unit made up of persons of common descent counted unilineally, then given exogamy, a woman born into one patrilineage cannot become a member of another patrilineage by marriage. Therefore when the woman becomes a member of her husband's *tabinau* she is not becoming a member of it as a patrilineage. This follows from the definition of the patrilineage as a descent unit. She may be joining a patrilocal extended family or a compromise kin group in some way, or something else. But that is another matter. She cannot become a member of a descent unit by marriage.

There is a literature which speaks of the assimilation of a woman into the lineage of her husband; the loosening or severing of her bonds to her natal lineage and the strengthening of her bonds to her husband's lineage as she becomes assimilated to it (Freedman 1958; Fallers 1957). Insofar as this literature specifies that the woman's tie to her husband's lineage is an affinal bond and she cannot become a full-fledged member of her husband's lineage, this literature is perfectly correct. But if it is suggested or implied that she becomes a member of her husband's lineage, her position equal to that of any other member, then that literature misuses the term *lineage* and misconstrues the concept of descent: by definition a person cannot become a member of a descent unit by marriage but only by birth, adoption, or by affirming a tie to a common ancestor.

This point is of some significance. If we were to accept the view that a woman could belong to both the lineage into which she was born and the lineage into which she married, then there would be no reason to regard the *tabinau* as anything but a patrilineage. But it is precisely because a descent unit, by definition as an analytic construct, can only be made up of members by birth, adoption, or descent from a common ancestor, and the *tabinau* includes women who are members by marriage, that the first description cannot describe the *tabinau* as a descent unit. Its constituent parts must be distinguished. One is a patrilineage, the other is a patrilocal extended family.

This solution keeps the notion of descent intact, but in the process raises another question. How much should we concern ourselves with the fact that the Yapese define one cultural unit, while we analyze this as two units, thus creating distinctions which Yapese culture does not recognize, while ignoring distinctions which Yapese culture insists on. The first description thus departs importantly from what the Yapese say and do, that is, from Yapese formulations of their own cultural units.

One might argue that the importance of this point lies in the distinction between description and analysis. The description must depict the *tabinau* as a single cultural and social unit; the analysis must break this down into its component parts. If, however, we try to introduce a distinction between description and analysis, we repudiate the very first premise on which this whole discussion is based: description *is* analysis in the sense that it depends on the observation of existential materials within the context of, and in terms of, a particular theoretical scheme of greater or lesser specificity and of greater or lesser explicitness and precision.

We cannot evade this problem by assuming it possible to produce an accurate, theoretically uncontaminated description of the facts as they objectively are. What has happened in this translation (the first description) is that we have, for theoretically unstated reasons, set aside as irrelevant the Yapese formulation of *tabinau* as a single cultural unit and chosen as theoretically relevant the view of *tabinau* as two differently structured units.

I return to the problem of descent. Thus far I have discussed it primarily in terms of recruitment (though much remains to be said about that yet). Consider now the second way of defining descent, that is, as an ancestor-oriented unit. Is the *tabinau* a patrilineage by virtue of the fact that its members claim descent from a particular ancestor or group of closely related ancestors? The first description says that the *thagith* are ancestral ghosts. If that is so, then the present, living members of the *tabinau* do indeed trace their descent from these ancestral figures, and therefore meet the criterion of being an ancestor-oriented unit.

But are the *thagith* ancestral ghosts? In order to be sure that we have translated that term correctly we must know how the relationship between the people who became ghosts and the living members of the *tabinau* is defined. Are the ghosts founders, antecedents, or are they ancestral in the sense that the living members are their descendants? *Thagith*, the first description says, include *citamangen* as well as *citiningen*. I will confine myself to the *citamangen-fak* relationship here and take up the *citiningen-fak* relationship in the next chapter.

The answer to the question of how the *citimangen-fak* relationship is to be understood will illuminate the question of whether the *thagith* are ancestors so far as *citamangen* are concerned. This in turn will clarify the question of whether the *tabinau* can be regarded as an ancestor-oriented unit. But at the same time it will open up the whole question of whether the term *citamangen* can properly be translated as "father," and this in turn will bear on the question of whether *tabinau* relations in general and *citamangen-fak* relations in particular can be considered to be kinship relations.

It should be noted that so far as descent is concerned, the criterion of recruitment and that of ancestor orientation merge to some extent in the question of how the *citamangen-fak* relationship is culturally defined.

I turn now to the problem of the *citamangen-fak* relationship for the light it will cast not only on the problem of whether there is patrilineal descent in Yapese culture, but also for the main point, that is, whether this relationship can be understood as a kinship relationship in any sense.

Leaving aside these *citamangen* and *fak* who are outside the *tabinau*, the second description pictures the relationship between the two as a relationship with regard to land which entails norms and obligations of a special kind of interpersonal relationship. The *citamangen* is a landholder, *fak* the person whose *citiningen's* work on *tabinau* land earns him the right to maintain a relationship of dependence, obedience, respect, and propriety, to take good care of the *citamangen* during the latter's old age, and then be given the land which the *citamangen* holds. If however at any time *fak* fails to behave properly (as defined above) then the *citamangen* can terminate any use rights or any other claims on the land and the *fak* can be "thrown away," the relationship terminated. Or the *mafen* can intercede and as "guardians of the land" do the same. Normally the *mafen* would only act if the *citamangen* were incompetent or dead.

The crucial point is this: in the relationship between *citamangen* and *fak* the stress in the definition of the relationship is more on *doing* than on *being*. That is, it is more what the *citamangen* does for *fak* and what *fak* does for *citamangen* that makes or constitutes the relationship. This is demonstrated, first, in the ability to terminate absolutely the relationship where there is a failure in the doing, when the *fak* fails to do what he is supposed to; and second, in the reversal of terms so that the old, dependent man becomes *fak*, to the young man, *tam*.

The European and the anthropological notion of consanguinity, of blood relationship and descent, rests on precisely the opposite kind of value. It rests more on the state of *being*, on the sharing of certain inherent and therefore inalienable attributes, on the biogenetic relationship which is represented by one or another variant of the symbol of "blood" (consanguinity), or on "birth," on qualities rather than on performance. We have tried to impose this definition of a kind of relation on all peoples, insisting that kinship consists in relations of consanguinity and that kinship as consanguinity is a universal condition. The genealogical grid of consanguineal relations is regarded as a universal statement of relations of substance, more generally, of *being*, of inherent quality, while performance, forms of doing, various codes for conduct, different roles, are seen as variables, secondary, attached as different possible meanings to the fundamental set of signs which the genealogical grid, as relations of being or substance, represent.

In 1947-48 I was told by Yapese that coitus had no role in conception.

Twenty or so years later Labby's informants gave coitus a role in conception. But the same cultural definition of the relationship between *citamangen* and *fak* obtained during both periods; authority, control over land and land-based resources (statuses and rank), the *citamangen* entitled to respect and obedience while the *fak* was dependent and his position as *fak* was insured by his respectful obedience and dependency.

The new conception of conception which had become established by the late 1960s and early 1970s is that the man plants the seed in the woman and the woman is like a garden. The planting of the seed by the man is defined as *magar,* work, and the woman as the garden protects and provides for the seed. The seed grows and becomes a human being. But that is not all. The spirit *marialang* controls this process just as it always did, and the process of conception cannot take place without that spirit's approval and active help. The approval and cooperation is obtained by the intervention of the *thagith,* the spirits of the dead of the husband's *tabinau.* The *thagith* will only accede to the prayers if the *thagith* feels that the woman deserves to have a child. That is, only if a woman has acted as a good woman, done her work well, and behaved according to the proper standards for a wife will the *thagith* take the necessary steps to intercede with *marialang.* The child is given to the woman as a reward for her goodness.

The introduction of the acknowledgment of the role of coitus in conception has changed nothing; it is the *doing* of the male and the *doing* of *marialang* and the active intervention of the *thagith,* the care and protection of the seed by the woman and the *performance* of the woman as a good woman which produces the child. This is all *magar, work.*

So far as the *citamangen-fak* relationship is concerned, then, even when coitus is recognized as a factor in conception it is not taken to "mean" anything radically new or different; it has not changed anything. It is simply not culturally significant. And most important, it has not introduced the idea of biogenetic attributes or shared substance. That is, even with the idea that coitus plays a role in conception, the Yapese definition of the relationship between *citamangen* and *fak* remains radically different from the European cultural conception of reproduction. It is also radically different from the scientific conception of kinship which is, obviously, almost the same as the European cultural conception of kinship. (For further detail on the relation of coitus and conception in Yapese culture see Schneider 1968.)

Here then is the crux of one difference between the two descriptions. In the first, it was reported that *citamangen* and *fak* were father and child, and therefore a relationship of agnation obtained between them. Thus the series father and father's sister, father's father and his sister, father's father's father and his sister, and in descending generations, son and daughter, son's son and his sister, etc., constituted a part of a patrilineage (the other parts being all other agnates such as father's brother, father's father's brother, etc.). In this description the translation of *citamangen* as "father" rests entirely on the presumption that a state of being, a consanguineal relation exists between him and his *fak*. That this presumption is erroneous emerges from a consideration of the facts which appear in both the first and second descriptions, but which are stressed in the second description and discussed in detail above.

If the relationship between *citamangen* and *fak* is in no sense a consanguineal relationship then it is equally not an element in any relationship of agnation and there are no agnatic relations in the *tabinau*. If there are no agnatic relations in the *tabinau* then there can be no patrilineal descent or a patrilineage in the *tabinau*.

Now, all of this depends on the specific conceptions embodied in Yapese culture. We may look at it from outside and say that we don't care much what the Yapese say or how they mystify the relationship between *citamangen* and *fak* because we know perfectly well that there is in fact, whether they know it or not, whether they like it or not, a biological relationship between them, and that an agnatic core can be perceived to be in fact embedded in the *tabinau*.

There is another way of cutting through the cultural conceptions of the Yapese and going straight to the heart of the matter. If we follow Malinowski (1913) and Goodenough (1970) among others and define the father as mother's husband, then the matter is resolved neatly. All of the complications which have been raised from the point of view of Yapese ideology become irrelevant. Is the *citamangen* married to the *citiningen* or not? If he is the *citiningen*'s lawfully wedded husband, then he is, by Malinowski's and Goodenough's definition, the "father" and there are no buts, ifs, or maybes about it. The burden of the question then turns on the definition of marriage, of course, but for the purposes of this discussion we can accept that certain *citamangen* and *citiningen* are married to each other, or were at the time of the child's conception and birth, even if they were not before or are not later.

I do not mean to imply that Malinowski or Goodenough have imposed an arbitrary definition on us or that they have acted capriciously. Quite the contrary. Their position is reasoned and, as we will see later, there are grounds for arriving at this definition. Be that as it may, the result is that a considerable body of the conceptions, formulations, and constructs of Yapese culture which I have just reviewed become irrelevant to answering the question of whether *citamangen* is father, whether there are agnatic relationships or whether the *citamangen-fak* relationship is one of kinship.

But if we take such a position where is it to stop? At what point does native ideology and native constructs cease to have any significance for our attempts to understand or analyze the culture? This simply raises the point of what it is we are setting out to understand and analyze. Are we aiming to understand and analyze Yapese culture? If Yapese culture consists in *their* constructs, *their* formulations, *their* mystifications, *their* conception of conception, *their* groups and how *they* structure them, then we must abide by that aim. This is certainly my aim and the only aim that I regard as legitimate in anthropology. This does not mean that the problem is one concerning only their conscious ideology, precisely formulated and clearly articulated into an explicit whole. By the same token, it is not a problem of a structure of which they are either not conscious or cannot in the nature of the case be conscious. Neither of these particular problems are at issue here. The native conceptions, formulations, and definitions must be comprehended by the observer; they do form an ideology as a whole but not necessarily a perfectly logical or precisely articulated one. But at the other extreme, to formulate a structure wholly without reference to their understandings, formulations, and conceptions is certainly not the task either.

Another major difference between the two descriptions follows immediately from this one. The first description assumed that the rights of the *fak* in the *citamangen*'s land and so forth were rights based on their kinship or genealogical connection. But from the second description we learned that this was not the case at all. The right to stand first in line to succeed to the headship of the *tabinau,* and the right to play the proper role of *fak,* is earned by one's *citiningen*'s work for the *tabinau* and this right must be reaffirmed continually on the part of both the *citiningen* and the *fak. Fak* must continually exhibit obedience and respect, and must repay that dependency by caring for the aged *citamangen* when the latter is old and dependent.

To put it in another way, which many Yapese articulate explicitly, the position of *fak* is one which entails *constant exchange over a period of time;* the *citamangen* gives the material and other requisites to the *fak* and in return *fak* exchanges obedience, respect, and work, and eventually *citamangen* gives the ownership of the land.

This is the way in which the Yapese themselves phrase and speak of the relationship; this is the way in which they formulate the relationship. We can see that the relationship is more one of *doing* than of *being.* It is based largely on the interaction, the doing, of the exchange and less on the state of being, of having some substance, quality, or attribute.

So it is not only difficult to see how the *tabinau* can be regarded as a patrilineage, it is even more difficult to see how the relationship between *citamangen* and *fak* can be regarded as a kinship relationship. And if this is so then succession is not in any sense a function of kinship, and land relationships themselves are quite sharply distinguished from kinship relations. Kinship cannot be regarded as the "base" of Yapese society, nor as the idiom in terms of which land or any other relations between *tabinau* members are formulated.

This whole discussion has been biased by being put largely in terms of the problem of *tabinau* membership. That is, I opened the chapter by posing the problem of the constitution of the *tabinau* and asking whether it could be regarded as containing a patrilineal descent unit. I tried to show that by either of the two criteria for establishing a patrilineal descent unit—recruitment through the father or orientation to an ancestor or ancestors through agnatic links—the *tabinau* did not contain a patrilineal descent unit or patrilineage. But the implicit premise on which the whole question of descent or patrilocal extended family was based, and which biased the first description, is the notion that social structure consists of groups, their formal structural constitution and functional interrelationships. The rules governing group membership—be they the rules of descent or of residence or whatever—are therefore fundamental to such a view of social structure.

If the problem of groups and group membership is set aside, however, and we do not look at the Yapese data through this lens, the problem of the woman's relationship to the *tabinau* of her birth and marriage, as an instance of a class of problems, takes on a different complexion.

The Yapese say that a man "belongs to" his *tabinau,* or a woman "belongs to" or is "of" a *tabinau.* There are other ways of formulating this connection but as has already been indicated the fundamental premise of Yapese culture is that people belong to the land and not, as European culture has it, that land belongs to people.

Hence, the question in describing the Yapese *tabinau* must be one of who "belongs to" what land. Put this way, a man belongs to the land which is a particular *tabinau* and the landholder speaking on behalf of that land says that that man may take food and other resources from certain plots. By virtue of their common relationship to the same plots—one as landholder and one as land user, one as authority and one as dependent, and so forth—they are considered *nga tabinau* or *gidi ko tabinau,* that is, "of a *tabinau*" or "people of a *tabinau.*"

Who is allocated such rights in land? Who is held by the land? It does not depend first on being the *fak* to the particular *citamangen* who is the landholder. As had been said above, in the first instance a woman goes to live with a man and by virtue of sharing food with him, having sexual relations with him, and later on having a ceremony, becomes his wife. As his wife she works *tabinau* land. If he is the landholder she works land to which he belongs. If he is not the landholder she works land which he has been given to use by the landholder. By virtue of her work on the land, she earns the right for her children to also belong to certain plots of that land.

Further, his rights are claimed by the fact that he is "formed" by the *tabinau.* He has a name which belongs to the land and which, by being bestowed on him, ties him to that land; his very existence as well as his continued existence is at the pleasure of the *thagith*. Recall that an elder who gives a child a name of a *tabinau* different from that of his *citiningen* and *citamangen* thereby establishes that child's rights in the *tabinau* to which his name belongs.

Those who are attached to a single estate, made up of various plots of land dispersed throughout the village, are *nga tabinau* or *gidi ko tabinau*. Thus in the Yapese definition of the situation, membership in the *tabinau* as a group derives directly and only from common rights in the land.

To say that a woman has dual membership is not pertinent since group membership is not the significant issue in Yapese culture. As has been shown, *tabinau* means, in one of its senses, a connection or link between people through land, a relationship which is quite different from that of group membership. That is, people of *tabinau* may not form a group but only be linked together, one to another and then to another by their links to land thereby distinguishing them from those not so linked.

Further, a woman never loses her attachment to the land (*tabinau*) of her birth, but she can gain attachment to land (*tabinau*) by her marriage. If her marriage terminates without children she loses that attachment completely. If the marriage terminates after children have been born she retains ties to the land through her children, but not through her marriage.

The problem created by a woman's dual membership which required seeing *tabinau* as not one but two kin groups thus arises entirely as a consequence of the presupposition that what is at issue is group membership, group composition, and the rules governing recruitment to groups, all because social structure is conceived of as a structure of groups. But these are not the relevant conceptions of Yapese culture; they are the mystifications and distortions introduced by one theory through which Yap culture can be observed and described. But they shortcut that description by jumping immediately to the analytic level of groups without first going through the step of finding out how Yap culture is constructed.

As I have been suggesting all along, practically the whole of the first description is indicted on this ground alone. Instead of asking how Yap culture is formulated, what units it is composed of, how those units are defined and differentiated, what construction of reality and of how the world exists in Yapese culture, the first description sets up a series of a priori categories held to be analytically relevant and then attempts to fit them to the Yapese formulations. I have already raised the question of whether the *tabinau* contains a patrilineage, as that unit is analytically defined. What about the other group which *tabinau* is supposed to be composed of, according to the first description, the patrilocal extended family?

One problem with the analytic notion of a patrilocal extended family is that it is by no means clearly defined as an analytic construct in the first place.

Does the patrilocal extended family imply that its members are kin? If this is so, and if I am correct in suggesting that the relationship between *citamangen* and *fak* may not properly be translated as "father" and "child," and is indeed not even a kinship relationship according to certain definitions of that term, then on this technical ground alone there may be no patrilocal extended family. Does patrilocal extended family center on a coresidential group, a unit which dwells together, sharing the same dwelling or the same hearth or closely adjacent quarters? Then it is doubtful if *tabinau* can be a patrilocal extended family since there is no common dwelling and no common hearth. Indeed, the idea of a common hearth is itself an anathema on Yap since the food, the plots from which it is taken, the pots in which it is cooked, and the fire over which it is cooked must be different for a woman and her children from those of her husband, as well as different for old men and old women. Is a patrilocal extended family simply one in which people associated as related in some way live dispersed in different dwellings in different parts of the village? This is an unusual definition of a patrilocal extended family, if it is accepted by anyone at all. But if that is a patrilocal extended family then perhaps *tabinau* might be held to contain such a unit. But surely such a statement is at best trivial. It not only hardly exhausts what needs to be said, it leaves all that is culturally significant unsaid. Indeed, a woman moves from land of her *tabinau* to land of her husband's *tabinau* when she marries. This is not trivial. But its importance does not lie in who is associated by proximity or propinquity, as is implied by the analytic construct of the extended family. Its significance has to do with relations of *genung* to land through the relationship of the *genung* of the husband to the *genung* of the wife and then to her children.

8 *Genung,* Mother-Child, and Matriliny: Is This Kinship?

If there is some doubt whether the *citamangen-fak* relationship as it is defined in Yap culture fits the definition of a kinship relationship, there seems to be little doubt that the *citiningen-fak* relationship does. The *fak* is explicitly described as coming from the belly of its *citiningen.* *Wolagen* who come from the same belly are described by Yapese as different from *wolagen* who share the same *citamangen* but different *citiningen.* It is important to recall that having a child is not simply a matter of its coming from a belly. The spirit *marialang* and the ghosts of dead *tabinau* members, the *thagith,* play a crucial role, and only for the woman who by her actions deserves such a reward. Further, the child is formed as a person by *tabinau* name, etc. But coming from the same belly remains explicit in the cultural conception as something which entails special bonds of warmth, love, loyalty, respect, trust, and mutual help. For example, the adopted child is not told by its adopting *citamangen* or *citiningen* that it is adopted. This information is given the child as an act of cruelty by its peers. Furthermore, the child never loses its relationship to the *citiningen* whose belly it came from. Children may be given to others to raise or may be adopted, but the bond with the woman who gave them birth remains either as an important informal one or, in fosterage, as a formal one as well. Further, if the child is adopted by someone of a different *genung,* it not only assumes the *genung* affiliation of its adopter, but retains the *genung* identity and restrictions of the woman whose belly it came from. However, if a girl is adopted, she will transmit to her offspring only the *genung* affiliation and restrictions of her adopter.

Citiningen-fak are thus at once mother-child and persons of the same *genung,* since the *genung* affiliation of the *fak* is the same as the *genung* affiliation of the *citiningen.*

Where rank, hierarchy, and complex exchanges pervade *tabinau* and almost everything else in Yap culture, the stress in *citiningen-fak* and *genung* relations is on equality, sharing, trust, and mutual assistance. Persons of the same *genung* are *wolagen* and some may also be *citiningen-fak* or *wa'engen* to each other. *Wa'engen* may be translated roughly as mother's brother-sister's child, and consistent with the self-reciprocal nature of the term, their relationship is described as "like *wolagen.*" As has been noted, in certain contexts the mother's brother may also be described as *matam ko genung.* The use of the term *matam* here is, of course, quite inconsistent with the implications of the English word *father* as genitor. Rather, it suggests guardian, to care for, protect, watch over the welfare of, all of which are some of the meanings of *tam* and *citamangen*.

One final point. One's *genung* is not a subject for open discussion and is, in fact, kept secret insofar as this is possible. Certainly a mother informs her child of its *genung* and the prohibitions and other restrictions and obligations which such affiliation entails. Certainly a man and woman must know their *genung* if they are to marry without breaking the rule of *genung* exogamy. That a woman and her children are of the same *genung* is self-evident to everyone, but what that *genung* is—whether porpoise, rat, fungus, a particular spirit—is not subject for open talk and is often not known by others.

Surely, then, the *citiningen-fak* relationship and certain relationships of *genung* are kinship relationships in the traditional sense. *Citiningen* can perhaps be translated as "mother," for by Yap definition she may be the woman who bore the child or who stands for the woman who bore the child as its adopter (though there are other *citiningen* as well). The *fak* is her offspring, no matter how much the *tabinau* ghosts, *thagith,* may be involved with the spirit, *marialang,* in assuring the woman's pregnancy. The relationship between the *citiningen* who bore the child and *fak* is, by Yap definition, what could be called in English "biological" or "reproductive" in that it entails a commonality based on the body.

Although the relationship between woman and child is conceived of in Yap culture as at least in part biological, the notion of genetrix is not quite accurate. Western cultural constructs of kinship depend heavily not merely on the notion of biological relatedness, but also on the notion of creation, of responsibility for another's being, which is entailed in the idea of genitor and genetrix. God the father, the priest as father, Mary mother of God, and so forth, are all very closely involved with ordinary fatherhood and motherhood in European culture. This association is simply not possible where Yapese beliefs are concerned, even if the seed-in-the-garden image which Labby describes is considered. For European culture, in this respect, the view is that the seed is fertilized and nature takes care of the rest; it grows into a child. The Yapese view is that the seed or work by themselves are far less than the whole story, and not even the crucial part of it.

If we accept the idea of kinship, the kin-based society, the idiom of kinship and that kinship may or may not have some content, and turn back to our descriptions of Yap culture, a somewhat peculiar picture emerges.

The first description presents a very expectable, easily understood picture of a society in which double descent provides two complementary descent units, one deeply rooted in land, one free of land, one deeply rooted in hierarchy and rank and exchange, the other predicated on equality and sharing; a society which is practically kin-based and in which kinship is the idiom in terms of which political, jural, economic, ritual, and religious activities are phrased. I have tried to show, for point after point, that this picture just does not hold, for it is internally inconsistent and is based on demonstrably false assumptions. Close inspection of the constructs of Yapese culture suggests that there may be no double descent because the unit that was supposed to be a patrilineage is probably not a patrilineage as that is traditionally defined. The relationship of *citamangen-fak* did not conform to the traditional definition of a father-child or a kinship relationship by one definition, but did by the father equals mother's husband definition. There is no father-child relationship unless one accepts the argument that a man is a father by virtue of his being the mother's husband at the time she becomes pregnant. And since there may not be a father-child relationship, or any agnatic relatives or cognatic kin who can be traced through males, there may not be an ego-centered kindred in the traditional sense of that term, but only a set of matrilateral kin.

If there is descent, it is matrilineal. If there is kinship it consists in those *citiningen-fak* where the two are biologically linked or are treated as such by extension. Whether one considers descent as the use of a genealogical tie to recruit members or as an ancestor-oriented group, then the *genung* is a descent group.

If we have found kinship at last in Yapese culture, it is a problematic system but by no means unfamiliar. In important respects it is like the Trobriand and some Australian systems. But this is a picture which, as I have reported it, some anthropologists might find hard to accept.

I must once again address the problem of descent and whether Yap has double descent.

The distinction between descent and kinship which is made today starts with the fact that the terms were at first often used interchangeably. Writers in the mid- and late nineteenth century (and into the early twentieth century in some cases) often spoke of "kinship being traced through the father but not the mother" for patriliny and "kinship traced through the mother only" for matriliny. Some then took the next step of asserting that where kinship was traced through one parent but not the other, the child was not related by kinship to that other parent. For example, in matriliny, if kinship was traced through the mother, then the father and the father's sister were said not to be related by kinship to ego.

Rivers was the most vocal in attacking this formulation, arguing that if ego was a member of his father's patrilineal clan and took his father's totems he was nevertheless still related to his mother and his mother's brother by ties of kinship. Thus in a number of places (1907b, 1910a, 1915) Rivers goes to some length to clarify this distinction. For example, in a review of Thomas's *Kinship Organizations and Group Marriage in Australia,* Rivers says:

While on the subject of definitions I should like to express my dissatis-faction with Mr. Thomas's use of the term 'kinship', which he limits, though not quite consistently, to the relationship set up by common membership of a social group. In its ordinary use kin implies blood-relationship, and it seems to me a misfortune to apply it to such a relationship as that set up by the common possession of a totem. A very important problem in sociology arises out of the relations between the bonds set up by common membership of a social group and those dependent on community of blood and the discussion of this problem will not be facilitated by using for the second kind of bond a term which should properly denote one of the first kind. (Rivers 1907b:91)

For Rivers, where kinship was always traced through both the father and mother (and hence it was always a blood relationship, or community of blood, and so also was always bilateral), descent had to do with the assignment to the social group of the mother or of the father and hence must always be unilineal. By "social group" Rivers meant clans, moieties, totemic groups and what are now called lineages, though he did not use that term. But the rule of recruit-ment to the social group through one but not the other parent was to be distinguished from the tracing of genealogical ties through both the father and the mother and out through them. The first was descent, the second kinship.

In separating descent from kinship, Rivers implies that totemic groups, clans, moieties, and the like are not kin groups. His contrast between "the bonds set up by common membership of a social group and those dependent on a community of blood" makes this quite clear. Note that "*community* of blood" and "*common* membership" yield the same kind of linkage, while the genealogically *differentiated* network of kinship and *common* membership do not. Thus in the contrast/opposition between "community of blood" and "common membership," the first element of each, *commonality,* remains the same while the second element, blood and membership, differs. Rivers might have drawn the contrast differently. He might have contrasted common mem-bership with a network of differentiated ties which diminish in strength as genealogical distance increases. In the first, each member is equally tied to every other member. In the second, each member is differently tied to all other members, each tie depending both on the kind of tie (collateral, genera-tion, sex, etc.) and the genealogical distance between ego and alter. But he did not do this.

Let me pursue this point one step further. Where a descent group is culturally defined as a group which explicitly depends (in precisely Rivers's terms) on a "community of blood" or something very similar, and where kinship relations are culturally defined in those same terms, any distinction between kinship and descent must rest on some other feature. For example, one may distinguish between community or commonality and a network of differentiated ties. But the *kind* of tie remains the same in both cases. In such cases, then, kinship and descent are precisely the same in this particular respect, however much they may differ in some other respect.

As I have pointed out above, this is the case for Yapese culture. One kind of tie between certain *citiningen* and *fak* is that one comes from the belly of the other, and the tie between members of the same *genung* derives from the belly of the founding ancestress. Both of these would fall under Rivers's term *community of blood.* Hence in this particular respect Yapese culture does not distinguish between clanship and kinship: both are defined as one kind of relationship, the *genung* relationship, and both are made out of the same material. Whether they form different kinds of structures, one an ancestor-oriented pool of coequals and the other an ego-centered network of unequals, is a different question. Certainly it is an important question, but it should not be confounded with this one.

But Rivers's other question remains, that is, his point that kinship may be distinguished from descent, although the particular ground on which that distinction is made needs clarification.

Two other points can be made about the distinction between kinship and descent. First, if kinship is a network of genealogical relations which distinguishes categories and kinds of kin and thus different kinds of relations, descent has to do with common membership in an ancestor-oriented group or category, where membership depends on a link to a parent who is a member of that group (through the father or through the mother at least). Thus a culture can have a kinship system without descent or it can have a kinship system plus descent groups. Every society presumably has kinship, but only some have descent as well. This would not be the case where both kinship and descent were limited, for example, to ''the tracing of ties through the mother but not through the father.'' In Yapese culture it seems that there is both descent (the matrilineal clan) and kinship (ignoring the problem of the father for the moment).

Second, Goodenough (1955) first pointed out that certain structures were clearly ancestor-oriented, so that membership in the group, unit, or category is established with reference to a relationship to an ancestor. This is a descent group. Conversely,

If a society is to order social relations among its members by reference to presumed relations of genealogical connection . . . [one of these ways] is egocentrically, by focusing on each person individually and subdividing the totality of persons considered to be genealogically connected to him (his kindred) into a number of lesser categories—categories of kin. (Scheffler 1974:756)

Rivers (1924) had held, and Fortes (1945) and Murdock (1940) among others followed him in this, that in the nature of the case, descent must be unilineal while kinship was necessarily bilateral. His reasoning here was that kinship was traced through both the father and the mother (hence, bilateral), while descent, since it was a form of affiliation with a social group through either one parent or the other, must be either matrilineal or patrilineal. Even double descent fitted this conception, as was clear from Murdock (1940), for in each case the group was defined unilineally.

Goodenough's distinction between ancestor orientation and ego orientation, however, permitted the possibility of nonunilineal descent, that is, affiliation with a group defined with reference to an ancestor where the links to that ancestor could be traced from child to parent to grandparent, etc., regardless of the sex of the ascendant or the parent through whom the link was established. Nonunilineal descent groups could not exist with Rivers's or Fortes's formulation.

To compound the complications further, Fortes introduced the notion of filiation, the idea being that a child-parent link which was not extended to an ultimate ancestor or ancestress should be distinguished from one which did. Thus a claim based on the fact that one was the child of one's parent should be distinguished from recruitment to a descent group through one or the other parent. But this notion was seen by some as problematic: descent, especially in a group like a lineage where links to a presumably real ancestor were genealogically traceable, could easily be interpretable as what was called "cumulative filiation." The question arose as to how this was different from descent.

I do not mean to exhaust the matter of descent here, for much of it is not relevant to the major problems of this book except in one tangential, though interesting way. I have spoken glibly of "the conventional wisdom" and "current theory" and as if there was a sort of body of generally, if not universally, agreed-on notions surrounding kinship. The problem of descent shows immediately that such is not the case where descent is concerned. Instead, a state of chaos prevails, as demonstrated by literature on descent in the New Guinea highlands. Further, in considering descent on Yap and double descent in general, it is important to note that this is one of the most confused and contradictory areas in the kinship literature at this time, despite the fact that Fortes (1959b, 1969), Scheffler (1974), Goodenough (1970), and others feel that they have made the matter perfectly clear.

Two more points bear directly on the problem of descent on Yap. Radcliffe-Brown ([1924] 1952) and especially Fortes (1945) and Fortes and Evans-Pritchard (1940), among others, introduced a functional dimension into the descent-kinship distinction. They argued that descent units created politico-jural units while kinship created domestic, or domestic and economic, units. The idea that the clan is a political and jural unit goes back at least to Maine (1861), Fustel de Coulanges (1864), and Morgan (1877: pt. 2; 1901). Morgan uses the term *gens* instead of clan, which he takes from the Roman and Greek material where it is unquestionably a political unit. (W. Robertson Smith's 1885 description of the lineage in early Semitic culture was an important influence too.) Radcliffe-Brown followed Maine and Morgan and said that primitive societies of the simpler kind required unilineal descent to provide distinct segments which had political and jural functions and were capable of holding, using, and transmitting property and thus providing for social order within the whole tribe (1952:32–48). A tribe was made up of segments defined by rules of unilineal descent. Thus descent was seen by Fortes (1945), Evans-Pritchard (1940), Radcliffe-Brown (1952), and those who followed them as essentially politico-jural in function, while kinship, being always bilateral, gives order to the domestic sphere. Kinship is the domestic system, descent the politico-jural system. Hence the two are quite different both in rules of recruitment and function.

The distinction between descent and kinship also turns on the premise that relations of descent rest on the identity of members. That is, all members of a descent unit are equally related to the ancestor or ancestress and to each other. But kinship ties are ego-oriented and differentiated. They also diminish with distance from ego, so that, for example, a mother is closer to her daughter than to her daughter's daughter and closer to her daughter's daughter than to the daughter's daughter's daughter. Similarly, the divergence of collateral lines yields degrees of distance. And distance is the metaphor for the degree to which there is a sharing of identity where it is defined as of a biological sort; primary relatives share more than secondary relatives, secondary relatives share more than tertiary relatives, etc. The diminution is, of course, a consequence of the infusion of new and different "blood" through marriage outside the line. If incest were permitted and consistently practiced, in principle at least, kinship and descent would be indistinguishable in this regard. (See, for example, Fortes 1969:172 on this point.)

Now consider the problem of descent on Yap. First, is the *tabinau* a descent group, or does it contain a descent group? Second, what about *genung?*

The *tabinau,* as I have shown, cannot itself be a descent group by any definition that I am acquainted with on the following grounds. First, women gain membership in it by marriage. For this reason at least, their relationship to all other members is through affinity and not that of consanguinity or parent-child-sibling. That is, they cannot (and do not) claim descent from or even filiation with other members of the *tabinau* of senior generations. Second, although the *thagith* might by stretching the point be regarded as ancestral spirits or ghosts, and each *tabinau* has a pool of names which earlier members of the *tabinau* held, it is difficult to see the *tabinau* as an ancestor-oriented group. Though it may cite the deeds of one or another ancestor and its history may make claim to certain predecessors from whom certain lands, statuses or honors derive, it does not have a founder or even founders in the usual sense of this term. Its definition is an estate to which people are attached. Third, the membership of the child derives from the mother. The child's rights in the estate (and hence membership in the group which is held by the estate) derive from his mother's work for the *tabinau*, her diligence and proper behavior toward her husband's parents and, as the child grows older, from the child's respect for and obedience to his mother's husband. The child can be "thrown away" at any time by the mother's husband or at his death by being disinherited or later, in extreme situations, by the mother's husband's sister(s) and her (their) children (the *mafen*) for improper behavior. Therefore in no simple sense can it be said that the child becomes a member of the group by virtue of being the child of his mother's husband or his father. Even if we interpret the name giving and so on as confirming his entry into the *tabinau*, his continued membership depends more on doing than on being. On the other hand, being a member of a descent group is defined in terms of being: affiliation is normally automatic, and though one may lose that affiliation, it takes an act of grave offense to be disaffiliated. But so far as the *tabinau* is concerned, it takes the constant doing of the right things—respect and obedience—to remain affiliated.

There is an easy way out of this. We can assert that our purpose is only to analyze the situation in scientific terms suitable for comparative purposes. Thus although we may have great respect for the ideology and the cultural constructs of the Yapese, we can still choose to regard the *tabinau* as containing a patrilineage, the *citamangen* as the father by virtue of being the husband of the mother at the time she became pregnant, and the child as a member of his father's *tabinau*. The *tabinau*, or the patrilineage within it, consists of a set of brothers and their sisters and the children of the men, and the men's children, etc. This means that the lineage is shallow, of course, and its ancestor orientation, if it exists, is not its most conspicuous ideological element, but even a lineage of only three of four generations' depth is still a lineage. We can take a step further: the *tabinau* is not the descent group, but rather, the core of the *tabinau*, the patrilineage, is the descent group. As I have tried to indicate, if we wish to play fast and loose with the indigenous cultural constructs, where do we stop? If the culture does not define its group as ancestor-oriented, can we just go ahead and say it is anyway? If the culture does not contain any group, membership in which depends on some genealogical connection, can we just go ahead and say that it is so, even though the natives do not know it and perhaps even deny that it is relevant to their way of thinking? I am not raising questions *ad absurdum* here. Consider the literature on the "submerged descent line" and the "unnamed complementary descent group'' (Seligman 1928; Fortes 1949:54–55; Fortes 1963; Goody 1961:11, for examples) or implicit double descent (Lawrence 1937) or the "descent line" in the Murngin controversey (Barnes 1967:41–45; Scheffler 1978: 43–51).

So far as the *tabinau* is concerned, then, even though it might be possible to read a patrilineal lineage into it, this is not a culturally constituted nor culturally relevant nor culturally recognized group as such and therefore seems quite out of place in any description or analysis of Yapese culture.

If there is not patriliny in Yapese culture, there cannot be double descent.

Now the question of matriliny. Is *genung* a matrilineal clan? Few if any anthropologists would quarrel with the idea that *genung* is a matrilineal clan, and the fact that it is similar to so many such units found throughout the Caroline Islands and Micronesia generally would lend support to such a conclusion. It has a founding ancestress, it has certain prohibitions which enjoin its members from certain activities and foods, it has an origin myth and various other distinguishing features common to clans. Each member is said to derive—from belly to belly—from the founding ancestress, and membership automatically occurs because one's mother is a member. No problems of being versus doing confound this situation; it is clearly and unambiguously the state of being one's mother's offspring that makes one a member of a particular *genung.*

There are, however, some points which should be made about the relationship between descent and kinship, and the nature of descent, that arise from a consideration of the Yapese material.

To begin with, it will help to review once more the first description and those elements which have accrued to it during the discussion. First, *citiningen-fak* is clearly a relationship which, by its Yapese definition, involves a physical link between mother and child (though that is not held to be the case in Yapese culture for all who are related as *citiningen-fak,* for example, father's sister and brother's child). Second, all members of a *genung* are regarded as having the same ancestress, and therefore their relation to each other is of the same kind as the relationship between children of the same mother; they come from the same belly, they are physically linked. Third, not only do all members of the same *genung* have the same ancestress, but this same designation (*genung*) is used for a man, his sister, and his sister's children. Fourth, the ties between members of the same *genung* who live in different villages, separated by rank or physical distance from each other, are not close nor interdependent nor intense emotionally, but by formal definition they are all *wolagen.* And, indeed, the man, his sister, and the sister's children are at one and the same time *genung,* he is *matam ko genung,* the man and the sister's children are *wa'engen* to each other; that is, like *wolagen.* And the man and his sister are *wolagen,* though the woman and her children are, of course, *citiningen-fak.* Fifth, the woman and her children are *mafen,* guardians of the land, or protectors of property to the children of the woman's brother. And the children of the mother's brother are *fak* to the children of the father's sister, the father's sister being *citiningen* to their brother's children.

The view that descent can be radically differentiated from kinship in terms of its primary function, descent having to do with the politico-jural sphere and kinship with the domestic sphere just does not sit very well with the Yapese data by either description. As I have described the situation, insofar as the mother-child relationship is part of the domestic sphere, it is at the same time part of a wider unit which encompasses people from many different villages on Yap. The term *genung* certainly covers the politico-jural unit of land givers and land takers of the *tabinau* (for land goes from one *genung* in the *tabinau* to the next *genung* brought in by the inmarrying wife). But this hardly scratches the surface of the politico-jural domain. The villages, with their organization of chiefs, priests, chiefs of the old men, chiefs of the young men, parts of the villages, chiefs of parts of the villages, chiefs in charge of certain kinds of fishing, etc., just begin the process. The ranked relationship between villages into two "castes" and two sides, the association of more than 120 villages into three major alliances—all of this testifies to the fact that if the unilineal descent unit, the *genung,* has any politico-jural functions, they are but a part in a very complex total political system almost entirely divorced from notions of descent.

By the same token, *genung* is as deeply engaged in domestic affairs as is possible. It is the woman and her children who garden together, eat together, cook together, gather food together, share quarters together so long as the children are prepubertal. This is because *genung* is the relationship between a woman and her children as well as all those who trace their relationship to each other through their common ancestress. Indeed, recall the point that *genung* is a kind of relationship as it is culturally constituted in Yap, and that that relationship includes what we might distinguish as the domestic from the descent group, but which the Yapese do not so distinguish.

There are two distinct points to be made here, then. Whatever the formal analytic definitions arrived at by the duly constituted authorities who make the decisions on how these concepts should properly be defined, so far as Yapese culture is concerned, *genung* is a relationship. This relationship, first, is one which encompasses both kinship and descent and makes no distinction between them. Any distinction of that sort must be imposed on the Yapese cultural conceptions and thus distorts if not destroys them. Second, the *genung* relationship is one which makes no distinction between politico-jural and domestic functions. It is only by assuming that those kinship relations which occur in the family are different from, and the base from which, the politico-jural relations are extended and formulated in the idiom of kinship, that this functional distinction can be maintained.

The problem of kinship versus descent and the *genung* has certain features in common with the problem of *wolagen* which I put aside above. To recapitulate briefly, the problem of *wolagen* is this. Using the classical definition of kinship the kinship system of Yap concerns the relationship between a woman and her children, the *genung* as an ancestress-defined unit where all members are *wolagen* for the same reason that the children of one mother are *wolagen*. If this were all, the matter would be simple and there would be no problem; *wolagen* would mean those who are related by being the offspring of one woman, the immediate mother or the ultimate ancestress— whether she was a porpoise, a spirit in human guise, a fungus, or a rat. But *wolagen* cannot have that meaning alone since it is used for the children of the same *citamangen* but different *citiningen,* and it is used for the children of *wolagen* who are men (*wolagen ni pumo'on*) whether they are *wolagen* by the same mother or not. Thus some *wolagen* are kinsmen and some are not. On the face of it, this is common throughout the world. I could put the matter crudely and erroneously by saying that *wolagen* are the children of the same mother, the same father by different mothers, members of the same clan, of two brothers or two sisters, and so on. That would sound like good common sense. If *citamangen* could be translated as father it might hold. But I have gone to some lengths to show that the translation of *citamangen* as father is open to question. Kinship, defined as a biological relationship, real or putative, which is culturally valued, and only applies, if it applies at all, in Yap culture, to the relations of *genung,* mother-child, and the children of the same mother.

The problem of *wolagen* is replicated in the problem of *citiningen-fak.* I have been translating this relationship as mother-child, meaning *mother* in the English sense of that term; the woman who bore the child. But in Yapese culture the term *citiningen* also includes the relationship between ego and the *citamangen*'s *wolagen ni pin* (mother's husband's sister) and her *fak* that is, crudely, the "father's sister's child." It also includes the *citiningen*'s *wolagen ni pin.* (But her child is *wolag.*) If the woman who was *citiningen* divorces ego's *citamangen* and leaves, returning to her place of origin, she should properly not be referred to or counted as, nor may she act as, a *citiningen* anymore. If and when the *citamangen* remarries, this new wife becomes the *citiningen.* Hence the term is translatable as "father's wife" but not "mother."

To translate *citiningen-fak* as "mother-child" is also not correct, for not only are persons other than the English "mother" and "her child" included in this relationship, but this relationship is terminated if the "mother" divorces, leaving the child with the child's *citamangen.*

A solution to this problem seems to present itself immediately if we argue that *wolagen* is a word or concept, that words and concepts have many meanings, and that certain of these meanings are primary or referential while others are extensions of them. For example, the word *father* in English has the primary meaning of genitor. But the word *father* is also used for time (Father Time), for the priest (Father John), and so forth. The latter two usages obviously (it is said by some) derive from the former and not the other way around. They derive from the former by extension. That is, certain connotations are shared by time and by the priest with the genitor and so the term *father* is extended to them. For Yap the argument might be similar. The primary meaning of *wolagen* is offspring of the same mother and or the same ancestress. All other uses of the term *wolagen*, uses which apply to persons who are not so related, are extensions. Or, these other *wolagen* are called "classificatory" rather than "true." Hence there is nothing wrong or surprising or confusing about the fact that the term and concept *wolagen* is found to apply to far more than merely offspring of the same mother or ancestress. This is precisely the problem of all so-called "classificatory kinship terms." The problem is to determine which are the primary or denotative meanings and which the extensions made on the basis of shared connotations.

This way of dealing with the problem of *wolagen* raises more problems than it solves. First, it entails a theory of meaning which rests on the distinction between primary meanings and those which are derivative, perhaps by metaphoric extension or some other process, and a distinction between denotation and connotation which is at least debatable. For us the difficulty centers on the assumption that where kinship terms are concerned (and let us assume that *wolagen* is a kinship term) their primary meanings are the kin types closest to ego which then are extended outward. They are extended, first, to kin types more distant from ego, and second, to objects which are not kinsmen (Father Time, the priest).

Now, this is simply another way of assuming the primacy of kinship, or the privileged position of kinship. It is a special case of that view, but it is basically the same. One form which it takes is the assumption of the primacy of the nuclear family and the extension of all kinship out from the nuclear family, a position Malinowski (1929, 1930a, 1930b, 1932) and Lounsbury (1965:147) take. This can then be joined to the notion that the domestic unit or nuclear family is in some sense basic to, or structurally prior to, and fundamental to the rest of the sociocultural system. This semiotic theory merely resuscitates in another form the very assumptions which were discussed earlier and shown to be at least debatable.

There is another way of looking at this problem. The terms *tabinau, citamangen, citiningen, fak,* and so on are cultural constructs having to do with kinship, economics, religion, and politics. Let us call the latter the different meanings of the former. The problem has been framed as a question of the relationship among these different meanings. Is kinship privileged? This view takes meaning to be an attribute, a fixed feature of the construct. Instead, let us assume that meaning is more or less dependent on context. That is, the different meanings (kinship, economics, politics, religion) occur in conjunction with those signs in different contexts. Speaking of the *citamangen-fak* relationship as multifunctional or versatile, for example, simply ignores the relevance of context. But if the *citamangen-fak* relationship is such that meaning 1 occurs in context A, meaning 2 occurs in context B, meaning 3 occurs in context C and so on, then we have specified the context within which each different meaning occurs, as well as those from which it is excluded.

One further assumption. Contexts in a culture are not random. Contexts themselves are culturally defined and form clusters within which they are culturally interrelated. In certain contexts the particular construct, or its sign, can be understood to aggregate two or more meanings which in different contexts would be distinguished. Thus in context X meanings 1, 2, and 3 may be encompassed by one of greater generality and when the construct or its sign is used in context Y, then some meaning which specifies meaning 2 but not 1 or 3 may be entailed. This is a simplified way of speaking about markedness.

The question of whether kinship is a privileged system or not assumes that kinship "is," and has, a static set of attributes, that is, a certain set of meanings, where the multiple meanings must also be viewed as fixed, context-free, static attributes.

By viewing the situation in terms of markedness, however, we can get away from the notion of the static, fixed set of attributes and see the different aspects or meanings as context dependent. It would then seem unnecessary to designate meanings as privileged or not, as denotative or connotative, primary or extensions. Rather, they could be seen as more or less marked. In this view, the multifunctional meanings might be regarded as the unmarked meaning of the *citamangen-fak* relationship (for example), or the relationship among *tabinau* members. An economic, political or religious, or even possibly a kinship meaning might then be seen as specially marked. If, for example, the question concerns the political functions of the *tabinau,* the term *citamangen* might, in that context, have to do with political action. This would be its marked meaning in that specified context.

If we consider kinship in the frame of marking, then the conventional wisdom would have kinship as the unmarked sense, while land, religion, economics, and politics become the marked meanings comprehended within the general kinship sense, as special kinds or aspects of kinship. And it is in these terms that we could understand the versatility or the multifunctionality of kinship. It is not so much that kinship is a privileged system, but rather that it is culturally defined so as to include a variety of other related meanings within its purview.

This raises the question of kinship in yet another way, which might well be more productive, but in the end it leaves us with the same question with which we started. Is it specifically kinship that is unmarked and comprehends the others, as is the case with the construct of "man" in English, which "means" human being and so includes both men and women? Or is the unmarked meaning of *citamangen, citiningen, tabinau,* etc., just not easily translatable, or not yet translated properly, and kinship is nowhere involved? Or is kinship only one of the marked meanings of *citiningen?* If kinship is indeed the unmarked sense, why is it kinship that is unmarked?

There may be certain advantages to posing the problem in terms of markedness, but the problem remains. The concept of kinship seems to fit, but roughly, some of the material from Yap. Shall we say that Yap culture is unique and can best be dealt with by setting it aside since it does not fit the paradigm very well? Or can we say that on the evidence of this one case the concept of kinship needs reconsideration?

Not yet; but we can at least say that thus far something is wrong. The concept of kinship obfuscates more than it clarifies our understanding of Yapese culture.

The Relationship between the
Facts of Sexual Reproduction
and the Cultural Constitution
of Kinship

Introduction to Part III

I have proceeded as if the only relevant definition of kinship postulated some sort of direct biological relatedness, real or putative, which may or may not be explicitly encoded in cultural terms in any particular society. But this definition is really too crude, for it masks some very important differences among students of kinship and ways of studying kinship.

The crux of the problem is the different ways in which the facts of sexual reproduction, real or putative biological relatedness, or reproduction without the "sexual" are held to be related (or in no way related) to the cultural constructs of kinship. The ever problematic father is a good example. Shall we define kinship so that the man who is the biological progenitor is the cultural father? In this case kinship becomes the social or cultural recognition of what we in our twentieth-century scientific wisdom know to be a biological fact—or, to use the classic formulation, kinship is the social recognition of biological facts. Since we have been given to understand that in some societies physical paternity is denied, should the relationship be stated so that the father is the mother's husband—a particular kind of member of the family perhaps, and kinship is not so much the cultural *recognition* of biological facts as it is a necessary and special adaptation to them which may even ignore, deny, or be unaware of certain of them but focuses on "reproduction"?

I have not strayed from the question of whether kinship is a privileged system, and if it is, just why. This is still one of the central questions. But an answer to the question might be found in the way in which the relationship between physical and social kinship is formulated. For example, if the argument that social kinship is determined by, formed by, and an adaptation to, the scientifically demonstrable facts of reproduction, and that a very special kind of system of social relations is thereby created which differs from all other kinds, this might be a way of demonstrating that kinship is indeed a privileged system, and just why and in what way it is.

9   A History of Some Definitions of Kinship

The definitions of kinship centering on relationships which arise out of human sexual reproduction have yet to be examined with care. It is to this problem that I turn now, to explore the different ways in which physical and social or cultural kinship have been related in the conventional wisdom of kinship studies. I will do this by first undertaking a brief historical review, by no means exhaustive, but representative I believe, and sufficient to fairly represent the development of thinking on this problem.

To begin with, the term *kinship* is used to refer to both the biological system of relations, quite apart from any sociocultural aspects, and also to the sociocultural aspects. I will purposely use the term *biology* loosely here to mean what laymen think of as physical relatedness as well as those relationships which arise out of the facts of human sexual reproduction, but which need not imply a sharing of biological substance.

What is problematic in the definitions of kinship is whether the sociocultural aspects can be set apart entirely from the biological aspects or whether any concern for the sociocultural aspects necessarily implicates the biological aspects. If so, just how?

For Lewis H. Morgan, the problem was simple.

The family relationships are as ancient as the *family*. They exist in virtue of the law of derivation, which is expressed by the perpetuation of the species through the marriage relation. *A system of consanguinity which is founded upon a community of blood, is but the formal expression and recognition of these relationships.* Around every person there is a circle or group of kindred of which such person is the center, and the Ego, from whom the degree of the relationship is reckoned, and to whom the relationship itself returns. Above him are his father and mother and their ascendants, below him are his children and their descendants; while on either side are his brothers and sisters and their descendants and the brothers and sisters of his father and of his mother and their descendants as well as a much greater number of collateral relatives descended from common ancestors still more remote. To him they are nearer in degree than other individuals of the nation at large. *A formal arrangement of the more immediate blood kindred into lines of descent, with the adoption of some method to distinguish one relative from another and to express the value of the relationship, would be one of the earliest acts of human intelligence.* (Emphasis added. 1870:10)

97

It followed that in distinguishing the *descriptive* from the *classificatory* system, it is the descriptive system which Morgan called a ''natural system'' precisely ''because it is founded upon a correct appreciation of the distinction between the lineal and several collateral lines and of the perpetual divergence of the latter from the former. Each relationship is thus specialized and separated from every other in such a manner as to decrease its nearness and diminish its value according to the degree of distance of each person from the central Ego'' (1870:14, 142–43). The *classificatory system,* on the contrary, as it is used among American Indians and others, Morgan said, is contrary to the nature of descents, confounding relationships which are distinct, separating those which are similar, and diverting the streams of the blood from the collateral channels into the lineal. *Where, for the descriptive system, knowledge of the lines of parentage is necessary to determine the classification, just the opposite is true for the classificatory system; a knowledge of parentage is quite unnecessary.* It is impossible to explain its origin on the assumption of the existence of the family founded upon marriage between single pairs; but it may be explained with some degree of probability on the assumption of the antecedent existence of a series of customs and institutions, one reformatory of the other, commencing with promiscuous intercourse and ending with the establishment of the family, as now constituted, resting on marriage between single pairs (paraphrased and quoted, with emphasis added, from Morgan 1870:143).

Thus for Morgan, the mode of classification of kinsmen derives from and describes the peoples' own knowledge of how they are actually, or most probably, biologically related to each other. This knowledge depends on their form of marriage. For Morgan, marriage consists quintessentially of a sexual relationship between male and female. The processes of biological reproduction make the married pair the parents of their biological offspring and the offspring of such a mated pair siblings. The links which are recognized culturally, or marked in the mode of classification of kinsmen are the links of descent among these people as they may be known, which in turn depends on the mode of marriage.

The mode of marriage is the crux of the matter. For Morgan, as for many of those writing from around 1850 through the early decades of the twentieth century, the intellectual problems focused on the development of civilization and on the development of man. Of these, one central problem was that of the origin(s) and development of kinship, marriage, and the family. It was widely but not universally held that the earliest state of affairs was that of primitive promiscuity. But what social forms followed primitive promiscuity? Two general theories were offered—the patriarchal and the matriarchal. The patriarchal theory argued that somehow the unorganized, chaotic group of people became organized into groups dominated by men, and from this developed the *patria potestas,* that is, groups of people led by a senior male who held all members of the group under absolute control. "Kinship" was "traced" through males but not females. But the matriarchal theory offered, among other evidence and argument, the observation that it is very hard to be ignorant of maternity, while paternity is a much more difficult relationship to establish. Hence the earliest social bond must have been that which was easiest to recognize, the maternal bond, so that "kinship" must have been traced first through the mother. Only much later, when promiscuity was eliminated, could any kind of paternity, that is, a biological bond between genitor and offspring, be recognized. So an early stage was that of group marriage in which a group of men shared a group of women in common. At such a stage, though each child would know its mother, there could be no way for it to know which man was its father. Later when a group of brothers held a group of sisters in common, paternity could be narrowed down to that group of brothers.

It was apparent even before Morgan wrote that the cultural and biological relations of kinship did not always coincide even in the most advanced societies. But the biological relationship was treated as the reference point, the fixed position, against which all cultural aspects take their meaning. For example, Maine (1861:27) makes it clear that adoption is a "legal fiction" since the relationship between adopter and adoptee is not a true biological relationship. And the term *fictive kinship,* as it is still used today, follows this usage.

These early authors treated kinship as primarily a biological relationship with the cultural aspect the mere recognition of its existence with other features trailing along in second place. The difficulties with this formulation soon became apparent. For one thing, it was, after all, the *social* conventions of kinship, marriage, and the family that were the specific points at issue in trying to unravel the earliest stages of the development of civilization. It was the creation of a social order, however rude or mean, that was the question. Physical kinship remained the same as it had been during the period of primitive promiscuity; what had changed was the rules of who could copulate with whom, who had rights over whom, who had social bonds with whom. The problem was to understand and reconstruct the development of those social arrangements.

So, not long after Morgan published *Systems* . . . in 1870, the climate of opinion began to treat social or cultural kinship as the problem and to draw a sharp distinction between it and physical kinship. For example, Durkheim (1898), in his famous review of Kohler, starts from Morgan's assertion that kinship terms mark true biological relations and argues that this cannot be so since, for example in the case of the Omaha and Choctaw, a single term may often be used for persons standing in various biological relations to ego but who all stand in the same relation to ego so far as their totem, or what we would call their descent group, is concerned. These people regard each other as kin because they are all descended from the same totem. It is therefore this social convention of their kinship, not their actual blood relationship, that defines them as kin and that therefore defines kinship. Kinship and consanguinity (in the sense of real physical or blood connection) are thus very different things, and as an example Durkheim gives the fact that the natural child who is not recognized as such is not, in the social sense of the word, kin to his ascendants and has no family tie with them. He goes on to say that in Rome the child did not become a member of the family where he was born by the simple fact of his birth, but that the father had to receive him with appropriate ceremony. By the same token, the father could terminate all kinship with the child even though their consanguineal relationship remained and was known to everyone concerned. Durkheim then brings up the inevitable example of adoption, saying that the adopter and adoptee are kin even though no consanguineal relationship obtains between them, nor is any presumed to. He goes on to say that kinship is constituted of the jural and moral obligations that society imposes, that these individuals belong to groups where the members believe themselves to have a common origin. But even the belief in a common origin is not really necessary for the relation of kinship to obtain between persons, Durkheim says, for many considerations totally unrelated to any idea of descent may determine how domestic rights and obligations are assigned to different members of the family group, the family group being anything from a large group of consociates to the husband, wife, and their children. Further, some feature of the social structure, some religious belief, may make the child closer to one or another of its parents, more intimately involved in the life of his father's group or his mother's group, and so forth. And so, argues Durkheim, the earliest forms of kinship group or family were almost totally independent of consanguineal ties, these having only more recently been assigned social significance. He then anticipates Rivers by saying that to be a member of a family or kinship group, it is sufficient to have something of the totemic being, of the sacred quality that serves as the group's collective emblem. This can result from birth, but it can be gained in many other ways: by tattooing, by all the forms of food prohibitions, blood communion, and so forth. Even birth alone is not adequate to make the child an integral member of the group; religious ceremonies or some kind of social formality must be added. The idea of consanguinity is thus secondary and as a result of this the organization of kinship expresses something very different from genealogical or consanguineal relations. So, concludes Durkheim, all kinship is social for it consists essentially in jural and moral relations, sanctioned by society. It is a social tie or it is nothing. There can be but one kinship, that recognized as such by society.

In his concern to maintain the social or cultural character of kinship and deny that it is merely a physical relationship, Durkheim fails to specify in just what way this social or cultural relationship can be distinguished from all others. That it entails social and cultural definitions, jural and moral commitments, marks of group membership, and so on no one would deny. But how is one to distinguish such a group or membership in such a group, or such relations, from those of any other kind—economic, political, religious, or voluntary association such as lodges or sodalities.

Van Gennep, in 1906, took a similar view and with much the same difficulty. Kinship or descent, he said, is not determined by the certainty of birth by a particular mother or by any particular biological relationship to a father, for native theories of conception vary considerably and the fact of birth as well as conception and gestation has different meanings and definitions in different native theories. Thus, for example, in some Australian societies the woman is regarded as no more than a temporary receptacle and in no sense as having conceived the child (Van Gennep 1906:xxvi–vii). So Van Gennep implies that if kinship derives from the act of conception, then we must understand the native theory of conception before we can say that there is a kinship relationship between mother and child. This is helpful insofar as it tells us that kinship is not simply a matter of birth or the facts of biology. But, like Durkheim, Van Gennep fails to provide a positive definition of kinship free of biological referents.

There were numerous attempts to disentangle the social from the biological dimensions of kinship, focusing principally on the Australians who were presumed to be the most primitive peoples extant and some of whom did not associate reproduction with coitus. For example, Frazer wrote in 1910, "To the Central Australian father (fatherhood) means that a child is the offspring of a woman with whom he has a right to cohabit, whether he has actually had intercourse with her or not. To the European mind, the tie between a father and his child is physical; to the Central Australian it is social" (vol. 1, p. 336). And Malinowski in his review of the family among the Australian aborigines (1913: chap. 6) suggests, though somewhat tentatively, that among the Australian aborigines the family—consisting of a man, his wife, and their offspring—is the most important institution. His views followed those of Westermark (1891) in this matter, and if we accept the view that they are ignorant of the facts of physical paternity, then the father must be understood as the mother's husband. This is the position which Frazer took in the quotation above in 1910. But again it will be noted that no matter how social the role of the father is, for Europeans like Frazer and Malinowski, cohabitation is critical to the understanding of fatherhood, even though in individual cases the man who is the "father" has not exercised this right, and does not believe that cohabitation has anything to do with reproduction. This suggests that not only is the father related to the child through his relationship to the child's mother (thus the ultimate biological reference) but through *rights* in cohabitation even if copulation does not take place.

At about this time, W. H. R. Rivers still seemed to support Morgan's view.

> I have now investigated the classificatory system in three communities, and in all three it is perfectly clear that distinct ideas of consanguinity and affinity are associated with the terms. The correct use of the terms was over and over again justified by reference to actual blood or marriage ties traceable in the genealogical records preserved by the people. (1907a:322)

But at about the same time, Rivers tried to deal more systematically with a definition of kinship and stress its social or cultural constitution. Rivers first tried to clarify the distinction between kinship and descent. All too often these terms were used in an inconsistent and confusing way. He makes the points most concisely in 1908 (p. 654), but the fuller, more detailed treatment comes in 1910.

> Of all sociological terms there are none more important and at the same time used more indefinitely than "kin" and "kinship." In his book on the Melanesians, Dr. Codrington has spoken of a child as not being of the same kin as his father [p. 29]. Here Dr. Codrington has used the English word "kin" as the equivalent of the Mota word *sogoi* for those related to one another by common membership of a social group, in this case the *veve* or moiety of the whole population. Thus one of the meanings which has been ascribed to the word "kin" is membership of the same group, so that it excludes certain people related by consanguinity, and includes others with whom no genealogical connection can be traced. The same definition is implied, though not definitely stated, by Dr. Frazer when in his *Adonis, Attis, Osiris* he has used mother-kin in place of mother-right [2d ed., p. 384]. This title implies that a man is only kin with the members of the group of his mother, and the term has been used with this significance by others. The ascription of this meaning to the word seems to me to depart so widely from the customary, as well as the legal, meaning of the word in the English language that I cannot regard it as satisfactory, and I have proposed elsewhere that on the contrary "kin" and "kinship" shall be limited to relationships which can be shown to exist genealogically ["Report of Seventy-seventh Meeting of the British Association for the Advancement of Science," 1907 (*sic*):654; also *Man*, 1907:142]. The special point to which I wish to call attention now is that, as we have seen, the relationship between a man and his father's sister, which so far as

functions go is of the nearest, perhaps nearer than that of parent and child, is one in which, according to the view of some, the two persons would not be kin. Our ideas of kinship are so intimately associated with honour and obedience that it seems to me to be a pity to use the word in such a sense as to exclude the relative who is honoured and obeyed before all others. I think we shall be keeping much more closely to the general meaning of the word if we use it to denote genealogical relationship, and find some other word for the relationship set up by common membership of a social group. (1910a:58–59)

The matter of descent can be set aside simply. Rivers seems justified in objecting to the conflation of kinship and descent. His treatment of kinship as genealogical relations is clear for the moment. But his treatment of descent as membership in a social group creates further problems, some of which have been touched on earlier.

I leave Rivers, though only for a moment. N. W. Thomas, in 1906, was also concerned with the relationship between physical and social kinship and makes some points worth noting.

The distinction between *consanguinity* and *kinship* first demands attention; the former depends on birth, the latter on the law or custom of the community, and this distinction is all-important, especially in dealing with primitive peoples. With ourselves the two usually coincide, though even in civilised communities there are variations in this respect. Thus, according to the law of England, the father of an illegitimate child is not akin to it, though *ex hypothesi* there is a tie of blood between them. In England nothing short of an Act of Parliament can make them akin; but in Scotland the subsequent marriage of the father with the mother of the child changes the legal status of the latter and makes it of kin with its father. These two examples make it abundantly evident that kinship is with us a matter of law. . . .

Kinship is sociological, consanguinity physiological; in thus stating the case we are concerned only with broad principles. In practice the idea of consanguinity is modified in two ways and a sociological element is introduced, which has gone far to obscure the difference between these two systems of laying the foundations of human society. In the first place, custom determines the limits within which consanguinity is supposed to exist; or, in other words, at what point the descendents of a given ancestor cease to be blood relations. In the second place, erroneous physiological ideas modify the ideas held as to actually existing consanguine relations, as we conceive them. The latter peculiarity does not effect the enquiry to any extent; it merely limits the sphere within which consanguinity plays a part, side by side with kinship, in moulding social institutions. . . . In speaking of consanguinity therefore, it must be made quite clear whether consanguinity according to native ideas or according to our own ideas is meant. (1906: 3–5)

We will have occasion to take up the point made in the very last sentence of the quotation from Thomas as well as the similar point made by Van Gennep below. But Van Gennep had more to say which is relevant. Although he is speaking of Lang, this need not confuse us.

> Here Lang conflates notions which the Arunta distinguish, namely physical kinship and social kinship. Lang plays on the words "paternity" and "maternity" even though, being cognizant of the system of calculating degrees of kinship, he knows full well that the word "father" is applied to a definite category of persons who have in common only that they stand in a specific relation to their "sons," apart from any consideration of actual procreation. Moreover, each couple has become a social unit through the accomplishment of nuptial ceremonies. If there are rules of transmission within this unit, if certain property passes from the male spouse to the children, or from the female spouse, that does not mean that it is because the first is regarded as genitor, or the second as genitrix. It is therefore necessary to understand, when we are told that "the totem is inherited in the maternal line," that it is not a question of the mother in the sense we give to that word, but of the feminine element which, combined with a masculine element, socially constitutes a group (couple). . . . In other words the central Australians dissociate two notions (genitor and male spouse, or genitrix and female spouse) which our anatomical knowledge forces us to identify. Consequently the existence of inheritance rules in no way tells against this proposition: "the Arunta are ignorant of the blood tie."
> They are in fact ignorant of it. And they are not alone. . . . The northern and eastern Australians are at the same stage as the central Australians; their interpretations differ only in details, the fundamental idea always being that *procreation is not necessarily and uniquely the consequence of coitus.* (1906:lxiii–lxiv, trans. M. Francillon)

In both the Thomas and Van Gennep quotations there is much of value, but for the problem before us these quotations repeat the central point. By the turn of the twentieth century, the view that kinship was biology, and its social aspect was, in Morgan's words, the "recognition" of those existential biological relationships, began to give way. This appears in the affirmation of Durkheim that kinship is social or it is nothing. The same position is argued persuasively by Van Gennep who does not entirely lose touch with physical kinship, but explicitly defines it only in part as the particular indigenous theories of conception or the folk ideology of reproduction. Thomas takes the same position. Kinship is not, as Morgan would have it, the social recognition of "our biology," but is instead "their biology," if it is biology at all.

Thomas, Durkheim, Van Gennep, and Rivers have gone this far. They are intent on making clear that there is an important distinction between physical and social kinship, and that social kinship is by no means merely the (cognitive) "recognition" of the biological facts, or even their "recognition" for social purposes. It includes social facts which do not accord with the biological facts and it is the selective social recognition at best of only certain of the biological facts for certain social purposes. Thus certain facts of social kinship may have no biological referents while others socially recognize only certain of the biological facts.

But Rivers is not through nor are we through with Rivers. I have cited material from 1907 and 1910. In a two-volume work written not long after the 1910 paper, Rivers writes extensively of the Mota of the Banks Islands in the New Hebrides. There he says, "In these islands it would seem as if parents have little, if any, more right to their children than any other persons" (1914: vol. 2, p. 136).

In 1915, Rivers continues to move in the same direction as Durkheim when he says,

> The least satisfactory [way to define kinship] is *consanguinity*. Among ourselves such a relationship as that which exists between parent and child, or between brother and sister, can also come into existence by social conventions such as adoption (q.v.), but among many peoples this formation of relationships . . . may count for little or nothing unless it has been ratified by some kind of social process, or a social process may result in the formation of a relationship between persons wholly devoid of any consanguineous tie. Thus in the Banks Islands in Melanesia the relationship of parent does not come into existence by the facts of procreation and parturition, but it is such acts as the payment of the midwife, the first feeding of the child, or the planting of a tree on the occasion of a birth that determine who are to be the parents of the child for all social purposes. . . . Kinship cannot be determined and defined by consanguinity even among ourselves, still less among other peoples. . . .
> Nearly all, if not all, peoples of the world preserve, either in writing or in their memories, a record of those with whom they are related by consanguinity *or by those social conventions which, as we have seen, serve the same social purpose.* Among many peoples, and especially among those of rude culture, the knowledge of relationship thus genealogically determined is far more extensive than among ourselves. Pedigrees preserved in the memories of a rude tribe of cannibals may rival, if not surpass, anything which even the most enthusiastic

genealogist is capable of carrying in his mind. Among such peoples it is the facts recorded in the pedigree of a person that largely determine his use of terms of relationship and regulate all the social functions which those terms connote. . . .

The genealogical mode, therefore, is that which furnishes the most exact and convenient method of defining kinship. Kinship may be defined as relationship which can be determined and described by means of genealogies. As thus defined, kinship will be both narrower and wider than the relationship set up by membership of the clan or other similar social group. If, as is now customary (see *Notes and Queries on Anthropology*, 1912. London. p. 156), the term "clan" is used for an exogamous social group, it would be only members of the father's or mother's clan, according as descent is patrilineal or matrilineal, who would be kin if the term were used for membership of the social group. . . .

The definition of kinship as genealogical relationship will also exlude the metaphorical sense in which terms of relationship are often used by peoples at all stages of culture. (Emphasis added. 1915:700–701)

Parenthetically, the exclusion by Rivers of what he calls "the metaphorical sense" is puzzling. If kinship is genealogy, and genealogy is the affirmation of the natives that so and so are kin, and that relationship is not necessarily one of consanguinity, then how can one discover when metaphor is being used, even for kinship terms? The exclusion of metaphor is a dead giveaway, for if kinship is social and not physical, and metaphor is social, then this raises the question of what a metaphorical kinship relationship might be.

There are many important points made in this quotation from Rivers (1915) but for us here there are a few central questions. The first is the denial that consanguinity can be used as a means of defining kinship. His reasons for rejecting consanguinity are that, among many peoples, social conventions and not consanguinity serve to define who are kin to whom, and he gives Mota in the Banks Islands as one example (I have omitted the example of the Toda from the quotation). The second important point is the statement that genealogy is the best definition of kinship. Although it is not entirely clear from this quotation just what Rivers meant by "genealogy," it would appear that genealogy is the presumption of kinship relationship as this is stated by the natives. That is, if the genealogy says that X is the daughter of Y, and Z the father of X, then that is all that there is to it. X may be the daughter of Y because of some social convention like paying the midwife, planting a tree, or an adoption ceremony as in our own society. It is the social convention as ratified in the genealogy which makes them kin.

Rivers's rejection of consanguinity as the defining feature of kinship is thus but the other side of the coin from his choosing genealogy, and in this he is (as Durkheim did before him) arguing for the primacy of social kinship and the irrelevance of physical kinship. Indeed, he seems to be putting the weight of the matter entirely on social convention—whether it be paying the midwife, planting the tree, or any such conventions which may be precipitated in the assertion of the genealogical relationship in the memory of the natives. In other words, different societies have different social conventions which define a genealogical relationship. Whatever these may be, they are summarized in the genealogy. Hence it is genealogical relationship that defines kinship. Rivers does not say so specifically, but it would seem that the limiting condition would be where a society defines consanguinity, or physical kinship, as the very social convention which establishes a genealogical relationship and thereby kinship. But such would be a limiting case.

Rivers's attempt to shift the burden of the definition of kinship onto social convention and away from the social recognition of the existential facts of physical kinship as Morgan and others of his time had formulated it was fertile in that it led to a considerable volume of work which focused on the social conventions. But in the end it created confusion and, as I will suggest, the confusion remains to this day.

I have pointed out elsewhere (Schneider 1972) that a close inspection of what Rivers actually meant and what he actually did in collecting genealogies were rather different from his very general statements about them. That is, his 1915 statement would lead one to believe that Rivers agreed with Durkheim, Van Gennep, and N. W. Thomas in arguing that kinship was a matter of social convention and not biological fact or fiction, and that these social conventions could all be summarized in the genealogy. Every genealogy contained a parent-child relationship, but that parent-child relationship might be understood in very different ways in different societies. Whatever the folk beliefs might be, and they were surely variable, they still postulated relations of parent and child, siblings, ascendant and descendant, and so forth, and it was these genealogically specified relations that constituted kinship.

But Rivers did not face two problems. The first I specified in detail in 1972. That is, that when collecting and using genealogies Rivers insisted on the "proper," that is, the English meanings of the relationships. Thus he makes it clear, "Care had of course to be taken to limit these terms (father, mother, child, husband, wife) *to their English sense.* The term which was open to the most serious liability to error was that of father, but *I was able to make the natives understand very thoroughly that I wanted the 'proper father'* " (emphasis added, Rivers 1900:75). Hence despite the eloquence with which he rejected consanguinity as the definition of kinship, he used it anyway, for there is no question—even in Rivers's mind it would seem—but that the English sense of these terms is of a consanguineal relation.

The second problem was simply this. If each society had a different social convention for establishing a kinship relationship—Mota by payment of the midwife, Toda by the bow ceremony, elsewhere the planting of a tree, and so forth—by what logic were these all considered to be *kinship* relations since each constituted a different relationship? If paying the midwife, planting the tree, the bow ceremony, were all different ways of establishing the same relationship, then one can see that it is the sameness of that relationship that is the kinship relationship. But Rivers never faces this question; he never tells us what this relationship consists of. He simply affirms that to pay the midwife made one a father; that to plant the tree made one a parent; that the bow ceremony established who the father was to be. What, then, is a "father," since he is clearly NOT the genitor, the procreator? If he is the social father as distinct from the physical father, what does it mean to be a social father? How can one distinguish a social father from a social mother or a social thinguma-bob? Rivers simply took the terms *father, mother, brother, sister, husband, wife, child, parent,* and so on and used them as if their meaning was self-evident, when his whole purpose would seem to have been that of making the self-evident explicit by defining precisely what they were socially, and why they were not definable by consanguinity, that is, by their physical relationship.

As if that were not enough, Rivers used his own ethnography to bolster his argument, but provided enough of it to destroy his own case. It is true that no one challenged him (to the best of my knowledge) for about fifty-five years; but when, in 1970, Scheffler did, it was to show not only the looseness of the argument and the ambiguous use of concepts such as adoption, con-sanguinity, and so on, but also that contrary to Rivers's general assertions about paying the midwife in Mota establishing parenthood, this payment was only part of the story. The whole story, from Scheffler's reading of the Mota ethnography, included the fact that if the parent who paid the midwife was not the husband of the woman who bore the child he was not (contra Rivers) the "parent for (all) social purposes"; that Mota posit genitors and genitrices and therefore posit the same relationships that English speakers posit and desig-nate by the words *parentage* and *parent;* that adoption in Mota, as among ourselves, creates a fiction of kinship but not kinship itself; and so on (Sche-ffler 1970:372–73).

By the third and fourth decades of the twentieth century kinship re-mained defined by reference to physical kinship though the center of attention was the social aspects of relations so defined. Close attention was paid to the organization and structure of the social aspects of kinship, even though physi-cal kinship always remained its defining feature in much the same way that some sort of belief in the supernatural has remained the touchstone of all that is called "religion."

An example of the stability of the ultimate physical or biological reference for kinship, as well as the confusion generated by Rivers's insistence on the supposed independence of social from physical kinship, appears forty years later in John Barnes's article on kinship for the 1955 edition of the Encyclopedia Britannica.

> Two persons are kin to each other when they are linked by socially recognized bonds of descent or marriage or both. Man is a bisexual animal, so that every infant has both a physical father and a physical mother. The young child may grow up in the care and protection of its physical parents, but in human society it may sometimes be reared by people who are not its physical parents, and it may take its place in society as the child of others. Everywhere a person derives his position in society in some measure from his parentage. He is expected to act in a specific way toward certain people merely because they are his kinsfolk. He is classed with them by outsiders whether he likes it or not. In most societies the adult status of a child is comparatively little dependent on its physical ancestry or its rearing; it is social parentage which determines where it may inherit, to what offices it may succeed, who are its kinsfolk and to what kin groups it belongs.

Barnes reiterates a point made by Rivers.

> Writers on kinship therefore distinguish between the physical parents, genetically related to the child, and the foster parents who care for it while it matures; and between both of these and the social parents in whom it acquires rights and privileges, duties and obligations, who, as it were, give it its social personality. The interpersonal ties linking the child to its social parents are repeated for its brothers and sisters, thus linking it to them; and since every child is potentially a parent, these ties are extended through the generations. Thus social parenthood generates a web of links between persons which we call cognatic or consanguineal kinship. Two persons are said to be cognates when they trace descent from a common ancestor. . . . anthropologists refer to the social parents as the pater and mater, in contrast with the physical parents, the progenitor and progenetrix. (Barnes 1955:403–4)

Just as in Rivers's discussion, kinship starts off with a firm definitional reference to physical kinship, which soon distinguishes physical from social kinship using the idea of "socially recognized bonds of descent" as a bridge between the two. But soon social kinship drifts off as a thing in itself, the only link between physical and social kinship being the use of the same terms— *kinship, parenthood, mother, father, brother, sister*.

Barnes's discussion can only make sense if kinship is understood as physical kinship, and it is on that basis, in terms of that model, and with reference to that system of relations that social kinship is defined. In Barnes's discussion, as in Rivers's, social kinship is separated from physical kinship but is not defined except by reference to rights and privileges, duties and obligations; it is not described; it is not distinguished from anything else in its essential character or by contrast with what it is not, nor are the particular rights and duties specified. The pater can only make sense and only has meaning with reference to the genitor or progenitor; the mater has no meaning except insofar as it refers to the social aspects which normally accrue to the progenetrix.

One important point for this discussion emerged in the debate on the nature of kinship in a series of papers by Gellner (1957, 1960, 1963), Needham (1960), Barnes (1961, 1964), Beattie (1964a), and Schneider (1964). In Barnes's comment on Gellner (Barnes 1961 and his further clarification in Barnes 1964), he makes a significant advance on his 1955 formulation by explicitly taking into account some of the problems raised by Durkheim, Van Gennep, N. W. Thomas, Rivers, and others who argued that different native theories of procreation made the concept of purely physical kinship irrelevant. Barnes draws three distinctions, one of which is new. First, there is the genetic father, the man who supplies the sperm which fertilizes the ovum. He is for all practical purposes unknown and unknowable in most societies of the world, and even in our own with the best tools of modern science it is only possible to exclude certain persons but never to positively identify any particular person. Second (the new point), there is the genitor. The genitor is the man who according to the particular cultural theory of the particular society we are concerned with is held to be the man by whose actions the woman was caused to be pregnant. Thus where the genetic father is a purely scientific concept (in the sense of Western science, of course), the genitor is defined in terms of the folk beliefs of each culture. It is conceivable, and Barnes seems to think it is possible, that such a status may be absent in some cultures. I would take it that these would be such places as are said to deny physiological paternity or the role of coitus in conception. Finally, the third concept is that of the social father, or the pater. The social father need not necessarily be a man. Thus in cases of leviratic marriage, woman-woman marriage, and so on, the culture may explicitly recognize and accord different rights, duties, and status to the (socially recognized) genitor and the pater, each different persons. It is with the genitor and the pater that anthropology is concerned and not with the genetic father. The same distinctions can be made between the genetic mother, the genetrix, and the mater, of course, and can be taken to include theories of reproduction. Thus there is genetic kinship in the sense of what the science of genetics seems to have established and there is the particular set of folk beliefs and indigenous theory of reproduction characteristic of a particular society. Finally, there is the set of social conventions which consist in roles, norms, rules, rights, duties, and so forth which are attached to the culturally distinguished statuses which are embedded in the indigenous theory of reproduction.

The simple distinction between biological and social kinship is thus insufficient. Biological kinship is always and everywhere a set of cultural conceptions. But these are of two kinds and their import is different. The first is that set of cultural conceptions called "science" in European culture. The second are the folk science or ethnoscientific conceptions of all cultures, including European. Even in European culture there may well be a difference between the beliefs of science and the generally held beliefs about the reality of reproduction. It is with respect to the latter that kinship is studied, and only in very special ways is it the most authoritative form of science, as in the studies of population genetics and some of the recent concerns of sociobiology.

But once again it must be noted that the second and third of Barnes's distinctions, that between genitor and pater, genetrix and mater, are inextricably linked, for the pater and mater can only be located or identified with reference to some idea about genitor and genetrix, for it is the social and cultural concomitants of genitor and genetrix that constitute pater and mater.

Scheffler and Lounsbury (1971) are quite clear in their definition of kinship. They rest the distinction between physical and social kinship on the cultural conception of the processes of human reproduction, and this is the defining feature for their understanding of kinship. "Let us simply state that by 'genealogical connection' we designate those *culturally posited* forms of interpersonal connectedness that are held to be direct consequences of processes of engendering and bearing children that have the property of indissolubility" (p. 37). They then set these in relation to each other saying, "Relations of genealogical connection or kinship proper, are fundamentally different from and are logically and temporally prior to any social relations of kinship. . . . The *social* relations normatively entailed by kinship are not conceived as congenital or indissoluble, no matter how binding they may be in law or morality" (pp. 37–39).

Needham and Maybury-Lewis (Needham 1971:13; Maybury-Lewis 1965) and some others use the phrase *relationship system* in place of *kinship system* or *kinship terminology system* but this has not gained wide currency and I suggest for the same reason that *social kinship* could never be completely freed of its defining feature, human sexual reproduction or the folk theory of it. The reason is that to do so would have required that kinship be wholly redefined and its redefinition would have made it largely unrecognizable, robbing it of the very essence of what was deemed to be its significance: biology, procreation, conception, gestation, parturition, seen either as "the real thing'' or the folk theory of it. To do this would have been as much as to take all the sense of the supernatural out of the idea of religion. Robbed of its grounding in biology, kinship is nothing; robbed of its grounding in the supernatural, religion is everyday life (Schneider 1965).

10 Some Fundamental Difficulties in the Study of Kinship Exemplified by Scheffler and Lounsbury

The term *biology* can be used only loosely where Scheffler and Lounsbury (1971) are concerned. Indeed, a careful look at what they say raises the question of whether they are talking about biology at all in their definition of kinship.

Barnes and Scheffler and Lounsbury make the important distinction between scientifically established genetic relations and native or folk theories of reproduction. Is it *our* theory of reproduction or *their* (the natives) theory of reproduction that kinship is concerned with? Van Gennep (1906), Barnes (1961, 1964), and Scheffler and Lounsbury (1971 as well as the important paper by Scheffler (1974:744–56) say that kinship is about *their* theory of reproduction.

Our (scientific as well as folk) theory of reproduction is a biological theory, but "their" (non-European) cultures may have theories about reproduction which do not imply biology in any accepted sense of that term. The distinction between biology and human reproduction is therefore vital to the discussion.

As I have pointed out, Morgan and his contemporaries defined kinship quite explicitly in biological terms, treating reproduction essentially as a biological process. Even later, many of the discussions of the relationship between social and physical kinship treated physical kinship as essentially biological.

Now the question I want to begin with is whether the definition of kinship provided by Scheffler and Lounsbury (1971) and Scheffler (1974) is about biology at all. Have they indeed departed from the traditional definition of reproduction as a biological process?

Scheffler seems to be clear on this point when he says,

> Therefore, one of the things the term [*genealogical connection*] should *not* be taken to mean is relations of biological or genetic connection *as such relations are understood in the science of biology* because such relationships are unknown to (i.e., not posited by) the vast majority of the world's peoples, and so they could not possibly serve for those peoples as criteria for the ordering of their social relations. (1974:749).

I say that Scheffler *seems* to have explicitly ruled out biology, but in fact, as

113

the above quotation shows, he has ruled out only what was already ruled out by Barnes (1961, 1964) and by Scheffler and Lounsbury (1971). This is biology in its *scientific sense*, not in the sense that all folk-cultural theories of human reproduction are biological and human reproduction is culturally defined as a biological process. The distinction here is between biology and genetic relationship as it is formulated by science, and biological relationship and processes as formulated by the folk theory itself. Hence the question is whether Scheffler and Lounsbury have shifted their definition of kinship away from biology and to the general process of reproduction, however this may be conceived in the local, folk-cultural theory.

With reproduction as the defining feature of kinship, a wide variety of folk theories of reproduction can be accommodated, only some of which might be predicated on consanguineal relationship. Kinship, then, is genealogical relations as these are defined by the folk theory of reproduction.

But is biology really excluded except where it is part of some particular folk theory? First I will quote Scheffler and Lounsbury (1971:37–38) with only minor omissions. I will then discuss their definition of kinship, and raise the question of whether biology has really been eliminated in favor of reproduction from their definition, and whether this really makes any significant difference. I think that it does not make any great difference, but the reasons for this judgment will appear in due course.

The critical term is "genealogical." The problem of defining it, and thereby "kinship," in a way that is cross-culturally useful has given anthropologists considerable difficulty. . . . let us simply state that by "genealogical connection" we designate those *culturally posited* forms of interpersonal connectedness that are held to be direct consequences of processes of engendering and (p. 38) bearing children and that have the property of indissolubility.[5] To phrase this another way, genealogical connection is employed here as a general cover term for a wide variety of culturally postulated forms of *congenital* relatedness between persons.

So defined, genealogical connection may entail an enduring and indissoluble relationship of "sharing" of one or another component of a person's being with those two parties presumed to have been responsible for bringing that person into being. "Body," "bone," "blood," "flesh," "soul," and even "appearance"[6] are some of the more common culturally posited shared components of being. In some cases, however, the enduring and indissoluble relationship is only vaguely defined; it is simply a matter of two persons' being jointly responsible for another's being, with no particular aspect (or aspects) of the other's being singled out as somehow critical. The terms of this stipulative theoretical definition of genealogical connection only require that, in local theories, sexual intercourse is considered necessary to the processes of engendering and bearing children. They do *not* require that local theories regard sexual intercourse as *the* sufficient condition for the initiation of these processes.[7] Beyond this, the processes may be (and are) conceived in a variety of ways.

[Footnote 5 reads: We do not assume that concepts of genealogical connection as they are defined here, are a cultural universal, but we suspect that they are far more common than much of the ethnographic and theoretical literature might lead one to believe. Few if any of the numerous cases of "ignorance of physiological paternity" (or even "maternity") or of "the (*sic*) role of sexual intercourse in reproduction" can withstand detailed scrutiny.]

[Footnote 6 reads: Malinowski's account of Trobriand beliefs make it clear that each person is presumed to resemble his or her presumed genitor in facial appearance, and Powell's . . . account reveals that the Trobrianders are no more "ignorant" of "the role of sexual intercourse in reproduction" or of "physiological paternity" than are most other folk who know nothing about the sciences of physiology or biology. The Trobriand theory is like many others in that the component of being that a child is thought to share with his presumed genitor is different from but complementary to that which he shares with his presumed genetrix.]

[Footnote 7 reads: Most well-documented folk theories of human reproduction hold that sexual intercourse is a necessary part of the process, not merely that virgins cannot conceive. It is not always held to be sufficient for conception or pregnancy because, for example, it is widely appreciated that not all acts of sexual intercourse result in pregnancy. To account for this fact many folk theories hold that other-than-human or "supernatural" agencies may also play a part. According to some theories . . . certain spiritual entities *activate* the foetus which itself results from events or processes associated with sexual intercourse.]

Attention should first be directed to the qualifier "that have the property of indissolubility." This is a note that we have not encountered explicitly in any definition of kinship, and it is most important. The linking of "congenital" and "indissoluble" seems significant here; is it because they are congenital, biologically inherent, that they are indissoluble? Or is it that they are just culturally conceived of as indissoluble? Scheffler and Lounsbury might well want to have it both ways: genealogical relations are indissoluble by definition whereas norms, roles, etc. are not; so too, genealogical relations are indissoluble because they are congenital and of such a (biological) nature that they cannot be dissolved. Either way, the linking of congenital and indissoluble as defining features is clear. But they never explain why they include these features in their definition.

Scheffler and Lounsbury affirm that it is the *"culturally posited"* and *"a wide variety of culturally posited forms of congenital relatedness"* that constitute kinship. They go even further, however, saying that genealogical connection may entail all sorts of shared components—body, bone, flesh, blood, soul, and even facial appearance, which according to Trobriand native theory does not derive from genetic continuity as European theory would have it, but derives from the mechanical aspects of sexual intercourse, that is, from mechanical rather than genetic processes. But this is still congenital.

They are equally adamant that although they cannot be sure that concepts of genealogical connection as they define them are universal, they suspect them to be far more common than much of the ethnographic literature might lead one to believe. They go on to say that few if any of the numerous cases of alleged ignorance of physiological paternity or the role of sexual intercourse in reproduction can withstand detailed scrutiny. In a more recent publication (1978:5–13) Scheffler reaffirms this position for the Australian aborigines. So far as one of the more famous cases is concerned, their position is plain: not only is the Trobriand child "presumed to resemble his or her *presumed genitor,"* (emphasis added), but they flatly deny that the Trobrianders are ignorant of the relationship between sexual intercourse and reproduction, citing Powell as their authority for this view. So the Trobriand "father" is a father by either or both of two ways: by virtue of the shared component of congenital relatedness of facial resemblance, or by virtue of the fact that the Trobrianders are well aware of the relationship between coitus and conception. Therefore, by Scheffler and Lounsbury's definition, the Trobriand father is as much a father as any other father in most, if not all, other societies.

Another feature of the definition provided by Scheffler and Lounsbury is the condition of *"culturally posited* forms of interpersonal connectedness that are held to be direct consequences of processes of engendering and bearing children . . . it is simply a matter of two persons' being jointly responsible for another's being." Here we seem to be back to the old notion of two people, if not "creating," at least being "responsible for" or "engendering" another and that some kind of culturally posited interpersonal connectedness is thereby established. Thus if a folk theory says that in no way whatsoever is a child engendered or brought into being by anyone but a single person, then the only genealogical or kinship relationship is with that single person. Note, however, Scheffler and Lounsbury's interesting distinction between the existence of the foetus and its vivification. The vivification may be accomplished in any of a number of ways, but the foetus must be the product of those persons who engendered it. Once again, engendering and being responsible for another's being is not quite enough; "bearing children" or birth is included in this process of engendering *by definition*. Thus, as before, if engendering and being responsible for another's being will not do it, then birth will. If folk theory merely affirms that a relationship exists between one person and another or that one was born to the other, this is sufficient to qualify a relationship as one of kinship. Certainly the idea of birth as a mode of relationship is as old as the idea of consanguinity. But we must be careful to be precise here. If the natives recognize that a child is born of a woman but deny that this fact creates any "culturally posited form of connectedness," then it would seem that this might exclude this from the notion of a kinship relationship. But this is not so for Scheffler and Lounsbury. Other parts of their definition make it mandatory that even when culturally posited forms of connectedness are denied to the act of birth, nevertheless the culturally posited existence of a congenital relationship requires that this be admitted as a kinship relationship. So too does the fact that the theory accounts for the fact that women bear children makes it admissible as a kinship relationship.

This very same problem arises with the explicit specification that "the terms of this stipulative theoretical definition of genealogical connection only require that, in local theories, sexual intercourse is considered necessary to the processes of engendering and bearing children." The local theory may say that sexual intercourse does not create any connection between the man and the woman's offspring, that is, no *culturally* posited form of connection is attributed to sexual intercourse. But this possibility is exempted from the general constraint that the local theory be decisive. According to the definition, all local theory has to do is to concede that sexual intercourse is *necessary* (not sufficient, not causal, not in itself creative) to the processes of engendering and bearing children. *The problem is that the definition is such that if one part does not apply, another will, even at the sacrifice of the native theory.*

Scheffler and Lounsbury's definition of kinship rests on the ideas of a congenital relationship and that sexual intercourse is believed to be a necessary part of the reproductive process. Congenital refers to the prenatal state which implies pregnancy, which in turn implies childbirth so that once again any local theory which includes any one of these conditions qualifies the relationship as one of kinship. But why stipulate "congenital" or that "sexual intercourse is necessary to reproduction"? Is not any local theory of reproduction enough, however farfetched, however mystical, however it departs from scientific dogma? Scheffler and Lounsbury claim that kinship is defined not by *science's* notions of genetics, but by the "folk-cultural theory designed to account for the fact that women give birth to children''; that is, it is *their* theory of reproduction, not *ours,* that is at issue. But they give with the right hand only to take away with the left, because they stipulate that the folk theory is a kinship theory only if it includes a congenital as well as a genital feature. We are further assured that most, if not all, probably do include these features, and if there are any exceptions they have yet to be clearly demonstrated.

Let me put the problem in another way. Of all of the imaginable and of all the well-known features of folk-cultural theories of reproduction, what reason do Scheffler and Lounsbury have for insisting that kinship relations are those relations predicated on birth and on the relation between sexual inter-course and reproduction and further have the character of indissolubility? Scheffler and Lounsbury offer neither explanation nor rationale for these three remarkable a priori conditions of their definition. In fact, they are simply bringing *our* biology (I do not mean genetics) back into what is presumed to be *their* (the natives') cultural theory of reproduction, and so they restore the Morganian definition.

To recapitulate, what Scheffler and Lounsbury (1971) and Scheffler (1974) seem to have done is to have shifted the definition of kinship away from simplistic notions of biological relatedness of the sort posited by Morgan and workers of his time, as well as most anthropologists since his time, and treated kinship as having to do with reproduction. After the almost inchoate efforts of Rivers and others, they seem to have joined Barnes (1964) in defining kinship in terms of the folk-cultural theory of reproduction. Not only, then, did they get away from the scientific notion of genetic relationship, but they put the burden of the definition on the native theory of reproduction. The question I raised was, had they really gotten so far away from biology and the notion of biological relatedness? In the course of raising that question and examining the Scheffler and Lounsbury definition closely, it appeared that not only did the question remain as to how far they had gotten away from biology, but important questions still remain. Why do they include certain features in their definition which seem to go against their avowed intention of putting the weight of the definition on the folk-cultural theory of reproduction? The question, to put it another way, is whether they really have shifted the burden of the definition of kinship from *our* theories to the natives' theories of reproduction.

The Scheffler and Lounsbury definition of genealogy, and hence kin-ship, is one of the most recent, more sophisticated and explicit that I know. It differs from the traditional definitions and understandings by being quite explicit on a number of points where the earlier definitions were vague. It also differs in that it introduces a few points which many of the earlier definitions lack. How widely accepted it is among anthropologists today, I cannot say.

(My guess is that most anthropologists have paid little attention to it because they do not care, preferring the more vague traditional views.)

Nevertheless, the Scheffler and Lounsbury definition is useful for the present discussion precisely because it is explicit. Since it is not a radical departure from the conventional wisdom, it can serve as a useful point of departure for further discussion.

For example, if we ignore the definition of father as mother's husband, the *citamangen-fak* relationship in Yapese culture is not a kinship relationship. But with the Scheffler and Lounsbury definition the situation is not so simple. This relationship is not a kinship relationship prior to the time the Yapese changed their view and adopted the idea that coitus was necessary to pregnancy and brought in the idea that the man plants the seed in the garden (the woman) and that she grows the child. At precisely that moment in time, the *citamangen-fak* relationship became a kinship relationship, and the *citamangen* became a father to the *fak,* his child. Just as soon as the idea that through sexual intercourse the man plants the seed, one of Scheffler and Lounsbury's conditions for the definition of genealogical relationship was met, namely, that sexual intercourse is considered necessary to the process of engendering a child. Where this whole area had not been kinship, in the change of a single belief, kinship appeared. Once the *citamangen-fak* relationship becomes one of kinship, the former the father, the latter the child, then the groundwork for agnatic relations is laid, the *tabinau* can be viewed as containing a patrilineal lineage, and so on. With this one change, the whole *interpretation* of the first description is restored! All of this the consequence of a change in this one belief.

This is truly amazing! With one single shift in the belief system, suddenly a whole segment of a kinship system that did not exist suddenly comes into being, and with it a whole new form of social organization appears. Was it really not there before? Using the generally accepted understandings of kinship loosely, it was not. Even using the new Scheffler and Lounsbury definition, it was not. But with the Scheffler and Lounsbury definition it suddenly appeared where it never had been when *one* belief changed. I will return to this remarkable situation shortly.

I want to turn now to the Doctrine of the Genealogical Unity of Mankind, which is central to Scheffler and Lounsbury's work, as it has been to Morgan's, Rivers's, and almost all contemporary students of the subject. This doctrine rests on three assumptions. The first is that all human cultures have a theory of human reproduction or similar beliefs about biological relatedness, or that all human societies share certain conditions which create bonds between genetrix and child and between a breeding couple. For Scheffler and Lounsbury it is the natives' theory of reproduction with certain additional stipulations. For Morgan, McLennan, and others it was biological relatedness. For Malinowski, Goodenough, and other functionalists it is the mother-child tie and the bond between the woman who is mother and the man most likely to have been the genitor of the child.

The second assumption is that these genealogically defined categories, in their primary meaning, are comparable regardless of the wider context of each culture in which each is set. A mother is a mother the world over, even if mothers vary in certain ancillary respects. So too a father, a son, a daughter, a brother, a sister. The third assumption is that differences in the specifics of different theories of reproduction, in concomitant beliefs about biological relatedness (whether the relationship is through blood and bone, blood alone, flesh, physiognomy, etc.) are distinct and do not really matter, that is, they do not affect the fact that an abstract genealogy can be postulated which applies to all human cultures, or, as I would have it here, to all mankind.

The first assumption can be dealt with briefly. When I say, "all human cultures have a theory of human reproduction," I mean that we have an analytic category which corresponds to the cultural category which is called "their folk theory of human reproduction" (or biological relatedness). If, in the native culture we are examining, there is nothing whatever that corresponds to our analytic category, then our analytic category is not applicable. But it is specifically assumed by Scheffler and Lounsbury that most, if not all, cultures do have such a theory and that such a theory fits their definition of genealogy. On the face of it it would seem that since human reproduction is universal, it is likely that all peoples will have some theory about it. Scheffler and Lounsbury think that most will include the criteria they stipulate, such as sexual intercourse, the sharing of physical features, and indissoluble relations.

The second and third assumptions concerning the comparability of genealogical systems, should give us pause, for they seem faulty in two important respects. First, there is no specification in the definition of kinship (whether it be that of Rivers, those in common use since Rivers, or that of Scheffler and Lounsbury) of the *value* or *significance* of the particular folk theory within the context of the total culture or even within those parts of the culture most immediately relevant. Second, even though the definition of kinship acknowledges that beliefs about human reproduction can differ significantly in their various details, it overrides the differences by appealing to a level of generalization where all are equivalent as modes of genealogical relatedness.

These two aspects of the assumption of the comparability of kinship, regardless of the wider cultural context in which each is set, are so closely related that they must be dealt with at once. The point of separating them above was to make clear at the outset the component elements of the criticism that I am raising.

It is one thing for a culture to have a theory of reproduction. It is quite another to determine the value and significance of the different elements of that theory in the wider context of that culture as well as in the narrower context of the particular theory of reproduction itself. This is particularly relevant to those criteria of the definition of genealogy which are central to all of the definitions of kinship from Morgan through Scheffler and Lounsbury: sexual intercourse and the notion of biological or congenital relatedness.

Not only is Yapese culture the specific case before us, but the place of coitus in reproduction in Yapese culture is also a particularly good example of this problem.

In discussing Yapese culture I have already indicated that whether or not sexual intercourse is considered a necessary condition for pregnancy, *the cultural definition of the relationship between* citimangen *and* fak *does not in any way depend on this fact*. This fact is largely irrelevant to what the Yapese hold to be the significant conditions which relate one person to another. The significant conditions center on an exchange relationship in which land plays a central role. That the child is given a name from the *tabinau* is critical in defining who he or she is as a social person. That name in turn relates that child to the *tabinau* in the sense of a group of persons who are all related to each other by various ties to the same plots of land. That name in turn places the child with respect to the *thagith* by memorializing the name of one who has already been related to that land, thereby affirming the child's relationship to the land. The fact that there is a biological relationship to the mother is of *some* importance, as I have indicated. Here it is less a relationship of doing than of being and it is not a relationship of exchange but of sharing. In the mother-child relationship the fact of *biological* relatedness is important, but its particular importance and the magnitude of its value and the specific meaning or significance it has are insufficiently spelled out merely by the general statement of important–not important, valued–not valued. The precise array of meanings, how they are related to each other and to their evaluative position in the total context must be stipulated. I have done this to some extent elsewhere (Schneider 1962) and need not repeat those details here.

When the belief changed and coitus was considered a necessary though by no means sufficient condition for pregnancy, the image was used of the man planting a seed in the garden which was his wife, and this constituted work, while his wife nurtured that seed as it grew as in a garden. Now, of all of the images which the Yapese might have produced, derived from the Spanish, Germans, Japanese, or Americans who occupied that island, forced their languages on the Yapese, forced their ways and schools and school-teachers on the Yapese, shall we say that it was a mere matter of chance and of no significance that the image the Yapese use is one which involves both work and land in a productive relationship? Would it be too much to say that this image was *over*determined by what has been stressed already as the high value which the Yapese place on work, on the high value they place on land, on the high value they place on the cultivation and growth of food which comes from that land, and on the elaborately ramifying meanings of these? I think not. The image is not that of the woman holding the fetus and the man feeding it by injecting semen regularly. It is not a belief that says that the man and the woman create the child jointly, with parts of their bodies (blood and semen), and that all they need is God's blessing for this natural occurrence to take place.

Not only has almost nothing changed from the time before coitus was held irrelevant to the time it was held relevant, but in those most important respects, the epitomizing symbols or images of high value in Yapese culture have been maintained and applied to the new conception. After more than fifty years of unrelenting Spanish, German, Japanese, and American pressure to give up their whole belief system, they did make a token concession. But they perverted the new idea so as to keep it within the scheme of their old meanings and significations.

I have tried to make two points here, but properly conflated them into one. One is that in the Scheffler and Lounsbury, as well as the traditional (from Rivers on), definition of kinship, the defining criteria are simply stipulated in terms of a present-absent scheme; value is assumed, assumed to be positive and assumed to be universally the same. I called this the Doctrine of the Genealogical Unity of Mankind. Second, that there is no place for meaning in the sense of significance, what it relates to, the place it has as central or peripheral to the larger scheme of things. I have, that is, separated value from meaning and significance, which is quite arbitrary and justified here only for expository purposes. There is no need to argue whether value and meaning should be kept separate as a matter of general principle. It is sufficient to affirm, as I have done, that to merely say that kinship is genealogy and is defined by the presence of certain criteria as in the Scheffler and Lounsbury definition, is just not enough.

Before 1948, the Yapese did not say this. After 1948, the Yapese did say this. But do they give it any value? What significance do they attach to it? What does it mean for them? I have suggested that the answer to all of these questions is "very little!" Further, when they do acknowledge the relation between coitus and pregnancy, they do so *in their own terms,* in images that mean something to them and that effectively destroy the meaning which that relationship has to the Europeans who gave it to them and who analyze "their kinship system."

But the point is more general than Yap alone. From Rivers to Scheffler and Lounsbury, it is simply assumed that for all human beings, for all cultures, genealogical relatedness (however defined) *is* of value and *is* of significance; not merely *en passant,* but as a central value of extraordinary significance. That is, the Doctrine of the Genealogical Unity of Mankind has prevailed. Otherwise, how could one believe in a kin-based society? How could one believe that the idiom of kinship was so important to so many non-European societies? And yet, where in the contemporary literature does one find a serious or extended discussion of the value and significance of biological or genealogical relationship, or the question, "What value does biological relatedness have for the particular people concerned?" All we have from the immediately recent period is the recognition that different peoples have different beliefs about how babies are made and which account, as Scheffler puts it so simply, "for the fact that women give birth to children." It is assumed that this relationship, of birth or blood or biological relatedness, or arising from reproduction, is self-evidently of high value, that it is of great and grave significance—that it is, in short, privileged. I was sometimes forced to make reasonable guesses as to why such an assumption was made because the literature is either silent or nearly incoherent on these questions.

I could proceed with further examples. The Trobriands are an important case in point. Let it be granted that the Trobrianders do believe that coitus is necessary for pregnancy. Whether they know this deep in their hearts or deep in their unconscious, they do know. What they say about making a baby by opening the passage, and then closing the cervix so that the blood will not come out—all this can be taken as given. So what? Is it *this* that relates the Trobriand "father" to his child so that the normatively prescribed relationship of love (Malinowski's "father-love" that he contrasts so dramatically with "mother-right") can then be attached to what Trobriand culture seems to hold as an inconsequential and meaningless "fact"? (Recall, for Scheffler and Lounsbury the genealogical relationship is *by definition* prior to the social relationship.) I, myself, cannot see it. Is the fact that the "father" opens the passage considered by the Trobrianders of such signal significance that it can serve as an idiom for political, economic, religious, and all sorts of other relationships? I doubt it. How does the fact that a child has the obligation to suck his dead "father's" rotting flesh from his bones relate to the fact that his "father" opened the passage or closed the cervix of his mother? Nowhere is this explained to us—neither by Malinowski or Scheffler and Lounsbury. But in European conceptions of kinship the fact that the father "created" the child and that they are of the same flesh and blood ties in directly and explicitly with a host of obligations between them. It is given as *the reason* why the child *owes* his father obedience and love and loyalty, and it is replicated in the relationship between man and the Diety who created him.

The mere existence of a theory of reproduction is not enough to create a kinship relationship as that has been defined for the purposes of the first description. If there is a bond created in the process of reproduction, that bond must be culturally significant to count for anything. Moreover, if it does count for something, the question then is, "What does it count for?" What is its significance? This is no more than to say that meaning and value cannot be omitted from any definition of kinship. The fact that it has been consistently omitted is a serious defect of those definitions and all of the work that has been based on them.

Once we have introduced the question of value and meaning into the problem, we are forced to return to the assumption which is made from the mid-nineteenth century through today, the Doctrine of the Genealogical Unity of Mankind. For those of Morgan's time, genealogy stipulated real biological relatedness; for those from Durkheim, Van Gennep, N. W. Thomas, and Rivers onward, it stipulated real or putative biological relatedness as confirmed or sanctioned by social convention. For Scheffler and Lounsbury the genealogical relationship is constant from culture to culture; it is just that each culture has a different way of defining parenthood and all of the genealogical relations which derive from that. We are forced to assume that genealogy for the Yapese is comparable to genealogy for the Americans, which is the same as any other genealogy in the world so long as that culture's folk theory meets the conditions laid down in Scheffler and Lounsbury's definition.

Are all genealogies equal? I offered the traditional wisdom before when I said that that was the claim. It is now obvious that not all genealogies are equal, and for two very good reasons. One is that the defining features of the genealogy may be variously valued and have different meanings or significance in different cultures. The other is that when the nature and content of the genealogical relationship is taken into account—and these are known to differ from one culture to another—then the assumption of the equivalence of the parent-child relationship is brought into serious question.

If red, yellow, and blue and so forth are all colors, and colors are those segments of the wavelength spectrum visible to the human eye, then we can speak about the way in which different colors are classed and the total spectrum segmented. A set of standards in Munsell color chips has been established, and these can be shown to different people from different cultures who can group them in terms of their schemes for classifying colors. All value and significance is implicitly assumed to be constant in this formulation of the standard, even though systems of color classification vary. Is it not the same with genealogy? All conceivable kin types can be specified, the outer margins lopped off as being beyond question, and we can ask of each culture, "How does it partition genealogical space?" just as we ask "How does it partition the spectrum of colors?"

It is possible, even probable, that the facts of genetic relationship, like color, are the same the world over and can be defined in precise, scientifically established terms. Different degrees of genetic relationship can be specified with respect to ascendants and descendants. In this respect, a genealogy which is in fact a statement of genetic relationship, or even a statement that has a high likelihood of being as close to the real genetic relations as possible, can be regarded as equivalent to the wavelengths that define the color spectrum. But Barnes in 1964 made it perfectly clear, if it had not been perfectly clear before, that there was a radical difference between genetic relations as defined by the criteria of "science" and what are culturally regarded as kinship systems. Even Scheffler and Lounsbury do not opt for *genetic* relations as the criterion for genealogical relationship. They opt for the local folk theory of reproduction.

Although color can be defined simply in terms of wavelength, genealogy *cannot* be defined simply in the terms that Scheffler and Lounsbury suggest. The reason is that the different theories of the relationship between the "parent" and "child" are not comparable in the same way that color is presumed to be. Variation in value and signification are not part of the wavelength spectrum, but they are an inalienable part of the culturally defined genealogical grid. At least at that level it must not only be shown that two different cultures postulate a relationship between parent and child, but that their value and significance are also the same.

The notion that one can separate a genealogical system at one level from the various particular folk theories of reproduction rests on the Doctrine of the Genealogical Unity of Mankind, the thesis that at one level all genealogies are equal to each other, or can be treated as dealing with the same thing and so are comparable. Insofar as a relationship is based on a relationship to land in one culture and on the presumption that a man was one of the creators of the child in another culture and had no direct relationship with the child's being in yet another culture, then it would seem that all genealogies cannot be equal to each other. If all colors consist of waves perceived by the eye and measurable by spectroscopes, all genealogies do not consist of the same thing and there are no "genealogoscopes."

By including the specification of the particular value and meaning in the definition of genealogy it can be argued that we have now destroyed the standard which permits the kind of comparative analysis of different cultures which is one of the anthropologist's fundamental tasks. That is so. That point brooks no dispute. But by the same token it can be said that to nullify a false and misleading mode of comparison will save anthropology from reaching innumerable false conclusions and save anthropologists from pursuing demonstrably false problems.

We must return to part II of this book, where we accepted genealogy and accepted the traditional definitions of kinship and tried to work out why or on what ground it could be argued that many if not all non-European societies were kin-based, what the content of kinship might be, how it could be imagined that kinship could be an idiom in terms of which politics, economics, religion, and all sorts of other things were expressed. The implicit assumption in all of those discussions was that genealogy was the same the world over, at some level at least, that kinship meant the same thing in each and every culture, that kinship had the same significance in all cultures. My point has been that these are patently false assumptions in general, and I have tried to show that it is false in the particular example of Yap.

Therefore I must insist that the first description is faulty in that it failed to specify the value and meaning of kinship. It simply assumed that the value was of a certain quality and magnitude and that its meaning was self-evident. A close look at the material showed that the particular value that kinship was assumed to have, as kinship was traditionally defined, was wrongly assessed, and that the meaning which kinship was traditionally assumed to have was also wrong. The very interesting fact that Yapese changed their belief in regard to the role of coitus was most illuminating in this analysis. It showed that the belief that sexual intercourse is a necessary though not sufficient condition for pregnancy, contrary to so much of the thinking of the mid- and late nineteenth and early twentieth centuries, was not necessarily important as a defining feature of kinship; more important was the question of the *value* and *significance* of sexual intercourse as it related to pregnancy.

One parenthetical note. Two extensive discussions in the literature have helped inform not only my discussion, but I believe to a great extent the definition provided by Scheffler and Lounsbury (1971) and Scheffler (1974). One is the "nature of kinship" debate to which I referred in the last chapter. The other is the "virgin birth" controversy. The latter includes Leach (1966), Spiro (1968), the extensive correspondence in the journal *Man* for 1968 and 1969, and Montague (1971), which Scheffler may have seen in manuscript form. At the time they wrote their 1971 statement, Scheffler and Lounsbury could not have seen the further papers (Spiro's reply to Montague in Spiro 1972, Derrett's 1971 paper, or those of Monberg [1975] and Tonkinson [1978]) in formulating their 1971 definition. But I of course had the benefit of these later papers.

11   A Note on the Significance of Definition

What difference does it make whether we define kinship in terms of folk theories of biology or in terms of folk theories of reproduction? Scheffler and Lounsbury are silent on this subject. They do not discuss the advantages of shifting—if they really do shift—from biology to reproduction. Indeed, they do not justify their definition, but merely assert it.

I have posed the problem as *our* biology versus *their* theory of reproduction, but this must not prevent us from seeing that in the end it is really *our* theory because *we* choose to define kinship. We do so the moment, and in the very process, when we formulate it as an idea. Whether it be sexual intercourse that is crucial, or reproduction in the sense of those who engender, we, in the role of analyst, in the role of those who define kinship as an analytic construct, stipulate what it is that kinship is about. The ultimate definition is still ours to make, and we make it.

This point deserves careful consideration. Scheffler puts the matter quite clearly when he affirms that "the foundation of any kinship system consists in the folk-cultural theory designed to *account for the fact that women give birth to children*" (emphasis added, Scheffler 1974:749). He is not asking how kinship should be defined; he is defining it. This is not a matter of right or wrong; it is entirely his option to define it in any way he chooses. We may criticize the definition, offer a different one, show the advantages of one over another, but that is all beside the point. The point is that as analysts we define kinship; it does not come to us already defined, nor do we go out and "find it" and "describe it like it is."

Scheffler's definition, like Rivers's and the conventional wisdom in general, does have certain advantages, it would seem. It does provide us with a generalized, standard, constant frame of reference within which comparisons can be made. That is, kinship is genealogy. This simply means that there is a relationship of parent and child (no matter how this may be defined in any specific culture), which gives rise to all other genealogical relations. By thus separating the fact of genealogical relationship from the details of each specific native theory, the highly variable folk theories become comparable. So we can see how different cultures constitute and differentiate genealogical relations, what role genealogical considerations play in group membership, access to office, inheritance, and so forth. Conversely, comparison can proceed in the opposite direction by holding genealogy constant, and correlating different theories of reproduction with gender relations, modes of production, descent rules, and so forth.

127

So far so good (though the question will arise later of the legitimacy of this procedure). But at this point I am still concerned with the implications of the definition of kinship as genealogy.

Another implicit feature of the first description, and a point which is emphasized by Scheffler and Lounsbury (1971:38), is the distinction between kinship as genealogy and kinship as a set of norms, roles, values, groups, categories, or social relationships other than genealogical. Given that distinction, there is then the question of priority—structural or logical—of the first over the second. It will be recalled that Scheffler and Lounsbury are explicit on this point.

Relations of genealogical connection, or kinship proper, are fundamentally different from and are *logically and temporally prior to any social relations* of kinship. Relations of genealogical connection may be described as components of "ethnoscientific" (sometimes "ethnobiological") theories. In contrast, the social relations of kinship consist of any rights or duties, or privileges and obligations, that a culture ascribes between kin in general or between the particular reciprocal kinds of kinsmen that it distinguishes. Anthropologists recognize and distinguish such rights and duties—those of kinship—not by their "content," which may be economic, political, religious, or whatever, but by means of the criteria for their distribution or allocation. . . . Where the distributional criteria are genealogical and egocentric, we speak of relations of kinship. The *social* relations normatively entailed by kinship are not conceived as congenital or indissoluble, no matter how binding they may be in law or morality; it is a matter of some concern to many of the world's people that one *cannot* choose his kinsmen whereas he *may or may not* choose to fulfill the duties and obligations of being a kinsman or a particular kind of kinsman. (Emphasis added. 1971:38–39)

If kinship is by definition a set of genealogical relations, this definition says almost nothing about how persons who occupy these genealogically defined positions—mother, father, etc.—should behave or what their social role should be. The role of the father for example may be harsh and authoritarian or it may be warm, indulgent, and hold little or no authority. Yet both roles may attach to the same genealogical position—that of father. This is only to say that the distinction between genealogical position on the one hand and norm, role, value, etc., can be drawn. It is an analytic distinction, of course, for in every real case a real person is father and also plays a role which contains normative elements and values and so forth. But the analytic distinction can be applied.

The distinction is important because it *seems* to permit us to say as an absolute fact that genealogy is structurally or logically prior to norm, role, value, etc. (This is Scheffler and Lounsbury's position cited above and in Scheffler 1972:115.) This seems to be so for exactly the reason given in the above example and quotation. To provide another: a chief may have authority and a father may have authority. There is nothing in the nature of authority that makes it an aspect or quality of kinship. It can attach to any status. Hence the status of father must come before the authority of the father, and the whole frame of kin types which goes to make up the genealogy has structural or logical priority over the roles, norms, values, social relations, and so forth of the total kinship system. It is because the father is the father that he can play an authority role; he is not father because he plays an authority role. By the same token anyone can play a warm, supportive, nurturant role, but that does not make that person a mother; it is because she is a mother (in some cultures) that she can and does properly play that role.

Yet a further word should be said about value and role, or social rela-tions as Scheffler and Lounsbury put it. If kinship is defined as genealogy, and genealogy necessarily is ego-oriented and involves degrees of closeness and distance, and in addition, certain alignments of genealogical positions are culturally marked, then by those very facts certain evaluative commitments have already been made. There must be something more than merely the stipulation that two genealogical positions are closer than two others, for closeness and distance must mean something in the way in which they are evaluated at least and very likely in the ways in which they are supposed to act in some respect. The value of the male line for certain purposes in patriliny, for example, is embodied in that genealogical ordering; the equal value of male and female for certain purposes may be embodied in double descent, and so forth. Two aspects of value may therefore be distinguished; one which attaches to norms for roles, the other which attaches to the particular classifi-cation of genealogical positions in a particular culture. But a further distinc-tion is important; genealogical distance implies something about social rela-tions. And one final point: genealogy and reproduction, on which it rests, may well entail specific role components or aspects of social relations, or what has sometimes been called "content of kinship," especially when contrasted with non-kin relations, but I will leave this matter for another time. The point is that the radical distinction between "genealogical connection or kinship prop-er" (Scheffler and Lounsbury 1971:38) and "social relations" cannot be as sharp or mutually exclusive as Scheffler and Lounsbury suggest. Whether the radical distinction is tenable or is only a distinction of degree rather than of kind need not detain us now.

I said that the distinction between genealogy and norm or role *seems* to permit us to say that genealogy is structurally or logically prior to norm or role. But that priority follows directly from the definition of kinship as genealogy and not from any empirical or independent consideration. It is purely a matter of definition. The structural and logical priority of genealogy is built into the premises embodied in the way in which kinship is defined. There is nothing "structural" about it. There is nothing whatever in Yapese or any other ethnography that helps us evaluate this question. Thus, to argue that the social role is just as important, or even more so, than the genealogy is beside the point. If kinship is defined as genealogy, then and only then can one begin to associate social roles or norms to the former, and not the other way around. That is shown once again by the fact that it is not only father's and mother's brothers who play authority roles, but chiefs, headmen, policemen, and a host of others, none of whom need be fathers to play such a role.

This seems a simple point but it has created problems for those who unconsciously shift the burden of the discussion first from the definition of the kinship system to what they then see as the more interesting or even more important questions. It is obviously not possible to assert that the genealogical system exhausts all that there is to know about a kinship system. It is likewise impossible to assert that the roles which kinsmen play toward each other, the ways in which they are formed into groups, categories or networks, the ideology of specific reproductive beliefs, the values associated with particular kinds of normatively defined interpersonal relationships are the most important part of any kinship system. These can only be established on the framework fashioned by the initial definition of kinship as genealogy. This makes the question "Why reproduction?" even more important.

If kinship were defined in some other terms—for example, as the axiom of prescriptive altruism—then genealogy would become structurally and logically secondary. It might still be quite important, but it could not have the logical priority it has now. We would be bound first to establish that the axiom of prescriptive altruism obtained and second to correlate different factors, such as genealogy, with the defining criterion.

This last point has taken on added significance recently since some anthropologists have argued that in some societies "kinship" is defined in native conception by a combination of both biological and one or another criterion. Silverman (1970), for example, suggests in his "mud and blood" hypothesis that for the Banabans, kinship is defined in terms of both landholding and blood relationship. For other societies it is argued that kinship is defined in terms of some special code for conduct such as the axiom of prescriptive altruism.

But here again the solution seems simple. It is *we* who define kinship. We can adhere to the traditional definition of kinship as the relations arising out of reproduction, in which case the Banabans and the other societies do not have "kinship." Or we can expand the definition of kinship to include both biological relatedness and some other feature or features. This last solution is no more than to change the definition of kinship. But either solution creates a conceptual revolution of no small magnitude.

Yet is anything gained either by agreeing that many societies do not have kinship as it is traditionally defined or by changing the definition so that those societies can be brought in? If we follow the first course, we restrict "kinship" so radically as to change beyond recognition our understanding of it and of its importance in human society. On the other hand, if we redefine kinship then we not only make future studies discontinuous with previous studies but we also protect a concept of kinship from those criticisms which are not dealt with by a change of definition.

As noted earlier, Rivers attempted to emphasize the social over the biological significance of kinship by recourse to the idea that fatherhood was established in the Banks Islands by paying the midwife. If Rivers had stuck to this position he would, of course, have radically changed the definition of kinship. But in the end Rivers stayed with genealogy as the defining feature of kinship and this Banks Islands episode stands as a lapse in his otherwise consistent position.

The matter is quite simple. Given the definition of kinship as genealogy, by definition genealogy has priority over related phenomena. If this definition proves inadequate to the study of some societies, then we are forced to three alternatives. We can exclude the societies to which the definition of kinship does not apply, we can change the definition of kinship, or we can abandon the whole notion of kinship. But we *cannot* smuggle in new criteria by which kinship is defined, such as sharing land or altruism, and still think we are dealing with kinship as genealogical or biological relatedness.

Earlier I made much of the fact that our definition of kinship—the conventional wisdom—stressed *being* while Yapese culture stressed *doing* in certain of its important relations and that this made for a poor fit between the conventional wisdom of kinship study and the way in which Yap culture was constituted.

This point should be related to the present discussion. The stress on *being* correlates with the separation of genealogy as a system of interconnected positions (all "indissoluble" by Scheffler and Lounsbury's definition) from the roles, norms, and values assigned to a genealogical relationship or category. And as I have just shown, this distinction is in turn a consequence of the definition of kinship as genealogical. And finally, the definition of kinship as genealogy presupposes that kinship derives from biological processes— reproduction, birth, and sexual intercourse—which yield indissoluble relations, that is, relations of *being, not doing.*

Insofar as relations are defined as *being* rather than *doing,* and those relations derive from reproduction, birth, sexual intercourse, etc., and these are all the culturally valued or culturally constituted elements, then we are faced with the same question I have just put so far as Yap is concerned. Does Yap have kinship or not? If it stresses *doing*, not *being*, puts little value on sexual intercourse as having anything to do with the bond between persons, places minimal value on reproduction as relating persons or statuses, then Yap does not seem to have kinship. Unless, of course, one wishes to follow Scheffler and Lounsbury and say that since they recognize sexual intercourse as having to do with the fact that women have babies, by that fact alone (with or without others) they have kinship by definition. But the point is clear; do we exclude the Yapese, do we redefine kinship, or do we just throw the whole notion of kinship out when dealing with cultures like Yap?

We can now provide one answer to the question of whether kinship is a privileged system or not, and if so why. The answer here is that it is indeed a privileged system *by definition*, for we cannot treat it as if it were a natural object with inherent qualities. It is privileged because of the way in which we define it and its functions. The problem, then, is not to try to evaluate its inherent features, but rather to study the implications of different definitions and different ways of conceptualizing the problem, and most particularly, of course, to see how it articulates with various data.

One further note on this point. Scheffler and Lounsbury say that genealogy is logically *and temporally* prior to any social relations of kinship. I have clarified the notion of logical priority; that is simply a matter of definition. They do not explain temporal priority. It is possible to work through Lounsbury's publications (for example, Lounsbury 1965) and guess that "temporally" refers to the so-called extensionist hypothesis, but this need not detain us here. Suffice it to say that the temporal priority of genealogy is never clearly explained by Scheffler and Lounsbury so far as I can see.

12 Malinowski's Legacy and Some Perils of Functionalism

As noted in chapter 9, many have said that kinship is a social and not a biological relationship, but have failed to specify what kinship is without the biological referent and what relationship exists between social and physical kinship. Malinowski and his functionalist followers provided just such a statement and established a framework within which the study of kinship could proceed.

I will speak loosely here of "Malinowski and his functionalist followers" and "Malinowskian functionalism." By this I mean Malinowski's work over his lifetime, and those authors who either accepted certain of his positions or tried to refine and develop certain of his views. I do not mean to imply that Malinowskian functionalism is a single, monolithic, and internally consistent doctrine. Rather, I use the terms to indicate a general theoretical position which derives from or through Malinowski.

Malinowskian functionalism provided a new statement of the relationship between social and physical kinship by shifting to a functional statement of that relationship. That is, social kinship became the ways in which certain fixed conditions of human existence, specifically those having to do with reproduction, were attended to. The physical features of reproduction, the nature of human nature, and the psychobiological nature of human beings as these are related to human reproduction are thus brought into the social sphere as the foci around which the social sphere is organized. It is the social regulation of action so as to meet the problems imposed by the biological, physiological, and psychobiological conditions centering on reproduction that defines kinship. This formulation of the problem implicitly redefines kinship from what "kinship is" to what "kinship does," so to speak. That is, it is redefined from being a kind of thing or cultural form (a relationship of consanguinity, for example) to a kind of function (the ways in which reproduction is regulated).

It is not only the biological facts of reproduction, the facts of sexual relations, the required care and feeding of infants if they are to survive, the psychological states involved, and so forth—the basic needs—that require regulation. Derived needs arise from the ways in which the basic needs are met. For example, the basic need for reproduction is met in part by the birth of the child. But since the society has to continue to exist, and since people are withdrawn by death and added by birth, a derived need arises from the fact that the child has to be placed in the social universe. This means that there

133

must be some customary way of doing this. The social position of its parents functions to locate the child. The conditions of reproduction and the universality of the family mean that a child has two parents and both parents are important to its social placement. The fact that sexual relations have to be regulated means that reproduction itself must be regulated. Women cannot become pregnant as the spirit moves them; they have to be socially defined as eligible to be mothers. So too, the relationship between father and child is based on the relationship between a man and the woman who bears the child, and this socially sanctioned relationship makes him eligible to be the social father. But eligibility is not enough; some social convention must confirm the new status. The father is not only a necessary part of the universal and indispensable family, but also a necessary part of establishing the legitimacy of the child and the way in which the child achieves his place in society as a member of a particular family, clan, class, and so on.

Instead of positing a single, substantial bond of some kind between kinsmen, Malinowskian functionalism uses the functional prerequisites of human nature, society, and culture. Kinship is defined as the institution whose primary function is to meet the needs of reproduction and the derived needs which arise from them. The bonds of kinship thus grow out of certain conditions and experiences rooted in the nature of sexual reproduction rather than consisting in a specific *thing* (like shared blood). Those bonds do not just appear; they must be socially formulated and confirmed and made part of the culture. This "value added" element is essential to the Malinowskian functionalist view.

For the functionalists who followed Malinowski, kinship is defined with reference to the biological conditions of human sexual reproduction, and in this respect is no different from any other definition discussed in chapters 9 and 10. But it differs in one important respect. The biological and other conditions of reproduction constitute conditions which have to be met: kinship is the way these conditions are met. For instance, given the functional prerequisite embedded in the conditions of sexual reproduction, the family, or a familylike unit, is universally the mediating element between those biological conditions and the total kinship system. It is in the family and through the family that many of the basic needs are met and it is through the social and cultural extension of familial relationships that social kinship exists. The family, for Malinowski, consists in a woman and the children she bears along with the man with whom the woman and the children are in a more or less stable relationship.

Malinowski's shift from a formal to a functional definition of kinship reflected some of his more general preoccupations, as well as being of particular interest itself. First, he was generally concerned with function as the major theoretical problem of anthropology. Second, he was convinced that the family was a universal and *the* fundamental institution of society. Third, he was interested in the so-called denial of physical paternity by certain Australian groups and the Trobriand Islanders.

Spencer and Gillen reported in 1899 that the Aranda denied the role of physical paternity, and similar reports from other Australian tribes followed soon thereafter. Malinowski published his book on the family among the Australian aborigines in 1913 and gave this problem serious attention, as it was given serious attention by almost everyone concerned. In the same book, he also addressed the problem of how best to understand kinship, though his views are stated there with great caution (Malinowski 1913: esp. chap. 6). It was here that he first defined the father as mother's husband (although, as I have already noted, he was by no means the first to do so). This definition followed from his profound conviction of the universality and fundamental importance of the family in human society. If the family could be shown to be an important part of the culture of the Australian aborigines, as his book aimed to show, and if the father is an essential member of the universal family, then the father must be defined as something other than procreator or genitor. The father could, instead, be defined as mother's husband. Shortly after the publication of the book on the family among the Australian aborigines, Malinowski worked intensively among the Trobriand Islanders, who also denied the role of the male in procreation. If physical paternity is explicitly denied by the natives, the substantive relationship between father and child as a cultural formulation was out of the question (though a substantive definition of the mother-child relationship could still be sustained, of course).

So far as kinship is concerned, then, kinship as a sociocultural system is still rooted in, and in part determined by, the nature of human nature. But the relationship between physical and social kinship is now formulated in functional and adaptational terms. This new formulation of the relationship between physical and social kinship has had profound implications for the study of kinship.

I will not speculate further on the relationship in Malinowski's work between the denial of physical paternity and the formulation of kinship in terms of its function rather than as a substantial bond. But even if Malinowski was not the first to define the father as mother's husband rather than as genetic father, or even as social father, he and the later functionalists certainly developed that position most fully.

From a functionalist perspective, there are a number of other answers that can be given to the question of whether kinship is a privileged system.

One is that kinship either is, or can create, a basis for solidarity which is stronger than all other kinds and which in turn can or does provide a foundation on which all other kinds of relationships are built. Without kinship as such a base, no other relationship can exist or even get started. Hence kinship is a prerequisite to any further differentiation, as it is a prerequisite for any relationship which can at the same time have undifferentiated political, economic, and other functions. Without the bonds of kinship there is no ground on which they can establish the solidarity and trust which is prerequisite to social relations.

I have been careful in the preceding paragraphs not to explicitly invoke the "extensionist" hypothesis, but it is implicit. I have avoided this since it is a long and complex problem which, though surely related, is not necessary to the problem at hand.

Another answer starts with an evolutionary premise, which is not inconsistent with Malinowski's functionalism. According to this premise, the family was the first form of social organization and so remains the cornerstone of society and culture. Thus the necessary precondition to any differentiation is a simple kin-based society. Even the evolutionary view, however, depends on the question "What makes kinship a privileged system such that it is the most elementary form of social relationship out of which all others evolve?" One answer might be, "Because kinship is rooted in certain especially fundamental and fixed conditions of the biological and psychobiological nature of human beings associated with human sexual reproduction." This answer leads back to Malinowskian functionalism. It did not begin with Malinowski, of course. Functionalism is as much associated with Durkheim and Radcliffe-Brown. But Malinowski initiated a particular functionalist view that has had great influence on contemporary students and is an integral part of the conventional wisdom of today.

Rather than recount further details of Malinowski's own position on kinship, the family, and functionalism, it will be more helpful here to consider the views of some of his more recent followers. Although Malinowski's followers or the adherents of functionalism are not unanimous in their views, those I have chosen are, I think, representative and well within the mainstream. These are Spiro (1977), Barnes (1955, 1961, 1964, 1974a, 1974b), Firth (1936), and Goodenough (1970).

Spiro (1977) starts with the Westermark and Malinowskian view, saying,

> Some formidable critics to the contrary notwithstanding, I share with Malinowski, Murdock, and Lounsbury (among others) the view that the nuclear family is the invariant core of every and any kinship system. (P. 2)

He goes on to add that "the universality of kinship, at least so far as its family core is concerned, marks man's affinity with many other mammals" (p. 3). If we ask just what Spiro means by "core," since it is so prominent in his view, we are told, the family, sometimes uniparental, sometimes biparental, is phylogenetically rooted, constituting the nucleus, and sometimes the whole, of mammalian societies; and despite the current fashion in some anthropological quarters of minimizing, if not denying, the biological basis of the human family and kinship, it is difficult to escape the conclusion that some of the same biological variables that account for the phylogenetic roots of the family also account for its persistence . . . . kinship is rooted in biology. . . . The roots of these similarities [between kinship systems] are not hard to discover. However much kinship systems must adapt to and are conditioned by variations in ecology, economy, demography, politics, and so on, they must all deal with certain invariant conditions of human social existence. That is, every kinship system must attend to certain ineluctable biological facts, among which I would stress the following. Human reproduction is bisexual, and conception is effected by means of heterosexual intercourse; humans are born helpless, and they remain physically and emotionally dependent on their caretakers for a prolonged period; children live, minimally, in biparental family groups, so that it is their caretakers (usually their parents) who, for better or worse, satisfy their dependency needs; dependency being the infant's prepotent need, feelings of affectionate attachment develop towards the agents of its satisfaction; satisfaction is always relative to frustration, so that these caretakers are simultaneously the first and most important objects of affection, as well as hostility; siblings are also part of the family group, and since affection is a scarce—and therefore competitive—good, they, like parents, are objects of these same conflicting emotions. (Pp. 3–4)

Barnes takes a position which is similar but not quite in line with that of Spiro, since it does not take the family as universal.

Cultural motherhood is a necessary interpretation in moral terms of a natural relation, whereas the relation of genitor is an optional interpretation, in the idiom of nature, of an essentially moral relation. Speaking more generally we may say that there is a real world we call nature which exists independently of whatever social construction of reality we adopt. The relation between nature and culture is contingent; some aspects of nature impinge more obviously and insistently on the human imagination than others. The constraints on the construction we make of fatherhood arise from our social lives as adolescents and adults; our concept of motherhood is more closely constrained by our lives in the womb and as young children while we are still largely creatures of nature. (1974a:72)

Firth takes essentially the same position.

The fact that there is no society without a kinship system of some kind means that in the first place there is overt allowance made for sentiments generated by parturition, sex union and common residence. . . . in the second place that these physical phenomena provide a simple base, easily recognizable and unusually unchallengable, on which other necessary social relationships may be erected. (1936:577)

Spiro, Barnes, and Firth agree that kinship is "based on," or "phylogenetically rooted in," simply "rooted in," or "constrained by" the "real world we call nature." My initial concern is with the use of terms like *base*, discussed at some length in previous chapters. Having introduced the notions of *base, rootedness,* and *constraint,* Spiro, Barnes, and Firth fail to clarify what these words mean or how those conditions work. So the meaning of *base* is no clearer here than it was in the notion of the "kin-based" society discussed in chapter 5. If, however, we accept this lack of clarity, we can pursue the implications of the "base in nature" as developed by Spiro, Firth, and Barnes.

The notion of a "base in nature" creates a self-justifying and untestable definition of kinship: "kinship" as a sociocultural phenomenon is, in the first instance, defined as entailing those "natural" or "biological" facts which it is at the same time said to be "rooted in" or "based on." The phenomena which are shown by analysis to be related are already related by definition. Since they are defined as related in the first place, it is no great discovery to find them to be related. If Barnes, Spiro, and Firth were to define kinship in such terms as were independent of what Barnes calls "nature," and then were to show that there is a relationship to what they can independently define as "nature," then the case could be examined to see if the correlation held, and if so whether the direction of the determinate relationship was as proposed by Barnes, Spiro, and Firth, namely, that biology and nature constrain kinship, and not the other way around.

So when Spiro says that "kinship systems . . . must all deal with certain invariant conditions of human existence" and then goes on to stipulate which ones these are, I can only ask whether kinship is or is not defined as ways of dealing with those conditions in the first place. A careful reading of Spiro suggests to me that he does so define kinship, and I am forced to conclude that his argument is circular.

Because of the circularity of his argument, it is not really possible to evaluate Spiro's contention that "kinship" deals with the invariant conditions of human social existence that he stipulates. This is because he does not tell us how these invariant conditions of human social existence are *actually* dealt with. That is, he does not offer a step-by-step analysis which can be examined in detail, but only asserts this to be his conclusion. If he were to list the invariant conditions of human social existence—say, conditions 1,

2, . . . *n*—one could then examine any given kinship system and ask two different questions: first, are conditions 1, 2, . . . *n* actually met (and if so, in part or in whole?) by the particular kinship system being examined, and second, are any of these conditions met in any significant degree by aspects other than kinship? That is, are the particular conditions which Spiro posits exhaustively met by kinship, or is kinship but one of an array of many different aspects of culture that meet these conditions? It might be argued, for example, that the condition of heterosexual intercourse, to which Spiro says "every kinship system must attend," is in fact attended to by many different aspects of culture—moral, jural, economic, religious, etc.—of which kinship is perhaps the least important.

If certain aspects of kinship could indeed be accounted for by the "ineluctable biological facts," while certain others could not, the question would arise as to the relation between them. Are those parts of the kinship system which are determined by the biological facts in some sense primary, while others are secondary and derivative? If, as Spiro says, "kinship systems must adapt to and are conditioned by variations in ecology, economy, demography, politics, and so on," do the biological facts have some priority or are they but one of the conditions, like ecology, economy, demography, etc., to which kinship systems must adapt? Take note: if the latter is the case, then kinship must be as much rooted in these other conditions as it is rooted in the ineluctable biological facts. So we are back to our main question: What is so special about the facts of human sexual reproduction that the economy, the ecology, demography, etc., do not share? Is kinship a privileged system? Does its special privilege reside in its roots in biology or sexual reproduction? If so, just how? Spiro answers none of these questions for us. Neither does Malinowski.

This point should be taken one step further. Spiro links kinship with certain invariant conditions of human existence: with the bisexual nature of human reproduction, the role of sexual intercourse in conception, the helplessness of newborns, and so on. Why should "kinship" be linked to the ways of dealing with *these* particular invariants? If kinship is defined as the ways in which these invariant conditions are met, then I can only repeat that Spiro's argument is circular. If, however, Spiro conceives of kinship as an independently defined set of relations, he gives no hint of this for he does not define kinship independent of its alleged functions. Thus even if we grant Spiro's contention that there are certain invariant conditions of human existence, and that every society and culture must cope with them, the problem is to show how they are coped with and *then* to determine the place of "kinship" (however that is independently defined) in the total array of ways which deal with those conditions.

Let us leave aside, for the moment, the untestability of their definitions and assertions, and consider the relation between those aspects of culture that are "based on" or "constrained by" nature and those that are not. Spiro, Firth, and Barnes concur on this point. According to Spiro,

> Some of the same variables that account for the phylogenetic roots of the family also account for its persistence. . . . I consider non-kinship relations more than . . . those of kinship, to stand in need of a high degree of symbolization. That is, the extension of the boundary of the interacting group beyond the network of consanguineally and affinally related kin depends crucially on symbolization for the conceptual basis both of group formation and social identity. At the cultural level, it is religion which, par excellence, depends on the human symbolic capacity, for it is symbolism that transforms personal fantasy, the wellspring of religion, into culturally constituted reality; it creates beings (spirits) out of non-beings and invests words and gestures with instrumental efficacy. This being the case, the universality of religion is not accidental, for as Robertson Smith and Freud (among others) observed long ago, much of religious symbolism is rooted in and is the metaphorical expression of kinship relations. More specifically, religious symbols often represent the transformation and elaboration of the cultural level of fantasies and cognitions at the psychological level, and these in turn are often produced by kinship relations at the social level. (1977:3)

For Barnes much the same picture emerges.

> Some aspects of nature impinge more obviously and insistently on the human imagination than others. . . .
> I argue that the mother-child relation in nature is plain to see and necessary for individual survival. An infant may be free to form attachments to mother-surrogates, but most scientists would agree that a woman's response to an infant after she has given birth is in some degree innate or genetically determined. Hence a relation of physical as well as social motherhood is always recognized culturally and institutionalized socially. On the other hand the evidence of the human father-child relation in nature has been, until the last hundred years in the West, slight and inconclusive. . . . the constraints on the construction we make of fatherhood arise from our social lives as adolescents and adults; our concept of motherhood is more closely constrained by our lives in the womb and as young children while we are still largely creatures of nature. (1974a:72–73)

Firth concurs, as the previous quotation of him indicates (1936:577), for he says that the simple physical base constrains any cultural construction since it is easily recognizable and usually unchallengeable.

Lévi-Strauss can be included in this discussion for he seems to take a very similar position, a position which, in part, accounts for the fact that he turned his attention from kinship to mythology in seeking the ways in which the human mind is structured by an examination of its products. Since mythology is a "pure," "unencumbered" product of the human mind in ways that kinship is not, it is therefore a better reflection of the structure of the human mind than is kinship (cf. Boon and Schneider 1974).

This position says, in brief, that insofar as symbolization and the sociocultural construction of meaning is concerned, kinship is relatively narrowly restricted by virtue of being so closely "rooted" in or "based" on, or "tied" to, the real, invariant, biologically given conditions of human reproduction.

This is an odd position for Lévi-Strauss to take, for he also says, "A kinship system does not consist of those objective ties of filiation or consanguinity given among individuals; it exists only in men's consciousness and constitutes an arbitrary system of representations, not the spontaneous development from a factual situation" (1963:50). I may, then, be in error in ascribing this position to Lévi-Strauss. Or, it may be that Lévi-Strauss has not been entirely consistent.

Spiro views meaning and symbolization in a remarkable way. If it is religion which, par excellence, depends on the symbolic capacity, this is so because it is not "based" on, "rooted" in, or constrained by those invariant facts of human existence that kinship is. Yet Spiro himself goes on to explain how religion is in fact just as deeply rooted in the invariant facts of human existence by showing how "much of religious symbolism is rooted in and is the metaphorical expression of kinship relations. More specifically, religious symbols often represent the transformation and elaboration of the cultural level of fantasies and cognitions at the psychological level, and these in turn are often produced by kinship relations at the social level" (1977:3). That is to say, the capacity to symbolize and attribute meaning is clearly an inherent human capacity; what is symbolized and the meanings attributed is not infinite but is sharply constrained by the source of the symbolization, which is largely kinship relations, which are themselves rooted in the conditions of human existence. Hence to argue that religion is largely symbolic because it is not constrained in the same way as kinship, yet kinship is largely the source of the symbolization and the things symbolized and the impetus for symbolization in religion is to state just the same sort of constraint on religious symbolism and meaning as is seen for kinship. Barnes seems to take a similar position when he says that more can be made symbolically out of the father than out of the mother because "our concept of motherhood is more closely constrained by our lives in the womb and as young children while we are still largely creatures of nature" (1974a:73).

Meanings and symbolic significance are neither inherent in, nor do they arise in a necessary or determinate way simply from the concrete facts of the human situation. They are cultural constructions, a system of representations which are attributed to what are in turn conceived of as the "facts" of the human situation. Religious beliefs, both insofar as these are the products of capacities inherent in the human being (phylogenetic) and insofar as they emerge from the human condition, are as much rooted in and based on invariant human capacities and conditions as are any other beliefs. As much constraint is imposed on religion by man's humanity as on anything else. By the same token, the capacity to use the so-called invariant facts of human existence, whether it be people's birth by women or people's ambivalence toward those with whom they are most intimately engaged in early childhood, as facts to which a very wide range of meanings and symbols can be attached, remains the same (Schneider 1976).

The problem, to summarize briefly, starts with the use of terms like *based, rooted in,* and so on. These phrases are not explicated by Spiro, Barnes, or their predecessors, Murdock, Malinowski, or Westermark sufficiently clearly and precisely so that they can be evaluated. They are pregnant with allusion, but every attempt to pin them down fails. The problem is compounded by arguing that the invariant facts of human social existence, particularly those of human reproduction, constitute a set of *constraints* on the kinds of meanings, symbolizations, and social forms which are possible. This assertion is simply insufficient; what is constrained? How does the constraint work? On what does the constraint work and how? Barnes says that we can make anything we want out of the genitor, but we are sharply limited in what we can make out of the genetrix. Yet the psychoanalytically inclined, like Spiro, for example, know that people can and do make the most remarkable objects out of the genetrix, and that these may be institutionalized in sacred images, folk tales, myths, as well as the nightmares of individuals. What limits are imposed by the facts of motherhood? On what? How do they work? Can it be shown that such limits are not there or are different for the genitor? Until this is spelled out the argument is unconvincing.

Even if we accept the Spiro and Barnes sort of argument that the "facts" of "nature" constitute a set of constraints, just what is constrained and how remains to be demonstrated. That is, if the newborn child must be fed if it is to live, then this requires that if a child is to live (other things held constant) then it must be fed. But within what social forms feeding occurs, what feeding means, how it is comprehended, what it represents, how it is conceptualized and symbolized are only constrained in one narrow respect; feeding the child is necessary if it is to live. Feeding may be conceived of as an act of generosity or of duty, of God's bounty or woman's nature, as the reward for observing sacred obligations, and so on and on. Indeed, feeding need not even be conceived of as "feeding," for feeding itself is a cultural construction. Is this what is meant by "kinship"? And indeed, what are construed as "facts," as the "invariant conditions of human social existence," are always more than that alone. They are also the reifications and objectifications of certain ethnoepistemological beliefs whose significance does not lie in their objective, scientific credibility, but rather in their signification as symbols and meanings of a cultural order. This is but to say that the "invariant facts of human social existence" only exist as such when so constituted culturally and thus made to serve as the vehicles for the meanings which are culturally assigned to them. But is it this that is meant by "kinship"?

If kinship is privileged because it is deeply rooted in and sharply constrained by the facts of human reproduction, of sexuality, of the needs of helpless infants, and so on, this has simply not been demonstrated by Malinowskian functionalism and certainly not by Spiro's exposition of it. This is at least in part because the attempt of Malinowskian functionalism to show how the social forms of kinship are determined by, shaped by, and given meaning by the conditions of nature on which they are based is quite inadequate. In fact, the attempt to relate physical and social kinship in a convincing and productive way, as it had not been related heretofore, by shifting from social forms to social and natural functions as the theoretical point of departure, was hardly even an improvement, much less a success, though it seemed to show a revolutionary promise.

13   Some Further Perils in the Study of Kinship as Exemplified by Goodenough

Spiro asserts that the roots of kinship are in the biology and psychobiology of human reproduction. Goodenough (1970: all page references in this chapter are to this volume) agrees but focuses his attention on providing a framework in terms of which description and cross-cultural comparison can take place. The universal facts of human sexual reproduction provide the framework within which universally applicable concepts for comparison can be formulated. Goodenough states this clearly on the very first page of his text. "Human societies, despite their many forms and diverse customs, are all alike in being expressions of mankind's common human nature" (p. 1). This requires that we go beyond the ethnocentric assumptions which tend to dominate our vision and "see human phenomena other than through the lenses to which our society's customs have habituated us" (p. 1). Because this is difficult, "we have to find some set of terms that will enable us to describe other cultures with minimal distortion from ethnocentric cultural bias. And we need some set of universally applicable concepts that will enable us to compare cultures and arrive at valid generalizations about them" (p. 2). Goodenough then goes on to quote with approval a passage in which Kluckhohn argues the classic functionalist position with regard to comparison, that is, that this can be done by taking invariant points of reference supplied by the biological, psychological, and sociosituational "givens" of human life. These invariant points and their interrelations determine the likenesses in the broad categories and general assumptions that pervade all cultures because the givens provide a focus around which and within which the patterns of every culture crystallize. Hence comparison can escape the bias of any distinct culture by taking as its frame of reference the natural limits, conditions, clues, and pressures of human existence. In brief, there are certain functional prerequisites to social life, conditions that must be met, or that every culture must cope with, if it is to persist, and because they determine what every culture must do, they can serve as a universally applicable standard of comparison.

So, for example, in discussing the ways in which marriage might best be defined, Goodenough says

> Gough has moved in the right direction in that she looks for a universal problem, one that all societies must handle; . . . to achieve a generally applicable definition of marriage we must find a universal human in-

145

terest that relates in some way to sexual reproduction. Sexual access is the only human concern I can find that meets this requirement. That it should do so is itself a reflection of several general human characteristics. One is the tendency to form continuing, affect-laden relationships. The reasons for this tendency are imperfectly understood, but the prolonged dependence of infants and small children on adults seems to be a significant consideration. This tendency carries over into sexual relationships, so that men and women tend to attach importance to the persons with whom they have sexual connection and tend to cultivate their relations with them. Associated with this is the universal tendency for males to be combative and competitive regarding sexual access to females. Finally, for a variety of reasons that are yet unclear, men and women who have grown up together as siblings tend not to establish sexual liaisons with one another. (P. 11)

This last brings in the incest prohibition, of course. But it is clearly grounded in a general human tendency of a psychobiological sort.

In the above quotation one learns that men and women tend to form stable associations, and that their offspring are included. This is the family, of course. Goodenough, like Malinowski, affirms that the relationship between the adult male and female is based on a sexual relationship. For purposes of description and comparison, Goodenough defines this relationship in terms of social rules governing sexual access and the formal announcement of their existence (p. 12).

Goodenough is moving toward a definition of marriage. His next step is to state that "Because rights and obligations other than those pertaining to sexual access can be vested in the sibling relationship, a definition of marriage that includes other than considerations of sex and reproduction cannot be applied universally—as long, that is, as we assume that marriage involves a transaction that links two persons in a manner they were not linked before" (p. 12). He then quotes Fortes with approval, who says, "anthropologists agree that what distinguishes the conjugal relationship from all other dyadic relationships . . . is the exclusive, or at the minimum privileged, sexual rights and claims of the spouses on each other. These rights and claims pertain to socially responsible procreative sexuality as opposed to irresponsible juvenile and adolescent sexual indulgence" (p. 12).

Goodenough then gives us his definition of marriage—a definition intended to be universally applicable and useful for comparative purposes (pp. 12–13).

> I myself would define marriage, then, as a transaction and resulting contract in which a person (male or female, corporate or individual, in person or by proxy) establishes a continuing claim to the rights of

sexual access to a woman—this right having priority over the rights of sexual access others currently have or may subsequently acquire in relation to her (except in a similar transaction) until the contract resulting from the transaction is terminated—and in which the woman involved is eligible to bear children.[8]

[Footnote 8: Whether or not she is capable of bearing is another matter. . . . The conjugal relationship established by a marriage may include many rights and privileges pertaining to other than sexual matters but they are irrelevant to the general definition of marriage.]

A further point is worth noting. "Arising from human nature and affecting the nature and distribution of rights and duties . . . (is) the universal tendency to male dominance over women and children" (p. 18). "This tendency gives men a proprietary interest in the sexuality of women and in the labor and services that women and children can provide. Men tend to treat these things as a form of property" (p. 22). It is this, of course, that requires the definition of marriage to be phrased in terms of rights of a man against all other parties to sexual access to a woman. If the person who has those rights has any duties, Goodenough does not find them to be universal and so does not include them in his definition. Correspondingly, the woman has no rights that Goodenough finds to be universal. This does not mean that the woman has the duty to provide sex on demand; she may or may not have the privilege of according that right herself. The right of sexual access is a right vis-à-vis others who may want that right. Because this right is associated with a relationship in which the woman is eligible to bear children, it plays a significant role in the ascription of jural paternity (Goodenough, personal communication).

The pattern is clear. There is a universal biological condition, an ingredient of human nature, related to sexual reproduction, which in turn creates a universal problem. This becomes a part of social kinship by constituting a constraining condition within which a jural definition, a statement of rights and duties, is formulated. This jural formulation must be applicable to all cultures, that is, it must be universal. This is guaranteed by the fact that it is generated by a universal human condition. The relation between physical and social kinship is perhaps more precisely formulated as a relation between the universal human conditions that bear on human sexual reproduction that must be met if society and culture are to persevere, while social kinship is the minimum universal cultural forms, or aspects of them, which meet these conditions.

The basic unit of any kinship system is the woman and her dependent children. Two kinds of family groups may be formed. The woman and child and her sexual partner form the elementary conjugal family; or the woman and her child joined by her brother(s) or consanguineal kinsmen form the consanguine family (pp. 18–19).

Goodenough makes it clear that it is the woman and her child that constitute the basic unit.

> Scheffler (1970) . . . derives jural parenthood directly from biological parenthood. . . . Scheffler correctly insists that what we recognize as jural kinship and parenthood in our own and other societies rests ultimately on a relationship involving biological procreation. But this anchoring relationship is that of the natural mother and her child, not the natural father and his child. Natural fatherhood can be reasonably inferred only in social arrangements in which men have close to exclusive rights of continuing sexual access to women, in arrangements I have called marriage. (P. 30)

This brings us to motherhood.

> We are dealing with a jural role, then, but can identify it cross-culturally not by its content but by some constant among the criteria by which people are entitled to the role.

> My suggested definition of marriage provides one such constant. A more immediately relevant constant is the fact that children are borne by women and, until very recently in human history, are dependent on the women who bear them for their survival during their first year of life. In these and perhaps other ways, as well, the nature of our species provides conditions that favor the close association of women and the children they bear. . . . we may say that jural motherhood consists of the rights and duties a woman has claim to in relation to a child by virtue of having borne it, providing she is eligible to bear it and provided no other disqualifying circumstances attend its birth. (Pp. 24–25)

Unlike motherhood, jural fatherhood cannot be derived from natural fatherhood.

> as a working definition . . . jural fatherhood consists of the rights and duties in relation to a child a person has claim to by virtue of his being married at the onset of her pregnancy to the woman who bore it, provided he is otherwise eligible and provided no disqualifying circumstances attend the child's birth. The same rights or a reduced version of them, may be claimable in some societies by the acknowledged genitor other than the mother's husband or by the mother's subsequent husband. Not being the genitor may or may not be a disqualifying condition. Ceasing to be the mother's husband may or may not be a dis-

qualifying condition. The rights and duties of fatherhood, as thus defined, may be very few; and they may even approach the vanishing point. . . . Nevertheless the only cross-cultural constant that provides a point of departure for systematic comparative study is provided by marriage and the jural relationship of a man to the child a woman conceives while he is married to her. (Pp. 28–29)

To put it simply, then, a parental relationship involves the allocation of newborn children to adults as dependents for the time it takes them to mature, and all societies make such allocation to married couples. The mother is the woman who bears the child, if she is eligible to bear the child—however that eligibility is stated in the particular culture. Those rights may be delegated to some other woman or transferred outright or surrendered in the case of fosterage, adoption, or divorce, but such rights derive from the rights of the woman eligible to bear the child (p. 25). And the father is the mother's husband, provided he is qualified or eligible (p. 28).

From here the definition of kinship is but a short step (pp. 22–23).

Consideration of the family inevitably leads to consideration of parenthood, and consideration of parenthood is obviously the key to any cross-culturally useful definition of kinship, as Malinowski (1930, 146) clearly saw. . . . kinship, at least consanguineal kinship, derives from a chain of socially recognized parent-child connections.[15]

[Footnote 15 reads: . . . Clearly what defines kinship as such is not the content of kin relationships, but the fact that the relationships, whatever their content, are based on a socially recognized chain of childbearing and childbegetting. The chain itself is a natural phenomenon, but all societies make something of it culturally. What they make of it is necessarily related to the pattern of dependence of human infants and children on their nurturing adults and everything that follows from it.]

Or, as Goodenough puts it a few pages later, quite formally (p. 29),

Kinship, I have said, cannot be defined without reference to parent-child relationships. Jural, as distinct from biological, kinship consists of the father-child and mother-child relationships, as jurally defined, and any other jural relationships that depend for their definition on the genealogical proliferation of jurally defined parent-child and husband-wife ties. Kin relationships can, therefore, be described as relative products of "parent," "child," and "spouse," together with whatever indications of age and sex may also be required in specific cases, as with the kintype notation used by anthropologists.[19]

[Footnote 19 reads: Buchler and Selby (1968, 35) have properly observed that the kintypes we designate by the anthropological notations F (father), M (mother), B (brother), MB (mother's brother), etc., are "sociological constructs, based in part upon biological considerations." I would add that for any particular society to which we apply them, they have meaning according to the cultural definition of jural parenthood in that society. The definitions of kin types that comprise a genealogy in one culture are not necessarily those that comprise it in the next; but the general definitions of fatherhood and motherhood I have given here show us how to arrive at these different cultural definitions in each case.]

This is as much as to say that there is a "core" of kinship which is directly determined by biological conditions of reproduction and is constant across cultures. Each culture adds features to that core which make it different from other cultures. All fatherhood is the same in those respects in which it is defined: but in any particular case it will be quite distinct by virtue of features other than those in which it is defined. Those features which are shared by virtue of being the defining features I will call the core features.

This core is the genealogical grid, of course: "the relative products of 'parent,' 'child,' and 'spouse,' . . ."; what I have called the Doctrine of the Genealogical Unity of Mankind. It is at once a universal feature of every kinship system and an etic concept in terms of which all kinship systems can be described and compared.

Goodenough's treatment of the relationship between the universal problems which man's nature and the requirements of social life entail on the one hand, and the kinds of definitions which are required for cross-cultural comparison on the other hand should be spelled out more precisely.

The general principle is that form does not depend on its function for its definition. Formal definitions are used when the aim is to equate things formally and see how their functions vary. Functional definitions are used when the aim is to equate things functionally and see how they vary formally. The anthropological concern with varying "forms of marriage," for example, requires a functional definition of marriage. An anthropological concern with the functions of the Eucharist among Christian societies requires a formal definition of the Eucharist. Thus by locating the universal problems which humans face as a result of their psychobiological constitution and the requirements for the maintenance of social life, the foci for certain universal cultural domains can be located and defined so that certain kinds of useful comparisons can be made. The requirement that children be formally assigned to persons who take responsibility for them is determined by the conditions of human reproduction: the long dependency of children, the need to fix responsibility for them rather than have it diffused among many different people, along with various other conditions. This requires parenthood, and parenthood provides the focus and definition of the domain of kinship. But the definition of parenthood for comparative purposes can in turn be set in either functional or formal terms, depending on the aim of the comparison. If the aim is to compare the forms of parenthood, the definition must be functional; if the aim is to compare the functions of parenthood, the definition must be formal. Definitions used in cross-cultural comparison, whether formal or functional, must be universally applicable. That is, they must depend on such features as permit them to be applicable to, and equatable, from one society to another. Any particular society will have a form of marriage, for example, which includes certain elements which it shares with all other societies and by which we know it to be "marriage" and not something else. This minimal or "common denominator" sort of definition permits both the description of uniform universal features plus a variable penumbra of elements which are more or less distinctive to particular cultures. (This is my interpretation of a personal communication from Goodenough. He is not responsible for any distortions which I may have introduced into it.)

Goodenough puts it this way.

> . . . comparison requires some set of common terms suitable for describing the content of each culture—a set of etic concepts. . . . But it requires something else as well: some basis for deciding what set of forms in culture A are appropriate ones to compare with a particular set of forms in culture B. . . . when we compare property relations in two cultures, by what criteria do we decide that we are dealing with something we can call "property" in each case? Or "marriage," "kinship," "religion," etc.? Clearly these do not pertain to the content of cultural forms but to the roles which these forms seem to play in peoples' lives. . . . These terms . . . reflect functional considerations. . . . Functional classifications enter implicitly, if not explicitly, into almost all comparisons of culture that anthropologists have made. They have provided the one set of presumed universals or common denominators of culture, taking for granted that all people everywhere have similar problems and concerns arising from their common humanity. (Pp. 119–20)

This quotation, which I think is a reasonable representation of the way the matter is actually set forth in the book, seems to me to bring form and function much more intimately together than the personal communication I cited just before it. But one thing is clear in the book. The precise definitions of the various aspects of kinship, such as motherhood, fatherhood, marriage, and so on, are put in strictly formal, not in functional terms. On the other hand, the domain of kinship itself is defined in functional terms, in terms of the universal human problem of reproduction, as well as formal terms as the system of relative products derived from marriage and parenthood (as in the quotation cited from p. 29). This suggests that Goodenough is more concerned in this book with formal description and comparison, taking kinship, as it is functionally defined, as a constant. That is, his descriptive and comparative focus is largely on form, holding function constant.

To be explicit about the way in which the different areas within kinship are defined in formal, not functional terms, while kinship itself is defined largely functionally, consider the following examples. The conditions of reproduction constitute a universal problem for human beings and their cultures. This defines the domain of kinship in functional terms, and kinship in turn is based on parenthood, the way in which human cultures universally deal with the problems created by human reproduction. But the definitions of motherhood and fatherhood are such that fatherhood need have nothing whatever to do with biological paternity. And motherhood need have nothing to do with the biologically necessary relation of intimacy between mother and child, the psychological requirements for the child's growth and development as a social person, or even the growth of the child inside its mother's body or its suckling at the mother's breast. These functional considerations are distinct from the problem of establishing a formal definition based on empirical observations of world ethnography. All known cultures are surveyed and only those formal features which fit the idea which is being defined—marriage, fatherhood, motherhood, etc.—that are found to be universal can be used to construct the definition of the cultural form. That some functional considerations may creep in, for example through the premises that are involved in the assumptions about the significance of universals, may be true but these seem consistent with Goodenough's statement that "functional classifications enter implicitly, if not explicitly, into almost all comparisons of culture that anthropologists have made" (pp. 119–20).

The definitions of features within kinship like marriage, parenthood, etc., do not derive from theoretical considerations but from empirical observations of what are believed to be universal features of the forms. They have one further important characteristic for Goodenough; they are restricted to rights and duties. That is, they are jural. Thus even if it were possible to show that affective or other aspects of cultural forms such as marriage, parenthood, etc. are in fact universal, these would be excluded from the definitions on the ground that Goodenough is explicitly concerned with jural considerations. In this respect the formal definitions are cognitive and thus in accord with Goodenough's famous definition of culture as that which one has to know in order to have one's actions accepted as proper—according to the rules—by the natives. (*Cognitive* does not necessarily mean "conscious," of course, so that the rules need not be formally codified or verbally explicit, though they may well be.)

The notions of "etic" and "emic" are central to Goodenough's treatment of kinship, as they are central to his general approach to culture. He starts with a clear commitment to such aims as "we have to find some set of terms that will enable us to describe other cultures with minimal distortion from ethnocentric cultural bias. And we need some set of universally applicable concepts that will enable us to compare cultures and arrive at valid generalizations about them" (p. 2). When discussing Truk, in particular, he says, "To start with the objects of residential choice as the Trukese perceived them, as they are defined by the standards of Trukese culture, results in a different structure from one arrived at by projecting on them an erroneous conception of their culture, the categories of one's own folk culture, or the categories of one's own professional anthropological culture" (p. 104). Goodenough's aim and his commitment to what he calls "emic" description and his concern that his etic concepts adequately and accurately describe the emic cultural forms is clearly stated (p. 123). But this commitment to getting the emics right must be understood within the limits of his conception of "etics" and "emics" as well as his conception of culture which is, as I have indicated, cognitive and explicitly confined to jural features. Thus what he might regard as an emically accurate depiction of some cultural form might differ considerably from what I or some other person might consider accurate simply because our conceptions of culture and the "emic" differ.

Goodenough, in a personal communication, seems to confirm this last point when he indicates that despite the apparently polar formulations of etic and emic, every emic statement is at the same time deeply entailed in etic considerations. That is, the selection of a topic for consideration requires a theoretical stance outside the particular culture being described; every definition which seeks to perceive a distinction embedded in a particular culture starts with an etic background consisting in the knowledge of known and conceivable distinctions, as well as certain formal definitions of the cultural forms involved in such description, and so on. Hence an emic description which is envisioned as a perfectly unbiased picture of a particular culture "as it really is," so to speak, is a fantasy: it is simply not possible. What Goodenough calls "emic," then, is a description formulated in etic terms which distinguishes a particular cultural form, or set of forms, from others with respect to some problem defined in jural and cross-culturally applicable terms. The etic is always embedded in the emic, just as the emic is embedded in the etic since the etic is built up on the basis of emic considerations; and both are formulated in terms of rights and duties.

Goodenough's book falls well within the conventional wisdom of kinship studies which treat the domain of kinship as a clear, self-evident, unquestioned and unquestionable domain based on, as well as defined by, the conditions of human reproduction and their social and cultural regulation. The domain of kinship is defined functionally and formally as the social and cultural manner of dealing with the universal problems of human reproduction by "parent," "child," and "spouse" and their relative products. "Clearly what defines kinship as such is . . . the fact that the relationships . . . are based on a socially recognized chain of childbearing and childbegetting. The chain itself is a natural phenomenon, but all societies make something of it culturally. What they make of it is necessarily related to the pattern of dependence of human infants and children on their nurturing adults and everything that follows from it" (pp. 22–23).

There are a number of points in this view of kinship which are problematic. The first is that the fact that there are certain biological "facts" and that every society makes "something of it culturally" still leaves the domain defined in a particular way. It is an *analytically* defined domain. Whether any society clearly marks this off as a distinct *cultural* domain is never raised as a question by Goodenough in this book (or elsewhere in his writings so far as I am aware).

There is a distinct difference between a domain which can be marked off in some way by an observer who wishes to use it for some analytic purpose and a domain which is marked off as part of the culture of some particular society. For example, the domain which I might define for some analytic purpose as that of medicine does not correspond to any domain distinguished in Navajo, Mescalero Apache, or Yapese cultures to note but three with which I am familiar.

There is nothing inherently wrong (or right) with defining a domain or problem area for analytic or comparative purposes, though there are a number of problems that must be controlled when doing so. But there is something wrong with confusing or conflating an analytic or comparatively defined domain with a domain which is defined or marked out as part of a particular culture. Goodenough, in conformity with the conventional wisdom of kinship studies, either assumes that kinship is a descriptively and comparatively useful analytic domain and at the same time one which every culture itself constitutes as part of its own culture, or he ignores this important distinction. That is, he does not distinguish the analytic from the culturally constituted domain. (See Schneider 1976 for a fuller discussion of this point.)

As was noted, the "emic" always entails the "etic" for the "emic" starts with a problem, an analytic formulation of the relevant variables of the problem, a set of categories in terms of which description and comparison can proceed, and then asks, in terms of that formulation of the problem and those "etic" concepts, how this particular culture formulates its distinctions and so forth. But one kind of problem which Goodenough does not seem to allow for, and the one set of variables which he does not seem to give consideration to, is the question of how particular cultures formulate their organizations, of how they define the domains that they conceive their universes as being constructed of, of how the domains which they define as the existent and relevant cultural formations are related to each other.

There is nothing inherent in the "etic-emic" notion that makes it inconsistent with the formulation of such a problem or the statement of such variables. Indeed, the whole problem can be fitted very neatly into a functionalist scheme if one assumes that a universal problem which all human beings must face and deal with is the formulation of life as a meaningful system, its symbolization and expression in terms of some ideology, and this includes their social life, its constituent parts (or domains) and how they interrelate. But Goodenough prejudges this issue, leaving no room for such a formulation by flatly formulating kinship as a domain which either conflates the analytic and the cultural or treats the latter as if it were irrelevant. Like all who subscribe to the conventional wisdom, he starts with the premise "kinship is" when the first question might better be, "Is kinship a cultural as well as an analytic domain in this or that particular society?" Or, more importantly, "Is kinship a useful domain at all, and if so, for what purpose?" To put the matter differently, the fact that "all societies make something of it culturally" (pp. 22–23) does not tell us whether what they make of it culturally is universally the same and constitutes the same clear-cut domain or system, with the same assumed importance which the anthropologist gives it when he analyzes it, or whether it is but a minor or major aspect of some larger (or smaller) domain of different dimensions and differently focused. For example, is it inextricably intermeshed with what this particular group of natives regard as their "ritual and ceremonial system," or that particular group of natives regard as their "political system, including property holding"?

If I am correct in saying that neither the "etic-emic" scheme nor a strictly functionalist position is inconsistent with the question of what domains are constituted within the culture itself, then it would seem to follow that any identification of domains must be labeled as being either analytic or "emic" in the sense of culturally constituted. It may well be that Goodenough regards kinship as so clearly and self-evidently an analytic domain that he feels it is not necessary to make such a statement explicit. As must be evident by now, one of the points that I have been making consistently throughout this book is that I am not convinced that kinship is universally constituted as an emic, or culturally constituted, domain, or that the genealogical grid is universally culturally constituted, though it may be possible to impose such an etic grid on all cultures by using carefully constructed etic definitions of parents, children, and spouses which are actually totally alien to the images, constructs, and native distinctions embedded in particular cultures.

If this is true, then kinship for Goodenough, as it is for many, if not all, practitioners of its study, is strictly an analytic scheme in the same sense that an analysis of natives' physical condition may show them to have an inadequate protein intake, or chronic helminthic infestations, or an analysis of their productivity may show their agricultural yields to be of some carefully measured magnitude expressed in European standards of measurement. It is not an analytic scheme which takes as its initial point of departure the question of how in the very first instance, and without reference to functionalist theory, the natives themselves formulate the domains or constituent parts of their culture, and how they themselves formulate the units of those domains.

This problem is exemplified in that bit of conventional wisdom which Goodenough shares with most if not all other students of kinship, the Doctrine of the Genealogical Unity of Mankind.

Kinship, I have said, cannot be defined without reference to parent-child relationships. Jural, as distinct from biological, kinship consists of the father-child and mother-child relationships, as jurally defined, and any other jural relationships that depend for their definition on the genealogical proliferation of jurally defined parent-child and husband-wife ties. Kin relationships can, therefore, be described as relative products of "parent," "child," and "spouse," together with whatever indications of age and sex may also be required in specific cases. (P. 29)

This definition of kinship and the genealogical grid composed of the relative products proliferated out of the primitives' "parent," "spouse," and "child" means that in these minimal respects, the genealogical grid and its constituent kin types are the same in every culture. This is because mother, father, spouse, and child are all defined in precise, formal terms which are universal. However fathers and mothers may differ from one culture to another, in certain ways they are, by definition, the same in all cultures. Otherwise they are not mothers and fathers.

This in turn means that when kinship is compared from one culture to another, certain features—the features that define the genealogical grid—are held constant, while all other features are variable. Obviously, if other definitions are used for father, mother, spouse, and child, or for kinship in general, a different set of features would be constant while certain of the constants under the previous definition would become variables.

Those features which are the defining features, the minimal features which distinguish a father from his friend, for example, are thereby accorded a privileged position. Whether that privilege implies causality, high cultural value, or a determinant quality may vary with the particular student of kinship. But the very fact of being used as a defining feature in terms of which any particular instance is either judged to fit, or conform to the type, or is dismissed as not fitting at least implies one thing; that the defining features have not an ordinary, but a special significance as compared with all other features. It is in this sense that the defining features are privileged.

The selection of certain defining features thus marks those features as having special value. Such features are not picked at random. Some justification must be provided for selecting them rather than others. The points that Goodenough makes which bear on this question are that the features of his formal definitions are selected empirically and that they must be universal. Their empirical universality seems to be the justification for the selection of the defining features of his formal definitions of fatherhood, motherhood, marriage, etc. This points in a general direction, but the grounds for the justification are not made explicit by Goodenough. If their universality is a sign of some special significance, what is that significance? When kinship is regarded as universal this also implies some special significance, but I can find no statement about whether it has more or less or different significance than any other universal response to any other universal human problem, and there are certainly many universal human problems which culture deals with. There is an extensive literature on the significance of cultural universals, but Goodenough does not refer to it, perhaps because he feels it is too obvious and well known to need such explication.

Another possible justification for selecting certain features in terms of which to define kinship, fatherhood, motherhood, marriage, etc., might well be their functional significance. Goodenough does not say this directly; indeed, except for kinship, his definitions of motherhood, fatherhood, marriage, and so on are all strictly in terms of form, not function. Further, he makes it clear in the personal communication cited above that form and function are independent except insofar as function sets certain constraints within which different forms may be possible. But those constraints are such that all imaginable forms are not possible. This justification might be related to that of universality. It is possible that a universal human problem might be met in such diverse ways that no universal formal features could be found among those different ways. Whether this just happens not to be the case, or whether there is some good reason why it cannot be the case, or there is some reason why it is not in fact the case is not evident from Goodenough's discussion.

The relationship between form and function for Goodenough is ambiguous in certain respects. A distinction can be drawn between a vital function and one which is not. That is, it may be possible to show that if this or that matter is not attended to, then the particular structure of the culture or society would be different or would become altered. These would not be vital functions. But like Spiro and Barnes, and Malinowski before them, Goodenough seems to be saying of such problems as are attended to by kinship, motherhood, fatherhood, and marriage, that without attendance to them human social life could not exist. These would be vital functions. Vital functions are necessarily universal, for human social existence depends on them. It is these vital functions that Goodenough's treatment of kinship is concerned with.

In principle, function specifies what *must* be done, but it does not specify *how* it must be done. Recall that Goodenough holds function constant when forms are compared, and holds form constant when function is to be compared, implying the independence of form and function; and that he views function as a set of constraints within which form may vary. But where kinship and family are concerned Goodenough often seems to suggest that function is one important determinant of form. If this is the case they are not entirely independent of each other.

There are at least three ways in which particular functions in the domain of reproduction seem to determine cultural forms. The first is by the well-known "social recognition of biological facts" as this concept is used by Morgan, McLennan, Radcliffe-Brown, Fortes, Firth, and Goodenough. The second, as stated by Goodenough, Malinowski (1930b), Wilson (1980), and Spiro (1977) among others is that certain patterns of behavior which humans tend to exhibit by virtue of their human nature alone are transformed into cultural forms, or aspects thereof. These two ways are not always distinguishable.

For example, Goodenough states that "men and women who have grown up together as siblings tend not to establish sexual liaisons with one another" (p. 11). Does he mean that this human tendency of those who grow up together as siblings to fail to form sexual liaisons becomes part of the incest prohibition? Or again, "Clearly what defines kinship is not the content of kin relationships, but the fact that the relationships, whatever their content, are based on a socially recognized chain of childbearing and childbegetting. The chain itself is a natural phenomenon, but all societies make something of it culturally" (p. 23). Here yet again is the social recognition of biological facts, of course. But Goodenough continues: "What they make of it is necessarily related to the patterns of dependency of human infants and children on their nurturing adults and everything that follows from it" (p. 23). Here the tendency toward certain patterns of action necessarily becomes cultural as well as natural. Or, another instance: "the tendency to form continuing affect-laden relationships carries over into sexual relationships, so that men and women tend to attach importance to the persons with whom they have sexual connection and tend to cultivate their relationships with them" (p. 11), which then presumably becomes part of the marriage relationship as it is culturally constituted. Here, as before, there is the celebration of a human tendency by bestowing social significance on it. Just why what people will probably do anyway requires social recognition or social signification is not discussed by Goodenough.

The third way in which particular functions determine cultural forms, or aspects of them, is by the interaction of a number of different functional conditions which determine a more complex cultural form. An example would be the conditions of pair-bonding, sexual interest, absence of estrus, the prerequisites to early socialization, and so forth all combining to require a familylike unit. Another example is Goodenough's treatment of motherhood. He says, "A more immediately relevant constant is the fact that children are borne by women and, until very recently in human history, are dependent on the women who bear them for their survival during their first year of life. In these and perhaps other ways, as well, the nature of our species provides the conditions that favor the close association of women and the children they bear" (p. 25).

I have used the term *determine,* but it is possible that I have not used a term which Goodenough himself would prefer. The question is of the relationship between the nature of human nature and the sociocultural forms of social living. The functionalist position in the most general sense states that whatever forms social life takes, they must meet certain functions prerequisite to human survival. Are function and form totally independent? That is, does a particular function require a particular form and only that particular form (or aspect of some form) or are there always a multiplicity of forms which can meet that function?

I do not always find Goodenough clear on this question. He says that function and form are independent and so he frames his definitions of parenthood, marriage, etc., in formal terms, while the general area with which the definitions are concerned (kinship) is located with reference to function. Thus, for example, the domain of kinship itself is functionally defined. "Clearly what defines kinship is . . . the fact that the relationships . . . are based on a socially recognized chain of childbearing and childbegetting. The chain itself is a natural phenomenon, but all societies make something of it culturally" (p. 23). Or "jural kinship and parenthood . . . rests ultimately on a relationship involving biological procreation" (p. 30). Or "a cross-cultural definition of kinship, which we have seen, derives in turn from a cross-cultural definition of parenthood. And definition of the latter, we saw, rested on certain facts of human nature that are a matter of universal concern" (p. 121). Much rests on the word *rests,* of course. But when motherhood is formally defined so that, among other considerations, the woman who bears the child, unless otherwise ineligible, is normally its jural mother, and when people have a tendency to form continuing affect-laden relationships which carries over into sexual relationships, I find it hard to see that this is wholly independent of the formal definition of marriage in terms of rights of sexual access and motherhood as the rights and duties a woman has by virtue of bearing that child. It seems to me that the nature of human nature, in this respect, goes a long way toward "determining" this form. The two are by no means independent: a significant aspect of social form "rests" on its vital function. Neither can I see these as merely "constraints" within which a wide variety of different forms is possible.

A number of statements throughout the book relate particular functions or particular states of human nature to particular social forms so that the former does much more than merely set limits constraining the latter; they directly determine the latter in one of the three ways that I have indicated. A further example may make my point.

> A cross-cultural definition of kinship, . . . derives . . . from a cross-cultural definition of parenthood. And definition of the latter, we saw, rested on certain facts of human nature that are a matter of universal concern. (P. 121)

Spiro (1977:3–4) is explicit in specifying the determinant role of biology in cultural form. A quotation from Barnes is also unequivocally clear on the determinant nature of function on form to compare with Goodenough's statements. Barnes makes much of the difference between physical motherhood and fatherhood, saying, "cultural motherhood is a necessary interpretation in moral terms of a natural relation, whereas the relation of genitor is an optional interpretation, in the idiom of nature, of an essentially moral relation" (Barnes 1974:72). Goodenough's statements in this matter are: "Scheffler (1970) . . . derives jural parenthood directly from biological parenthood. . . . Scheffler correctly insists that what we recognize as jural kinship and parenthood in our own and other societies rests ultimately on a relationship involving biological procreation. But this anchoring relationship is that of the natural mother and her child, not the natural father and his child. Natural fatherhood can be reasonably inferred only in social arrangements in which men have close to exclusive rights of continuing sexual access to women, in arrangements I have called marriage" (p. 30). "We are so used to thinking of parenthood in procreative terms that we easily forget that the acts of begetting and bearing children may not in themselves entitle men or women to any rights and privileges relating to children. *But I do not imply by this that procreation is entirely irrelevant to the definition of parenthood, either*" (p. 24, emphasis added). But what, precisely, is the relevance of procreation to the definition of parenthood?

If function specifies what must be done, not how it must be done, the relationship between function and form remains ambiguous for Goodenough.

He does not come out flatly, as Malinowski and Spiro do, and say that certain very specific social forms are required by and determined by certain very specific functional considerations. Though Malinowski and Spiro, to cite but two examples, put what few propositions they do make plainly so that one can take specific issue with their specific contentions, Goodenough does not do this. His treatment is different. Form and function are considered to be quite independent for certain purposes. But form and function are related so that function specifies some sort of constraints within which form can vary. Yet in certain respects, certain forms are very closely related to certain functions. The whole relationship is treated very amorphously, though function is discussed extensively in the book and plays a very prominent role in Goodenough's writings about kinship, of which this book is a major example. In brief, the treatment is unsatisfactory partly because it is not clear on just what the relationship between form and function is, and most particularly in its failure to specify just precisely what functions impose just precisely what constraints on which cultural forms, or just precisely what functions do determine just precisely which cultural forms, or even just where and why certain functions are independent of which cultural forms. This criticism applies equally well to Malinowski, Spiro, Fortes, Firth, and many other Malinowskian functionalists, but no less so to Goodenough.

It is difficult to separate Goodenough's theory of culture from the way in which he deals with kinship, parenthood, marriage, and so forth. His view of culture is very specifically formulated in both cognitive and jural terms—in terms of rights and duties—explicitly excluding affective or any other kinds of materials. This makes it a stronger and more systematically formulated theory than that of Malinowski or Spiro, for example, whose theories are far more diffuse. When Goodenough says that he is concerned to bar ethnocentric bias from description one must agree with him wholeheartedly. We are all, after all, against sin, and ethnocentric bias is *the* cardinal sin of anthropology. But when he defines culture in terms of rights and duties, and someone else defines culture in terms of patterns of and for behavior, and a third defines it as the system of adaptation of a human group to its ecological niche, and yet another sees it as a social formation which is the product of a particular historical process, and so on, then it is difficult to evaluate the ways in which kinship is handled without at the same time undertaking a general critique of a theory of culture. Nevertheless, Goodenough's position is well within the mainstream of those theories of culture which see kinship as a universal fact of social life and are concerned primarily with culture as a system of rights and duties. His cognitive bias sets him apart in some degree from the others, but his focus on the jural, on rights and duties, puts him squarely with Radcliffe-Brown, Fortes, Murdock, Malinowski, and the other eminent students of kinship.

Next consider the implications of Goodenough's work for the two descriptions of the Yapese material. Two points can be made from the point of view of Goodenough's position. First, the *citamangen-fak* relationship is indeed a father-child relationship, for the *citamangen* is the man who is married to the woman who bore the child, and was so at the onset of her pregnancy. This of course turns on the definition of fatherhood. If father is the genitor and must be the one who, in native theory, is responsible for engendering the child, then *citamangen* is not the father. If Goodenough's (and Malinowski's) definition of father as mother's husband is followed, then he is the father. It is as simple as that. Hence any argument that there is no patrilineal descent unit because there is no father fails according to Goodenough simply because there is a father.

Secondly, the second description is unsatisfactory because it is not stated in such etic terms as permit the description to be used comparatively. That is, the *citamangen-fak* relationship must start with the statement that it is a father-child relationship (this is its etic construction) and only then can it proceed to the details which are distinctive of Yapese culture, the emic features. By failing to use the etic guidelines, the emic details alone remain, and in the nature of the case are unique and hence not subject to comparative analysis.

There may well be, and probably are, other difficulties with the first description from Goodenough's point of view; but these, I believe, arise from differences between my understanding of certain etic concepts and Goodenough's understanding and use of those concepts, none of these being related to the fundamental problems of the study of kinship. An example would be our definition of descent and its distinction from kinship. Such differences all take kinship for granted and are concerned with specific applications or analytic concepts.

I will conclude, then, by reiterating the point made earlier. The question at the outset of this part of the book was this: What is the relationship between physical and social kinship as that has been understood in the conventional wisdom of the last hundred years or so? At first we saw the relationship put in terms of the social recognition of what were presumed to be biological facts of the utmost gravity and consequence; for Morgan, for instance, when primitive man first recognized the blood relationship and its significance, this was a major step toward the development of civilization, for such ties were self-evidently strong and binding. This followed from their substantive and instinctive qualities—they were natural, and their social recognition as such enhanced in some way their efficacy. But by the turn of the century, or just before, the point was made that such ties were social ties and were, in the Durkheimian phrase, *sui generis,* and should not be confused with biological relationships. But such a view, held by Rivers, Durkheim, and others, left kinship hanging in midair and essentially undefined. Without a biological referent, or some reference to the natural processes of reproduction, kinship was either nothing or almost everything, as in Needham's statement that "kinship has to do with the allocation of rights and their transmission from one generation to the next" (1971:3). Van Gennep's insistence that kinship centered on the native theory of procreation might have been a solution of sorts, but it was not generally recognized as such at the time. The matter was overtly ignored by most, though recognized as a problem by some for a time. The "discovery" that some Australian aborigines "denied physical paternity" only made the matter more difficult.

Malinowski and his version of functionalism seemed to offer a solution to the problem. The relationship between physical and social kinship became a relationship where the physical facts were functional necessities which determined the social facts, or at least, determined certain functionally necessary aspects of them. Culture in general, and kinship and family in particular, was seen as an adaptive mechanism (not a new or revolutionary idea since this idea had been implicit in much of the developmental anthropology of the earlier period). Culture was the way in which human beings had to adapt to certain ineluctable facts of life. These functions had to be fulfilled if humans were to survive and their society and culture perpetuated. But when this functionalist doctrine is examined with care, nowhere is there a clear, specific, and detailed analysis showing precisely what functions *determine* precisely what social forms, how they do so, or even what functions *constrain* precisely what social forms, or how they do so. Instead there are general statements of glittering generality which depend heavily on their presumably self-evident quality to compel conviction.

The net effect of all this is to once again impugn any statement of a relationship between physical and social kinship. In Goodenough's hands (as in the hands of all functionalists so far as I can see) the relationship between social and physical kinship is asserted to be based on vital functions arising from the facts of human nature insofar as reproduction is concerned, but the precise relationship between physical and social kinship is no clearer or more fully demonstrated than it was fifty, seventy-five, or one hundred years ago.

This last point must be stressed. The privileged position of kinship has been argued by functionalists of many particular persuasions, from Malinowski through Talcott Parsons, as one which is based on its vital functions. In the absence of a clear and compelling demonstration of precisely what those vital functions are and how they determine or constrain specific cultural forms, functionalism must be dismissed as failing to resolve that issue. The question of whether kinship is a privileged system and if so, why, remains without a satisfactory answer. If it is privileged because of its relationship to the functional prerequisites imposed by the nature of physical kinship, this remains to be spelled out in even the most elementary detail.

14   The Fundamental Assumption in the Study of Kinship: "Blood Is Thicker Than Water"

Why is kinship regarded as a privileged system? I have reviewed a number of answers to this question, but there is one more to be considered.

The clue to this answer comes from the fact that kinship has been defined in terms of the relations that arise from the processes of human sexual reproduction. Human sexual reproduction has been viewed by anthropologists as an essentially biological process, part of human nature, regardless of any cultural aspects which may be attached to it.

The question can now be rephrased; why has kinship been defined in terms of the relations that arise out of the processes of human sexual reproduction?

I suggest that it has been so defined because there is an assumption that is more often than not implicit, sometimes assumed to be so self-evident as to need no comment, but an assumption that is, I believe, widely held and necessary to the study of kinship. It is the single most important assumption on which the premise of the privileged nature of kinship and the presumed Genealogical Unity of Mankind rests. It is the assumption that Blood Is Thicker Than Water.

Without this assumption much that has been written about kinship simply does not make sense. Without this assumption it is difficult to understand why so many have written so much at such great length for more than one hundred fifty years about kinship. Without this assumption it is hard to understand why Morgan and McLennan, Maine and Bachofen, Spencer and Durkheim, among many others, put so much weight on the role of kinship in the history, evolution, or development of society and culture, as well as its maintenance and functioning, whatever its form. With this assumption it is easier to understand why Malinowski, Radcliffe-Brown, Lowie, Fortes, Firth, Eggan, Murdock, and Lévi-Strauss, among others, invested so much time in its study in the belief that it was *the* major institution of "primitive," "tribal," or "simpler" societies.

Because "Blood Is Thicker Than Water," kinship consists in bonds on which kinsmen can depend and which are compelling and stronger than, and take priority over, other kinds of bonds. These bonds are in principle unquestioned and unquestionable. They are *states of being,* not of *doing* or performance—that is, the grounds for the bonds "exist" or they do not, the bond of

165

kinship "is" or "is not," it is not contingent or conditional, and performance is presumed to follow automatically if the bond "exists." All kinship bonds are of essentially the same kind. *All of this is because kinship is a strong solidary bond that is largely innate, a quality of human nature, biologically determined, however much social or cultural overlay may also be present.* It is the biological character and the innateness in human nature and not the sociocultural overlay that largely accounts for the characteristics of the kinship bond. Finally, the strength of the bond depends on degrees of "closeness" so that each of the above clauses must be qualified by the phrase "more or less," depending on the closeness of the particular bond.

This assumption is largely implicit, often taken for granted and simply not discussed or, at best, only hinted at. Morgan is no longer able to testify on the subject. Many living anthropologists can give no more convincing testimony than Morgan, for I believe that many—though not all—are often not aware of the fact that they make this assumption. Yet however self-conscious nineteenth- and twentieth-century anthropologists are, their writings reflect the persistence of this assumption in the conventional wisdom of kinship studies.

McLennan, for example, treats the "thickness of blood" as if it were too obvious to deserve more than passing comment. He says,

> The earliest human groups can have had no idea of kinship. *We do not mean to say that there was ever a time when men were not bound together by a feeling of kindred. The filial and fraternal affections may be instinctive.* They are obviously independent of any theory of kinship, its origin or consequences; they are distinct from the perception of the unity of blood upon which kinship depends; and they may have existed long before kinship became an object of thought.
>
> What we would say is, that ideas of kinship must be regarded as growths—must have *grown* like all other ideas related to matters primarily cognizable only by the sense; and that the fact of consanguinity must have long remained unperceived as other facts, quite as obvious, have done. In other words, *at the root of kinship is a physical fact,* which could be discerned only through observation and reflection—a fact, therefore, which must for a time have been overlooked. *No advocate of innate ideas,* we should imagine, *will maintain their existence on a subject so concrete as relationship by blood.*
>
> A group of kindred in that stage of ignorance is the rudest that can be imagined. Though they were chiefly held together by the feeling of kindred, the *apparent* bond of fellowship between the members of such a group would be that they and theirs had always been companions in war or the chase—joint-tenants of the same cave or grove. To one

another they would simply be as comrades. As distinguished from men of other groups, they would be of the group, and named after it.

Hence, most naturally, on the idea of blood-relationship arising, would be formed the conception of *Stocks*. Previously individuals had been affiliated not to persons, but to some group. The new idea of blood-relationship would more readily demonstrate the group to be composed of kindred than it would evolve a special system of blood-ties between certain of the individuals in the group. The members of a group would now have become brethren. As distinguished from men of other groups, they would be of the group-stock, named after the group. (Emphasis added. [1865] 1970:63–64)

McLennan distinguished the ''ideas'' about kinship from the ''facts'' of blood relationship. The facts of blood relationship are such that ''there (never) was a time when men were not bound together by a feeling of kindred. The filial and fraternal affections may be instinctive.'' But the *ideas* about kinship are distinct from the *facts* of blood relationship. The facts exist in the nature of things. The ideas are, or derive from, the intelligent observation of these facts. And it is ideas about facts that become part of culture. Indeed, McLennan says, ''no advocate of innate ideas . . . will maintain their existence on a subject as concrete as relationship by blood.'' This appears to mean that it is the facts that are innate, not the ideas (as Bastian maintained), for the idea only arises when there is an intelligent recognition of the facts.

The facts of blood relationship are that they constitute bonds, feelings of kindred, instinctive affection. Such is McLennan's view. Morgan's formulation is remarkably similar. He says,

The family relationships are as ancient as the family. *They exist in virtue of the law of derivation, which is expressed by the perpetuation of the species through the marriage relation. A system of consanguinity which is founded upon a community of blood, is but the formal expression and recognition of these relationships.* Around every person is the center, the Ego, from whom the degree of the relationship is reckoned, and to whom the relationship itself returns. Above him are his father and mother and their ascendants, below him are his children and their descendants; while upon either side are his brothers and sisters of his father and of his mother and their descendants as well as a much greater number of collateral relatives descended from common ancestors still more remote. To him they are nearer in degree than other individuals of the national at large. *A formal arrangement of the more immediate* blood kindred into lines of descent, with the adoption of some method to distinguish one relative from another and to express the value of the relationship, would be one of the earliest acts of human intelligence. (Emphasis added. 1870:10)

Thus far, for Morgan, the facts of blood relationship exist; it is their recognition, the discovery of their existence, that constitutes an act of human intelligence. They are then put into formal arrangement—a set of ideas—as a system of consanguinity. But Morgan does not say what the facts of consanguinity entail, only that they exist, and their cultural constitution follows upon their discovery as existential, as facts. But of all of the myriad of facts is there something special about these facts? Morgan does address this question, but almost in passing, in the following:

> There is one powerful motive which might, under certain circumstances, tend to the overthrow of the classificatory form and the substitution of the descriptive, but it would arise after the attainment of civilization. This is the inheritance of estates. *It may be premised that the bond of kindred, among civilized nations, is a strong influence for the mutual protection of related persons.* . . . the protection of law or of the state would become substituted for that of kinsmen; but with more effective power the rights of property might influence the system of relationship. . . . In Tamilian society, where my brother's son and my cousin's son are both my sons, a useful purpose may have been subserved by drawing closer in this manner the kindred bond. But in a civilized sense *it would be manifestly unjust to place either of these collateral sons upon an equality with my own son* for the inheritance of my estate. Hence the growth of property and the settlement of its distribution might be expected to lead to a more precise discrimination of the several degrees of consanguinity if they were confounded by the previous system. (Emphasis added. 1870:14)

Here Morgan implies that if a man knows his own son, then he naturally wants to leave his estate to him. But if he cannot know that his son is indeed his own son, then he cannot have this desire. Notice that Morgan is discussing the father-son relationship. He and McLennan, and others, agreed that it was a wise man who knew his own father, and that unless and until there was monogamous marriage with restraints on sexual access, this state of uncertainty was unavoidable, and necessarily marked in the kinship terminology. Only with the advent of "marriage of pairs," that is, monogamy, was there a likelihood that the child of the wife was the child of the husband too.

Of the Iroquois Morgan says, "the League was in effect established and rested for its stability, upon *the natural faith* of kindred" (1901:86). Again Morgan seems to take the tie of kindred as natural, and for granted, needing no further stipulation. The fundamental assumption is implied in these quotations. Blood relationship constitutes a bond, a tie, "a bond of kindred," "a strong influence for the mutual protection of related persons." Similar ideas, similarly vague, can be found in Maine (1861:123–29).

There is an obvious problem with the view that the bonds of kinship are innate or instinctual: if they are innate, why did they not show themselves automatically and, if they are as self-evident as the color of the sky, why were they not automatically noted and immediately converted into those ideas of kinship which constitute what Morgan called a "system of consanguinity"? If, for example, there is indeed a natural tendency so that "it would be manifestly unjust to place either of these collateral sons upon an equality with my own son," how is it that a man does not naturally, automatically, feel the compulsion of the bond between him and his own son? Does Morgan mean that before a man can feel the bond of blood kinship, he must first know, as an intellectually established fact, that that bond actually exists? This contradiction seems to be true of both Morgan and McLennan. Let me put it in another way. If the earliest state of mankind was that of primitive promiscuity, followed by the social tie between the mother and child, that is, matriliny, because this relationship is so easy to see that it cannot be overlooked, and at the same time the tie between mother and child is so close physically and there is an instinctual love and affection and the tendency to protect her own child is so great—the maternal instinct, in a word—then the question arises as to how there ever could have been a condition in which the relations between mother and child did not constitute the condition of some kind of family organization, or at least, a strong relationship between mother and her child. And this indeed is very much the argument of those who denied that a state of primitive promiscuity could ever have existed. In the nature of human nature, the family built on the mother-child tie must have been the first set of existential relationships which were immediately translated into social forms as well. If I understand him correctly, this is Westermark's (1891) argument. But those who followed McLennan and Morgan rested their case on the separation of ideas from action: it is ideas that constitute culture. The relationship between mother and child as an instinctive one does indeed exist, but the *idea* does not necessarily exist at the same time. Indeed, this remains true even of those societies which have reached the state of patriliny: the mother-child relationship remains in force, but the social forms or ideas of descent are patrilineal, not matrilineal.

I think that neither McLennan nor Morgan, nor their followers, nor those who opposed their theories, questioned the fundamental assumption that the bonds of kinship were inherent in human beings, that they constituted solidary ties of greater or lesser strength. The argument was about when, where, and how the social forms emerged, about whether a self-evident fact of the relationship between mother and child could be ignored so that in some state of primitive patriarchy no social bond of kinship was recognized between mother and child, and so forth.

If in the nineteenth century the bond of kinship was treated as a biological given, a sort of instinct, a state that was inborn, by the third to fourth decades of the twentieth century the biological mechanism tended to be seen somewhat differently. The nature of kinship remained the same: it is a bond that derives directly from the nature of human nature. But the bond now emerges out of certain human predispositions and capacities that develop, mobilize, and emerge in interaction particularly during infancy and early childhood. There remains a notion of something like an instinct of motherhood, but this alone is not responsible for either the social constitution of the bond of kinship or the actual relationship which emerges between mother and child. The fact that the child is part of the mother's body at first, emerges from it, is cared for, nurtured, and fed by the lactating mother, all constitute essential parts of a process which takes place during the interaction between infant and then child and mother, and which in turn establishes and develops the bond between them. Freud's theory of the development of personality, which implicitly includes the social aspects, is one example of this point of view: it is in the nature of human nature to create the bond of kinship through the interaction of the relatively unformed infant with certain general predispositions, potentialities, and tendencies and the adult who cares for it and engages in an affectively intense and binding relationship with it.

Spiro's statement, which I quoted in chapter 2, highly condensed as it is, suggests this view that the bonds of kinship are in part developed out of the interaction and experience of the relation between adults and their offspring.

> every kinship system must attend to certain ineluctable biological facts, among which I would stress the following. Human reproduction is bisexual, and conception is effected by means of heterosexual intercourse; humans are born helpless, and they remain physically and emotionally dependent on their caretakers for a prolonged period; children live, minimally, in biparental family groups, so that it is their caretakers (usually their parents) who, for better or worse, satisfy their dependency needs; dependency being the infant's prepotent need, feelings of affectionate attachment develop towards the agents of its satisfaction; satisfaction is always relative to frustration, so that these caretakers are simultaneously the first and most important objects of affection, as well as of hostility; siblings are also part of the family group, and, since affection is a scarce—and therefore competitive—good, they, like parents, are the objects of these same conflicting emotions. (1977:4)

It is Malinowski's position which Spiro says he follows, though Spiro is far more sophisticated. But in its essentials, Spiro's and Malinowski's positions are the same. Malinowski is less clear on the interactional aspects, but more forthright on the relationship between culture and the innate or the nature of human nature. He says,

> We can also, now, define kinship as, in the first place, the personal bonds based on procreation socially interpreted; and, in the second place, as the complex system of wider bonds derived from the primary ones by the twofold process of direct extension and unilateral reinterpretation. . . . In the particular case of Kinship, we were able to show that cultural processes tend to follow the direction of innate biological drives, that physiological facts are made gradually to ripen into sentiments and these again lead to purely cultural institutions. (1930b:165–66)

Kinship is by no means only a cultural construct, but is always rooted in, based on, and grounded in basic human needs, tendencies, drives, and the nature of human nature. Physiological facts gradually ripen into (social) sentiments, that is, they ripen into "purely cultural institutions" (though what the word *purely* can mean here is not clear to me). But for Malinowski culture is itself an insignificant part of human needs, tendencies, drives, the nature of human nature. These drives, tendencies, and physiological facts are transformed into the sentiments of kinship that are cultural yet remain as the driving forces. Culture, and kinship in particular, is in large part what people as people must do or are most likely to do.

Most important for the problem here is Malinowski's view that kinship consists of bonds which are essentially psychobiological in nature. Culture can bend them, but only so far, and not very far at that. Malinowski's view of adoption makes this clear:

> Social and cultural influences always indorse and emphasize the original individuality of the biological fact. These influences are so strong that in the case of adoption they may override the biological tie and substitute a cultural one for it. But statistically speaking, the biological ties are almost invariably merely reinforced, redetermined, and remoulded by the cultural ones. (1930b:137)

A note on adoption is in order. Malinowski says that adoption is a case in which culture is so strong that it overrides the biological tie and substitutes a cultural tie for it. If this were true it would present a problem, and seeing this, Malinowski suggests that it is really no problem at all because ties like adoption are rare; that is, "statistically speaking, the biological ties are almost invariably merely reinforced, redetermined, and remoulded by the cultural ones."

The problem that Malinowski points to is this. If the blood relationship is presumed to have inherent qualities of its own which "are" and which "exist" and are so strong and take such precedence, then adoption ought not to be possible, or at most it should be unusual and rarely practiced. For adoption creates "kinship" where none in fact exists, that is, no real blood relationship exists. Hence there ought to be a clear cultural distinction between true kinship and all other kinds of relationship.

This is in fact the preponderant view. What is confusing is that adoption is confounded with the blood relationship by being called or treated as if it were the same kind of relationship. But in fact anthropologists have consistently treated adoption as something quite different from true kinship. For Maine, adoption was the first legal fiction, and as such allowed families to add new members by means other than birth. But there is no question that it is different from true kinship, blood relationship, the difference marked by the term *fictive*. Anthropologists have generally distinguished between "true" or "fictive" or "putative" or "classificatory" kin, or kin who are classed as kin by "extension." "True" or "real" kinship presumes that there *is* some biological relationship between persons so related. And adoptive kin were distinguished from "real" or "true" kin by Rivers (1904: vol. 5, p. 123) in his collection of genealogies in the Torres Straits and are so distinguished, generally, by most anthropologists.

Fortes seems to hold exactly the same position including the implicit recognition of the possibility for logical contradiction and the disinclination to pursue the matter.

> if a person who is not a kinsman is metaphorically or figuratively placed in a kinship category, an element, or at least a semblance, of kinship amity goes with this. It is conceivable—and I for one would accept—that the axiom reflects biological and psychological parameters of human social existence. Maybe there is sucked in with the mother's milk, as Montaigne opined, the orientation on which it ultimately rests. (1969:251)

In the end, then, the significance of interpersonal interaction in infancy and childhood experience (as often occurs in cases of adoption) does not seem to be held decisive by anthropologists; a bond of some intrinsically biological sort must be "there" for the bond of kinship to work. If the bond between the parent and the natural child and the adopted child were equally strong, of essentially the same quality or significance, then there would be no reason why the distinction between adoptive, putative, fictive relationship and "true" or "real" relationship should be so consistently drawn, as it has for the past hundred years or more.

Further, it is generally held that this distinction between "true" and "real" kinship and "extended" or "classificatory" kinship is universally made—it is found in all cultures. Malinowski's jibes against the ideas of "collective motherhood" and his insistence on "individual motherhood" is but one case in point. If every culture makes the distinction between "true" kinship and "classificatory" or "extended" or "fictive" kin, then that distinction must be of significance to all peoples. It is significant, presumably, because there is something fundamentally different about the biological fact of the bond and the social definition of a bond where that fact is absent or missing.

Lévi-Strauss pays almost no attention to the assumption that Blood Is Thicker Than Water, but hints that he subscribes to it, as in the following:

the value of exchange is not simply that of the goods exchanged. Exchange—and consequently the rule of exogamy which expresses it—has in itself a social value. It provides the means of binding men together, and of superimposing upon *the natural links of kinship* the henceforth artificial links . . . of alliance by rule. (Emphasis added. 1969:480)

Finally, the most recent, explicit, detailed, and developed commitment to the premise that Blood Is Thicker Than Water is made by the sociobiologists. They do this in numerous publications which need not be quoted here since they are so well known (see, for example, Hamilton 1964, Alexander 1979, Chagnon and Bugos 1979, and Wilson 1980).

I turn now to the qualifier "more or less" in the fundamental assumption: kinship consists in bonds on which one can more or less depend, which are more or less compelling and take more or less priority over other kinds of bonds, and so on. The qualifier, I said, depends on degrees of closeness.

Degrees of closeness can be calculated in various ways. Primary relatives are closer than secondary, secondary are closer than tertiary, and so on. Civil law, canon law, and genetics provide other modes of calculating closeness and distance, but for the problem at hand the differences between these methods are irrelevant. All depend on the assumption that what has been called "genealogical distance" is a crucial variable in the strength of the bond of kinship, and genealogical distance is a measure of the magnitude of the biological component and hence the strength of the bond. The closer two kinsmen are genealogically the greater the biological component of their relationship. For example, Murdock, discussing the criterion of collaterality, says, "The criterion of collaterality rests on the biological fact that among consanguineal relatives of the same generation and sex, some will be more closely akin to Ego than others. A direct ancestor, for example, will be more nearly related than his sibling or cousin, and a lineal descendent of a sibling or a cousin" (1949:103). It is "the biological fact" that Murdock says is decisive here. Malinowski puts it this way: "The primary and fundamental elements of the parent-child relationship—the fact of procreation, the physiological services, the innate emotional responses—which make up the family bonds vanish completely from the relationship within the clan'' (1930b:164). The fundamental assumption, then, postulates not only the presence or absence of a biological component, which is held to determine the bond that exists, but also that the strength of the bond depends on genealogical distance or the magnitude of the biological component. A further qualifier that I have not discussed is the difference in the quality between different kinds of kinship bonds. Thus, for example, women are assumed to respond to the biological component more strongly and with a different quality of relationship than men. But it is unnecessary to the point here to do more than note that this qualification exists and is also assumed to be a direct function of the biological constitution of the bond of kinship.

I have spoken of the Doctrine of the Genealogical Unity of Mankind as essential to the study of kinship. It states that genealogical relations are the same in every culture. If they were not, cross-cultural comparison would not be possible. It is precisely the assumption that Blood Is Thicker Than Water that makes the Doctrine of the Genealogical Unity of Mankind both tenable and forceful.

It is tenable because the assumption that Blood Is Thicker Than Water says that whatever variable elements may be grafted onto kinship relations, all kinship relations are essentially the same and share universal features. Hence the genealogical grid *can* be used as an etic grid: comparable things are being compared and analyzed by first establishing their identity and universality and holding constant the components that make them comparable. This is a necessary but not sufficient condition to the privileged position which kinship is accorded in the conventional wisdom of anthropology. The Doctrine of the Genealogical Unity of Mankind is so forceful and has a specially privileged position precisely because Blood Is presumably Thicker Than Water. This assumption makes kinship or genealogical relations unlike any other social bonds, for they have especially strong binding force and are directly constituted by, grounded in, determined by, formed by, the imperatives of the biological nature of human nature. They are the cultural formulations of what are held to be inherent, relatively inflexible conditions of the biological bases of human behavior.

It is no accident that the assumption that Blood Is Thicker Than Water is fundamental to the study of kinship. I chose the aphorism precisely because it is so commonly encountered in the daily life of our culture, at least since the eighteenth century, though the idea behind it is far older, I think. But it is an integral part of the ideology of European culture. I have spelled this ideology out in detail elsewhere (Schneider [1968] 1980) and there is no need to repeat it here. What is important to note is that the folk conceptions, categories, and ideology in general are carried over into the analytic scheme, the etic grid, with but minor modifications, and without subjecting it to critical examination or evaluation and precisely contrary to Goodenough's formulation of how an etic scheme should be constructed.

A further point should be made in this connection. First, this assumption is but a particular instance of the more general characteristic of European culture toward what might be called "biologistic" ways of constituting and conceiving human character, human nature, and human behavior. Man's humanity tends to be formulated in terms of his place in nature, with a few caveats about his free will, intentionality, conscience, and his (self-defined) extraordinary intelligence distinguishing him from other natural organisms.

Return to the rephrased question: Why has kinship been defined in terms of the relations that arise out of the processes of human sexual reproduction? The answer that I offer here should be no surprise. It is simply that so much of what passes for science in the social sciences, including anthropology, derives directly and recognizably from the commonsense notions, the everyday premises of the culture in which and by which the scientist lives. These postulates of European culture are simply taken over and put in a form that is customary for rational scientific discourse, appropriately qualified and made slightly more explicit in places and served up as something special, sometimes even in Latin. That is, the study of kinship derives directly and practically unaltered from the ethnoepistemology of European culture. It is hardly any wonder that the assumption that Blood Is Thicker Than Water is not often fully explicit. It is taken for granted as a fundamental truth of our culture and has remained so even when transformed into a part of a presumably rational, presumably explicit, presumably intelligently articulated theory.

This point applied equally well to two other features of the conventional wisdom of kinship; the idea that kinship forms a system, and the idea that kinship can be understood and treated as an isolable institution, domain, or rubric—that it is a distinct "thing."

I do not mean to imply that I have offered a complete, comprehensive, or exhaustive answer to the question of why kinship has been defined by anthropologists in terms of the relations arising out of the processes of human sexual reproduction. But I do mean to imply that such a definition is open to question on theoretical as well as substantive grounds. In this chapter the theoretical and substantive questions centered on the premise that Blood Is Thicker Than Water. But further, I have raised the question of whether this cultural premise applies beyond the bounds of European culture, that is, whether it is, as the Doctrine of the Genealogical Unity of Mankind would have it, universal. Quite apart from the theoretical and substantive justification for the premise is the question of whether it constitutes a premise universal to all cultures. This I seriously doubt.

In sum, for Maine, McLennan, and Morgan, among others in the mid-nineteenth century, kinship was taken for granted as, if not the very earliest, among the earliest forms of social organization of mankind. Why is kinship regarded as among the very earliest social bonds? The choice of kinship as the earliest or among the very earliest bonds on which social forms could be built was surely motivated. If these scholars saw it as the most primitive tie, why was it the most primitive? If it was the most basic tie, on which others could be built, what made it so? For later workers like Westermark and then Malinowski, society without the family was inconceivable. For Westermark there was no society before the family, for only with the family did social life truly begin. Once in place, kinship could then constitute a base on which other organizational forms could be built, but without such a base organizational development was impossible. For Malinowski the family was the cornerstone of society: extrafamilial kinship grew out of the family by extension, again, as for Westermark, the family served as the foundation for the invention and development of other social forms. Why is the family of such central importance? Why is the kin-based society the simplest and most primitive? What makes it possible for a society to be "based on" kinship? Why should kinship be the idiom in so many societies for political, economic, and various other organizational forms? Although economics, politics, and religion can serve as idioms expressing certain social conditions, they rarely serve as the all-purpose idiom that kinship is said to provide. How can this be? Why should adoption and other forms of "fictive" kinship be so clearly differentiated from true kinship—always for anthropologists, and allegedly for all societies?

The idea of the kin-based society, the idiom of kinship, the idea that kinship and the family are the cornerstone of all social life, that kinship is a specially privileged system, that kinship was the earliest, or among the earliest forms of social life—all of these make no sense without the fundamental assumption that "Blood Is Thicker Than Water." There is no doubt that however both physical and social reproduction are ordered they are functionally prerequisite to any form of social life, but so too are breathing, and sleeping. But no one has claimed that there are breathing-based societies, or that sleeping is the idiom in terms of which total social and cultural systems are phrased. Even where societies, like our own presumably, are economically based, kinship still retains a crucial and strategic position at least insofar as the family is a major constituent of kinship. Universality, functional prerequisitivity, may be important elements in answering the question of why kinship is so important, but they do not serve to distinguish kinship from other social forms, and as I have suggested, kinship is clearly distinguished by many anthropologists from other social forms as a specially privileged one.

My purpose in this chapter has been to suggest that there is a fundamental assumption on which all studies of kinship rest which, when recognized, makes sense of the privileged position which kinship has been accorded by

Maine, McLennan, Morgan, Rivers, Lowie, Eggan, Fortes, and others since their time; of the ideas of the kin-based society and the idiom of kinship, and similar features of the privileged status accorded to kinship. My aim was to make this assumption explicit and to offer some evidence for its existence, and the form in which it occurs, so that the suggestion cannot be treated as purely hypothetical.

Another purpose of this chapter is to suggest that insofar as the comparative study of kinship is tenable or a legitimate endeavor, it must be assumed that kinship is a unitary phenomenon (Needham 1960 notwithstanding) and this assumption rests on the fundamental assumption that "Blood Is Thicker Than Water." If kinship is not comparable from one society to the next, then it is self-evident that comparative study is out of the question. If the comparability of one kinship system with another does not rest on the assumption that "Blood Is Thicker Than Water," on what does it rest? That kinship concerns human sexual reproduction? On the universal functions which center on reproduction? If that is the ground for its phenomenal unity, then assumptions such as the kin-based society, the idiom of kinship, the presumably universal distinction between adoptive and real kin, fictive and true kin, and the privileged position of kinship among social institutions are left unexplained, as is the special position accorded to kinship by the mid-nineteenth-century theorists.

Finally, I have tried to suggest that this assumption is largely implicit, has not been carefully considered and evaluated, and is therefore as dangerous as are all implicit, unexamined assumptions. If the fundamental assumption does not withstand close scrutiny, then the comparative study of kinship must be either set on some other, firm ground, or abandoned.

PART IV

Conclusion

15   Institutions, Domains, and Other Rubrics

The quartet of kinship, economics, politics, and religion as institutions, domains, rubrics, or the building blocks of society or culture has been part of anthropology since its beginnings. In the mid-nineteenth century the problem for anthropology was to establish the history or development of civilization as this was embodied in European culture. Certain processes of historical development were assumed. Development proceeded from the simple to the complex, from the undifferentiated to the differentiated. European "civilization" was seen as the most recent, advanced, and highly differentiated form of social life known to man. To the extent that kinship, economics, politics, and religion were undifferentiated that society was "primitive," "simple," or "simpler."

An understanding of kinship must take into account the fact that it is one of this quartet of institutions, rubrics, or domains, with this long history, and that this quartet is treated as the most important set. Medicine, education, art, or myth, for example, are of lesser importance. Furthermore, there is a sort of theory of institutions which contributes to the ways in which kinship itself is formulated. The four distinct terms imply four distinct sorts of "things." This implies that each of these institutions constitutes a bounded unit. There is the further implication that each such bounded unit constitutes a system of some sort. Indeed, statements about "the economic system," "the kinship system," etc., abound. As "bounded" and as "system," it is implied that one can allocate concrete "pieces" or "parts" to one or another of these units, and that the institutions are to some degree concrete entities. Hence they can act as the "building blocks" of the society or culture.

Institutions, domains, and rubrics of this sort have been defined as organized around particular kinds of activities, or particular functions, and sometimes as combinations of the two. Religion, for example, is sometimes treated as that system of activities which embodies the ultimate values of the society (a Durkheimian view), sometimes as those activities that involve ritual, ceremony, and worship, and sometimes as anything having to do with a belief in the supernatural. The first stresses function, the second kinds of activities, the third a combination of the two.

Within this very general framework, institutions have been more specifically defined in a wide variety of ways by different workers over the last century and a half. The point is clear from the previous discussion of kinship. These different ways often articulate closely with particular theoretical positions, problems, and aims.

181

This leads to the next point. Whatever the particular task or theoretical stance—historical, developmental, evolutionary, functionalist à la Durkheim, functionalist à la Radcliffe-Brown, functionalist à la Malinowski, structuralist à la Lévi-Strauss, interpretivist à la Geertz, materialist à la Harris, Marxist à la Goody—the traditional quartet and the presumption of the special importance of the particular members of the quartet has survived intact. To put it in another way, the quartet of kinship, economics, politics, and religion has survived every shift of theoretical orientation, anthropological aim, and problem as well as every anthropologist (and I am sure it will survive me). This says something about the quartet which is worth stressing; it is so taken for granted, so embedded in the ways anthropology is performed, so widely used that there is no general theory of institutions but only the more or less implicit theories of particular persons or particular theoretical stances. If kinship can be studied and understood by Morgan, Maine, Malinowski, Radcliffe-Brown, Lévi-Strauss, and Friedrich Engels as if it were the same object, the same monolithic institution, the same "thing" about which each of these can "discover" something different and reveal different "truths," the implication is that there really is something quite real out there above and beyond any particular theoretician's peculiar views: a truth waiting to be revealed. Epestemes may come and go. Social formations may appear and disappear. Structure can mean different things to different people. A habitus may seize one but not another anthropologist while praxis may be fitfully fashionable. But kinship, economics, politics, and religion have been here for more than a century and a half and have survived as an integral part of the vocabulary of every—and I mean every—anthropologist (indeed, every social scientist) despite the most devastating criticisms.

For example, one of the most common criticisms is that when institutions are defined in terms of function the discreteness or unity of the institution simply does not stand up under examination. Kinship is a good example. Kinship has been defined functionally, for instance, as that institution which attends to the production and reproduction of persons, so that children are produced and parents are reproduced, or sometimes more simply as that institution whose primary function is to order and attend to the problems of human reproduction (see Malinowski 1930a:28 for example). Note that an institution by this definition has a primary function, which implies that it also has other, secondary or derivative functions.

The difficulty, of course, is that examination of the situation in any society shows that this primary function is taken care of by customary activities that spread throughout the whole culture and social system and which are not confined to what is normally considered kinship. At the same time, there is far more to what is usually considered as kinship than simply dealing with the problem of reproduction, even if we allow for the possibility that many if not all customs are multifunctional. On the other side, there are parts of what is traditionally defined as kinship that only remotely relate to reproduction, if they are related at all. Thus any given custom falls not into one institution or another, but spreads across all of them. This casts doubt on whether any institution can have a primary function at all. For example, if the primary function of kinship is ordering reproduction, and one problem is that of social placement, that is, setting the new member of the society in a particular nexus of social relations with a particular status, the difficulty is that there are a host of religious, economic, and political considerations which always enter into the system of social placement. The establishment of a son and heir to a sacred ruler is different from the establishment of a son and heir to a commoner, yet both entail not merely kinship considerations, but political, economic, and religious factors all of equal importance. Thus the boundedness of the notion of institution is dubious at best, and equally so any idea that institutions can be the building blocks of society or culture. Without some kind of boundedness and some degree of internal systematicity it is hard to see how society could be built of such amorphous blocks.

Let me make the same point in another way. Treating the quartet of institutions seriously has led to the consistent misinterpretation of the potlatch in terms of European notions of economics, which is as inept as the interpretation of Murngin as built on double descent with seven intermarrying lines or the view that Bali can be understood best as a centralized state headed by an absolute monarch.

I have slipped back into criticizing functionalism, which is all too easy. Is there any way of considering these institutions, domains, or rubrics without dealing with them functionally? Considered as forms of activity they again fail to make much sense. With bit after bit of culture the question arises as to whether this bit belongs to religion or to kinship, to economics or to politics? Is the reverence and respect that the Yapese *fak* pays to his *citamangen* a religious or a kinship matter? Or both? If both, what sense is there in distinguishing them by kind of activity?

The notions of the kin-based society and kinship as an idiom depend on the distinction between kinship, economics, politics, and religion. Where there are no such distinctions, there can be no way in which anything could be the special base on which a kind of society rested, nor can there be one form which serves as an idiom for the other forms. These two notions, kin-basedness and idiom, depend on more than just the distinction of kinship from all other aspects of culture and society. They also depend on the premise that at least four major aspects can be distinguished as functions for types of activity. If institutions, domains, rubrics like kinship, economics, religion, and politics do not stand up as analytic constructs, then it follows that kinship does not stand up either. Conversely, if kinship is accepted because it really is a fundamental, distinct, systematic, bounded sociocultural unit, then necessarily the next question must be: What other similarly constituted units might there be? That question need not be answered by "economics, politics, and religion," but whatever units there are will be conceptualized in ways which are congruent with the ways in which kinship is conceptualized, and thus ways which are similar to economics, politics, and religion.

There are other ways of constituting the units out of which a society or culture is fabricated. One of the simplest analytic devices, and the one which I personally favor, is to first establish the units which the particular culture itself marks off. For Yap it is the *tabinau*, the *binau, pilung/pimilingai,* and so forth. For another culture it will be other units which can then be compared with Yap or any other culture and we can then proceed from those.

The quartet of kinship, economics, politics, and religion derives, of course, from the spheres of life which European culture itself distinguishes. That is, they are metacultural categories embedded in European culture which have been incorporated into the analytic schemes of European social scientists. And they are the ideas which all social scientists fall back on under any sort of pressure, for they are ideas which everyone can understand. This is not intended as a critical statement, but as an observation. Theories come from somewhere. They are not made up out of thin air and without reference to the lives and experience of the theorists or those they speak to. That most of social science has its roots in the folk theories of European culture indicates its source but says nothing about its validity, utility, or applicability cross-culturally. On the other hand, experience has shown by now that to simply take the metacultural categories of one particular culture and use them directly as analytic tools with the assumption that they are somehow universally vital functions or kinds of activities just does not work. It is for this reason that I urge so strongly that the first step, prerequisite to all others in comparative work, is to establish the particular categories or units which each particular culture itself marks off; that is to say, the symbols and meanings of a particular culture. Once this is done, without being prejudiced by theories about functional prerequisites to social life or assumptions about universal activities, then comparison can begin and analytic procedures and tools can perhaps be developed.

The difficulties with the rubrics or institutions of kinship, politics, religion, and economics are legion and have been detailed more often than can easily be listed here, so I will list none of them. Suffice it to say that one further problem with the whole notion of kinship which I have barely touched until now is that it is embedded in a set of institutions, rubrics, or domains and that there is no satisfactory theory of these or any satisfactory way of justifying their existence or their distinction from one another, the primacy which the four major ones are given, the assumption of boundedness, of system, or the assumption that they constitute anything more than a valiant attempt to use the constructions of European culture as tools for description, comparison, and analysis. Much of this book has taken it for granted that kinship could be treated as a unit and a thing. The criticisms centered on how that unit or thing was to be understood. It is now time to face the fact that the very notion of kinship, like that of economics, religion, or politics, is essentially undefined and vacuous: it is an analytic construct which seems to have little justification even as an analytic construct. It is to this end that I devoted so much space to the ways in which kinship is defined in the conventional wisdom.

16   Conclusion

First I will review and summarize in highly condensed form the salient pre-suppositions in the study of kinship. Then I will try to state briefly what I see to be the difficulties with the study of kinship. I will conclude by touching lightly on the question of what might be done about it all.

The ideas of kinship as an idiom, the kin-based society, and much of the notion of the privileged position of kinship depend on the idea of kinship itself. But they also depend on another idea. This is the premise that simple societies can be distinguished from complex societies and that a scale of more or less simplicity/complexity can be established. Another way that this is often put is that societies can be distinguished as more or less differentiated. Undifferentiated is simple; differentiated is complex.

Simple/complex is often associated with theories of history, develop-ment, evolution, or growth. Such is certainly the case for Maine and Morgan for example. But the simple/complex dimension has also been associated with those who are avowedly antievolutionary and antihistorical like Malinowski and Radcliffe-Brown, among others. For these, the simple/complex and relat-ed dichotomies represent different modes of organization which have no necessary historical or developmental implications. But it is particularly the simple societies that are said to use kinship as an idiom, to be kin-based because many different tasks have to be done by a single, or a few very simple forms. It is in the nature of kinship—and it is here that kinship per se comes in—that it can and does serve as an idiom, so that the simple, undifferentiated societies can be, and indeed must be, kin-based.

Although the ideas of the kin-based society and the idiom of kinship may, for many scholars, depend in part on their evolutionary, developmental, or historical premises, it is the special qualities of kinship itself that give it its privileged position and that make it necessary, or at least very likely, that the society will be kin-based. The problem really comes down to the nature of kinship itself. How then is kinship understood in the conventional wisdom of anthropology?

First, kinship is one of the four privileged institutions, domains, or rubrics of social science, each of which is conceived to be a natural, univer-sal, vital component of society. Kinship takes its shape in part from being one of these institutions. It is a thing, or a focus of a constellation of varied activities, or it has a primary function, or it constitutes a distinct domain. It is taken as self-evident that it is distinct from the other major institutions, yet also related to them since they all constitute major building blocks out of

187

which all social systems are constructed. Further, kinship is the specially privileged of the privileged institutions, for it is kinship alone which can serve as idiom for, is the necessary prerequisite to, and out of which, the other three institutions are differentiated.

Second, kinship has to do with the reproduction of human beings and the relations between human beings that are the concomitants of reproduction. The reproduction of human beings is formulated as a sexual and biological process. Sexual relations are an integral part of kinship, though sexual relations may have significance outside kinship and sexual relations per se are not necessarily kinship relations.

Third, sexual reproduction creates biological links between persons and these have important qualities apart from any social or cultural attributes which may be attached to them. Indeed, the social and cultural attributes, though considered the primary subject matter of anthropologists, and of particular concern to social scientists, are nevertheless derivative of and of lesser determinate significance than the biological relations. These biological relations have special qualities; they create and constitute bonds, ties, solidary relations proportional to the biological closeness of the kin (though the correlation between the strength of the tie and the closeness of the kin may not be perfect beyond primary kin). These are considered to be natural ties inherent in the human condition, distinct from the social or cultural.

These, I think, are the three basic axioms used in the study of kinship, and all the rest follows more or less directly from them, though the particular formulation depends on the wider context in which the particular line of development occurs. For example, if the idea of the kin-based society is set in the context of a theory of evolution, it will differ in important respects from the same idea developed in the context of an antievolutionary theory. But the kinship part will trace directly back to these three axioms.

Another example is the Doctrine of the Genealogical Unity of Mankind. The derivation is simple. First, kinship is universal (axiom one). Second, kinship has to do with human reproduction and the relations concomitant to that process. Hence a system of relative products based on the primitives of father, mother, (parent), husband, wife, (spouse), son, daughter (child) is simply developed and extended from that nucleus (axiom two). The genealogy is also universal and follows from both axioms one and two. How far out the genealogy is extended, how it is partitioned, varies from culture to culture, and this follows from that special corollary that the strength of the bonds ("Blood Is Thicker Than Water") diminishes beyond the relations to primary kin. Every culture has a father, mother, husband and wife, son and daughter, but not all of them bother to count mother's mother's mothers' brother's son's daughters' sons.

The Doctrine of the Genealogical Unity of Mankind is one of the most important and explicit features of the conventional wisdom of kinship studies and as such it deserves special review here. This review will serve to emphasize features of the three axioms which are of strategic importance in evaluating the difficulties with the study of kinship. At the same time it will allow me to bring together some loose ends from the discussion of the relation between social and physical kinship and the chapter on "Blood Is Thicker Than Water."

Biological kinship has been distinguished sharply from social kinship by most anthropologists. This is true even for those few anthropologists who were able to see that biological kinship itself is culturally constructed. For the earlier workers like Morgan and McLennan the actual, natural, biological state of affairs remained constant and given. What changed was man's discovery of the actual, natural, biological state of affairs and his celebration of those as cultural facts as well. Once discovered, man could control those facts and change certain aspects of them. For example, once discovered man could eventually develop what Morgan called the "marriage of pairs" and so establish paternity with a fair degree of likelihood. But before he understood the processes of reproduction, at a time when promiscuity prevailed, there was no way of establishing paternity, nor indeed, could there be any interest in doing so, for the facts of paternity themselves were unknown. So Morgan says that the discovery of kinship was one of the earliest and greatest acts of human intelligence. In the phrase which was widely used later by Radcliffe-Brown, Firth, and Fortes, among many others, this was "the social recognition of biological facts."

In this view the social facts reflected, and thus were in perfect accord with, the biological facts. But with promiscuity, paternity could not be established and so it could not be socially marked. With group marriage, and with marriage understood as sexual relations, men of the group had sexual relations with women of the group and so they were husbands and wives to each other. There was a persistent problem with motherhood in that motherhood, unlike fatherhood, was readily visible and deemed too obvious to overlook. Hence the notion that the group of women married to the group of men could all collectively be "mothers" by virtue of their marriage to the group of "fathers" was inconsistent with the obvious fact of individual motherhood by virtue of pregnancy and birth. This was one of the points where it was obvious that social kinship did not simply mirror biological kinship. Further discrepancies between social and biological kinship were apparent and the forms of social kinship could not be accounted for as Morgan and McLennan tried to, by regarding them as the direct recognition of the biological facts. Where social kinship was different from biological kinship, this discrepancy required some attention. And indeed, it will be recalled that Durkheim, Rivers, and others went to great lengths to show that social kinship in certain cases did not correlate with physical kinship, though Rivers's argument was flawed in certain crucial respects. The discrepancy between social and physical kinship was not the only important thrust toward the separation of cultural and physical kinship. Durkheim was insisting with great vehemence and quite persuasively that social facts were sui generis, could not be reduced to other orders of facts but had to be accounted for or explained in social terms.

These may have been two important reasons for the move in the last decades of the nineteenth century and the early decades of the twentieth century to sharply separate social from physical kinship, but they were certainly not the only reasons. The social was more and more being differentiated from the psychological in general, and these were well along in being differentiated from physics, ethics, and philosophy in the general intellectual climate of the time. The growing sharp distinction between social and physical kinship was but one part of this more general intellectual movement.

Yet, as I have tried to indicate, there were really two tendencies working against each other to some degree. One was the recognition that social kinship did not simply mirror physical kinship and so the separation of social from physical kinship. The other was the persistent view that natural, biological processes constitute a major determinant, or at least a constraint on any direction that social kinship might take. A particularly well developed formulation of this was the Westermark, Malinowski, Freud view that social kinship was directly determined by the physical or biological conditions of reproduction, in the widest sense. Something more than a vague instinct of motherhood was postulated by Freud and Malinowski: they saw a pattern of interaction between the givens of nature, psychology, and biology and the kinds of experiences in the whole process of socialization and family living which were very convincing in giving a profoundly determinate role to biology, psychobiological processes, and what could be seen as the essential meaning of physical kinship. For almost all social scientists social and physical kinship could not be radically separated, because physical kinship was an important constraint on, or determinant of, social kinship. Not the only one perhaps, but certainly the most important.

In chapter 9 I stressed the problem which those who wished to separate social from physical kinship failed to even raise, much less cope with; if kinship was purely social and in no way physical, how was it to be defined, what was it, how was it to be distinguished from any other kind of social relationship? Durkheim and Van Gennep and Rivers never raised this question, and it might be interesting to speculate why. Speculation is required because to the best of my knowledge, none of these scholars said anything to explain it themselves.

One possible explanation is that I have posed a problem that was not seen as a problem by these men. Kinship was indeed about human reproduction, but social kinship was to be distinguished from its biological and psychological aspects for purposes of study in its own right. When Durkheim said that "kinship is social or it is nothing" he did not mean that it lost its roots in biology and human reproduction; only that it was now to be treated as a social fact, not a biological fact. Hence he simply assigned the biological aspects of kinship to the realm of the science of biology, just as he had assigned the psychological aspects of suicide to the study of psychology. When he subtracted the psychological aspects of suicide, he still had plenty of social facts left to explain; by setting aside the biological aspects of kinship he still had plenty of social facts to explain.

Second, one might speculate that Durkheim never escaped from the problem of motivation. His view of effervescence and of the functions of ritual and of the compelling nature of religion as embodying values toward which the actor felt (or just naturally developed) an attitude of moral authority all implied that however sui generis such social facts were, they required the cooperation of a motivated human being. Otherwise, like Lévi-Strauss's myths, they had to be seen as inexplicably working their inner logic out independently of any human beings or the involvement of any actors. And Durkheim's treatment of effervescence, ritual, and religion only depended in part on the workings of a cultural logic wholly independent of actors. By the same token, then, Durkheim implicitly depended on some motivating factor, some hidden motor behind kinship to make it work. That motor was probably biology in the form of the axiom that Blood Is Thicker Than Water. But it had to be kept implicit, as motivation was kept implicit while he focused on the social facts, on kinship as social relations.

A third factor which may have entered into Durkheim's position was his differences with Morgan. Where Morgan viewed kinship terms as direct reflections of the actual state of consanguineal relations, insofar as these were known or knowable by the natives, Durkheim rejected this view on the ground that what Morgan deemed to be the crucial relationship—consanguinity—was all too often not taken into account at all or taken into account, but accounted as having minor or no relevance at all. In many societies nonconsanguines are considered relatives and consanguines strangers to one another. Further, in many societies paternity does not exist as a social institution even where there is no doubt about the physical bond between the father and his children. Conversely, a man very frequently considers himself and is considered the father, in the moral and legal sense of the term, of children whom he has not engendered. He affirms that kinship in primitive societies is irreducible to consanguinity, that it depends on causes different from the simple acknowledgment of a specific physical link. This is so even with maternity, he argues, since among many peoples all births are attributed to the reincarnation of an external soul which introduces itself into the woman's body and becomes the child. The child is therefore much more directly dependent on the dead person of whom he is the reincarnation than on the woman who physically bore him. She plays the role of an intermediary in procreation; she is not the one the newborn child perpetuates. Thus the child is not attached to his mother's family, but to the one to which the dead person belonged during his life, and this is indeed what happens in a number of cases. In short, the social facts simply did not accord with the physical facts, hence the social facts could not possibly be accounted for or determined by the physical facts. (This is paraphrased from Durkheim 1913).

The social facts, however, were still very much the same as they had always been; they concerned domestic arrangements, representations, beliefs, moral and legal concerns with those social relations having to do with reproduction. For Durkheim, I suggest, the problem was to strip physical kinship away from social kinship, leaving kinship as a purely social system. If social kinship was based on anything, it was based on other social facts. And he says that domestic organization is based on fundamentally religious ideas and beliefs (paraphrased from Durkheim 1913). In sum, kinship and domestic arrangements and family remained modeled on the natural, biological processes, but their social aspects had to be treated in social terms and could not be explained by other than social factors. So biology still remained as a model and as a motivating force, just as psychology remained the necessary condition for social solidarity and its motivation.

The situation for Rivers may have been put in rather different terms, but was essentially the same. Rivers was concerned with the development of culture. He started as a confirmed evolutionist, then had a radical conversion to diffusionism. Insofar as kinship was nothing more than a set of biological facts which were only given social recognition, there was not only no problem, but that formulation itself was a major error. The history of kinship could help solve problems in the history of civilization—either with a developmental theory such as Morgan's or with a diffusionist theory such as G. E. Smith's. But biology was not culture. It was the cultural aspects that were the vital data for Rivers. Hence he had to separate social kinship, which was his problem, from physical kinship, which was not. Insofar as his was the most radical rejection of anything biological his was the position that most forcefully cried out for some statement of what exactly kinship was and how it was to be defined if it was not biology or modeled on biological processes. If consistency is the hallmark of small minds, Rivers was indeed a major thinker. In the end, then, the position which I think Rivers occupied, and not entirely consciously by any means, was rather like that of Durkheim. His primary concern was to free kinship from its simplistic formulation as a mere reflection of the state of biological relations of human reproduction and to study it as a social phenomenon—first following Morgan as a developmentalist, later following Smith and the diffusionists as embodying historical information.

I have already stated Malinowski's position fairly I think; social and physical kinship were quite distinct but the former was firmly rooted in the latter through the family and psychobiological processes of reproduction and socialization and the very specific psychobiological needs of human beings. Hence social kinship had to be defined in biological terms because it was largely determined by the facts of biology as these were part of human nature.

In sum, the focus of the efforts for Durkheim, Rivers, and Radcliffe-Brown was to isolate social kinship as a legitimate subject of study, to distinguish it from its biological aspects, but not to disavow the biological component nor to throw the biology out (except for Rivers, who threw it out but kept it in at the same time), but simply to set it aside. For Malinowski the problem was to show in general the ways in which social kinship were determined by its vital psychobiological functions.

In setting the biological aspects of kinship aside, there was no felt need to redefine kinship. It could still be defined as dealing with human reproduction as a social and cultural phenomenon. One could still assume that Blood Is Thicker Than Water but one need not dwell on that part of it. Indeed, for Malinowski and those who followed his sort of functionalism it was more convenient not to dwell on it, for to do so raised the whole question of precisely how specific social forms were constrained or determined by what particular biological conditions by what specific mechanisms, questions which they glossed over with glittering generalities.

As I have indicated, whatever the place of biology, there has been virtual unanimity in defining kinship in terms of human reproduction. Whether purely social for Durkheim, the social as dictated by biological circumstances for Malinowski, a reflection of the facts of consanguinity for Morgan, the social control over the means of human reproduction for Marx, or even the reproduction of social forms for some neo-Marxists or the transmission of rights from generation to generation, kinship is essentially about reproduction. One might say, well, that's how it's been defined. But one might also ask why it has been defined that way, asking at the same time, what is there about reproduction that makes it so salient that it is given a central place among the privileged institutions? Why not, for example, the customs surrounding eating, or a dozen other things universal to human beings and equally vital?

The short, quick answer is that kinship has been defined by European social scientists, and European social scientists use their own folk culture as the source of many, if not all, of their ways of formulating and understanding the world about them. Short and quick as that answer is, and it is essentially correct I think, it is too short and too quick. The longer, fuller answer is back to the axiom that Blood Is Thicker Than Water. This is certainly a very significant premise in European culture. This is not the place for a full, detailed analysis of this feature of European culture or of its place in the total configuration of that culture, but certain of its features may help to understand why it plays so important a role in social science.

What are called "blood ties" can be understood as the bonds of solidarity that are caused by or engendered by the actual biological connectedness, sometimes figured as genetic, sometimes hereditary, sometimes in emotional terms. Or the notion of blood can be understood as figurative, iconic, but still standing for the bonds of solidarity, bonds which are deeply affective, deeply binding, actually breakable but to be broken under the most unusual, tragic, unforgivable circumstances. Images of the mother's love for her child, and the child for her, of the father's innate or unconsciously dictated preference for his own real child come in also. Other features are closely associated, indeed, are inextricably intertwined. The perpetuation of the self in one's own children, the defeat of death in the continuity of the life one engenders are both images of the ties that bind and the continuity of life. Cooking and care may express these ties, and they also constitute the ties. Kissing and copulation may express these ties but they also constitute them. Obedience and loyalty may express these ties but they also constitute them.

I am trying to avoid any distinction between a kind of social relationship and the meaning of that relationship as expressed in symbols, or the implication that culture merely marks, in iconic or other form, the expression of some more fundamental social relationship which can be stated in abstract terms. Symbols symbolize something, of course. But what they symbolize is symbols, that is, each other. They do not symbolize essences, or deeper meanings, or more fundamental social forms. Even the words we use in analysis are no more "deep" or "fundamental" than that which is analyzed; all we have done is to reformulate in other forms.

So kinship is defined by social scientists, and anthropologists in particular, as having to do with reproduction because reproduction is viewable as a distinct and vitally important feature of social life. Its distinctness, its systematicity, are "given" in the analyst's experience of his own culture—they are demonstrable and self-evident and his not unreasonable assumption is that if we are that way, and if all people are people—deep down and underneath superficial differences of language, dress, and appearance—then all people most hold reproduction in as high value as we do. It is considered to be, after all, as vital a feature of social life as it is of human life itself. But the question is, is this really true of all people? I am not convinced that it is.

Whatever the historical situation may have been, the third axiom, that Blood Is Thicker Than Water, seems to me to be quite explicit for those who worked in the tradition of Westermark, Freud, and Malinowski. Not explicit in the very bald terms in which I have put it, but still clearly discernible. For many others it is more implicit as a necessary assumption about which little is said and consequently no systematic effort is made to bring this presupposition into line with the rest of the presuppositions in the study of kinship. But even for those who strenuously deny it, I think it can be shown to follow from the way in which their studies of kinship proceed. The fact that they deny some of their most important presuppositions should be no surprise, nor should it cause any special consternation. No one can make all of one's presuppositions explicit even in the most elegant theories, and surely there is not very much theory to kinship theory anyway. Finally, I have offered some evidence for the fact that many, from Morgan through Lévi-Strauss, make some explicit statements which suggest that they do indeed hold this premise and that it is indeed a part of their intellectual armory.

It is at this point that the Doctrine of the Genealogical Unity of Mankind can be understood to follow from the three axioms I have outlined, and why that doctrine is so vital a part of the explicit premises of the study of kinship. However sharply social kinship is distinguished from physical kinship, kinship is defined as having to do with human reproduction, and human reproduction is regarded as a biological process entailing sexual relations and some sort of biological or physical bonds between parents and offspring and siblings. It follows that all the time and everywhere there is at least that much that is the same. In these crucial respects fatherhood is the same in every culture; it is, as Scheffler and Lounsbury put it, a matter of engendering. Motherhood is the same in all cultures at all times and places because in its distinctive features, its definition, it is a matter of a child being born of, or engendered by, a woman. The Doctrine of the Genealogical Unity of Mankind is a necessary corollary of the way in which kinship is defined (as reproduction) and the way in which reproduction is understood (as a biological process following sexual intercourse), and the fact that ''Blood Is Thicker Than Water'' for all human beings (the third axiom). If motherhood differed from one society to another, if there were no universal aspects to fatherhood, there could be no standard genealogy against which to plot particular cultural variants.

So too the privileged position of kinship among the four most privileged institutions follows from the three axioms and their correlates, as well as from the way in which kinship is defined. I have not stressed the view that kinship is a universal of human culture and society partly because it seems to me to be so self-evidently held by so many. Its universality lies both in its functions and in certain of its forms. In this it differs from economics and religion perhaps, depending on how those are defined. But as the definition of kinship and the axioms themselves stress, the genealogy is built of relations which are the same the whole world over; the bonds of kinship are strong, particularly between primary kin, and are the same the whole world over (both culturally and biologically of course); the "grammar" and "vocabulary" of kinship (which make up the genealogy) are the same the whole world over and onto that framework can be grafted all sorts of disparate meanings and functions yet remain a constant, permitting cross-cultural comparison and yet allowing for the differences between particular cultures. Where politics is only constant in respect to relations of dominance and power, economics with respect to exchange of goods and services or however it may be defined, out of none of these can any "grammar" and "vocabulary" be constructed of the same kind as can be wrought out of the relative products of kinship.

So much, then, for what I see as the presuppositions involved in the study of kinship as it has been practiced by anthropologists since the mid-nineteenth century, if not earlier.

The difficulties which I see in the study of kinship derive from the major presuppositions which I have just discussed as these relate to the aims of anthropology.

Anthropology starts with the proposition that all human beings act and that their actions are in some important part related to the culture they share. A culture consists by definition, in the shared understandings of the ways in which the world or life is, the structure of its existence, which includes how people should act in such a world. Culture is thus a shared system of symbols and meanings; a system of categories and units and the ways in which these are designated and conceptualized; a conceptual scheme; a particular way of constituting reality or the multiple realities of life. This is not distinct from any realities that an observer may postulate. The relation between the reality postulated by the observer and that which is postulated by the particular culture is a separate issue, however important it may be. (For further elaboration of this way of defining culture see Schneider [1968] 1980 and 1976).

Anthropology, then, is the study of particular cultures. *The first task of anthropology, **prerequisite to all others,** is to understand and formulate the symbols and meanings and their configuration that a particular culture consists of.*

My difficulty with the study of kinship can be summed up simply: the assumptions and presuppositions which the anthropologist brings to the process of understanding the particular culture he is studying are imposed on the situation blindly and with unflagging loyalty to those assumptions and little flexible appreciation of how the other culture is constituted, and with it a rigid refusal to attempt to understand what may be going on between them. The anthropologist has, as part of his culture, his conceptual scheme, a way of ordering his experience of another culture, a way of constructing the reality he believes he is encountering, and he is not easily shaken loose from that secure, reassuring, comfortable, well-worn common language to which he is committed and shares with his community of anthropologists, and which helps to define his place in that community. The anthropologist lives by his culture just as everyone else does, and it is very unnerving to distance oneself from one's culture and community, for this leaves one without a firm anchor in some secure way of occupying a known place in a known world and ways of viewing that world.

The irony, of course, is that it is precisely the anthropologist who is committed to the idea of culture and formulated the one most sacred canon of his trade; to avoid ethnocentric bias; to be open and flexible and to learn and perceive and to avoid the blinding commitments which prevent his sensitive perception of, and appreciation of, the other and how he formulates his reality. This is supposed to be the sine qua non of the professional anthropologist.

More specifically, I have detailed throughout the book particular questions about the presuppositional baggage students of kinship impose on their task. The three axioms I stated earlier in this chapter seem to me to be insupportable. The division of the sociocultural world into institutions, domains, or rubrics of kinship, economics, politics, and religion which are presumed to be universally vital, distinct functions, and the major building blocks out of which all cultures or societies are made assumes a priori what should be the question: of what blocks is *this* particular culture built? How do *these* people conceptualize their world? What functions does *this* culture identify as being universally vital and distinct?

One of the common bits of intellectual legerdemain that the institutional divisions leads to is this: First we assume that kinship, economics, politics, and religion are distinct entitites. Then we proceed to define them so as to stress their distinction. We then approach a particular culture and describe it first in terms of one, then another, then another of these institutional entities. And then comes the great discovery! All of these institutions are inextricably interrelated and intertwined so that in any particular case they cannot be distinguished! What we carefully separate with the left hand we then discover with the right hand has been inseparable all along. At the risk of some exaggeration, it seems to me that this is just what Mauss's "total social fact" consists of: the arbitrary division of society into parts and the subsequent demonstration that the parts are really inseparable because they constitute an integrated whole. What was one to begin with is discovered to have been one all along!

The argument that is sometimes offered in defense of this procedure is that analysis consists of decomposing a whole into its component parts. There can be little to disagree with here. But without pressing the pun too far, it is one thing to decompose an object and quite another to discover what parts it is actually composed of. It is said that by smashing the atom we break it into its component parts and thus learn what those parts are and what they are made of. This may hold for atoms. But a smashed culture does not break up into its original parts. A culture which is chopped up with a Z-shaped instrument yields Z-shaped parts: a culture which is chopped up with tools called kinship, economics, politics, and religion yields those parts.

The second axiom, that kinship, by definition, has to do with human reproduction and that this is a biological process entailing sexual relations, fails not by reason of its definition, but rather because of the associated assumptions. These are that kinship is everywhere and always a culturally distinct, distinguishable, and highly valued entity. That is, the fact of engendering another human being (to use the Scheffler-Lounsbury phrase) is always a culturally distinct construct and is always given high cultural value. This could be treated as a question, a hypothesis to be tested empirically. But it cannot be done on the literature that is generally available to us today, for almost all of that literature assumes that these are the facts instead of asking if they are or not. I have spoken to many people who have come back from the field and been assured, most sincerely and without conscious deceit, that the people they studied really do have the constructs of kinship, as the second axiom defines them. But on close questioning I usually find that they did very much as I did when I returned to write up my material on Yap. They imposed the notions of kinship on their materials even while actually eliciting that material in the field. Their first unquestioned translations of terms and relationships "find" "mothers" and "fathers," "sons" and "daughters"— kinship—and this is then confirmed by being made consistent with their first assumptions. My own experience in this matter is most compelling, for I did just that and there is a record of publications which I have been required to repudiate here.

It follows from what I have said that the Doctrine of the Genealogical Unity of Mankind is insupportable for the reasons just given. This doctrine assumes that mother is mother the whole world over and that all mothers can be compared by holding one element constant (that they bear children) and then examining the variations. As an American observer, I certainly believe that women have children, and that to do so they must have had sexual intercourse, regardless of what other conditions may be required, such as God's will or being physically capable of conceiving and so on. I certainly believe that Americans, and those sharing European culture generally, as Americans do, believe that that relationship is, if not sacred, at least of immense value. But I am equally convinced that most anthropologists project that particular set of meanings onto all peoples everywhere and since they rarely if ever raise the question, there is no reason to believe that it is universally true as assumed. It has never been tested because it has been assumed to be self-evident.

Embedded in the preceding is a point which should be made explicit. One of the major difficulties with the study of kinship has been the failure to treat meaning and value as problematic variables which need to be discovered in each case, and that an important part of meaning is the context, the configuration of which the problematic element is a part. It is not only a question of the magnitude of the value which is placed on some culturally formulated element. It is the detail of *what* value and *what* meaning in *what* configuration of values and meanings that is the significant set of variables. I tried to bring this point out as strongly as I could in dealing with Scheffler and Lounsbury. It is one of the major shoals on which the Doctrine of the Genealogical Unity of Mankind founders.

The third axiom leads to difficulties which are in part similar to those I have just recited. Blood Is Thicker Than Water is not only axiomatic in studies of kinship, it is a fundamental axiom of European culture. Even if this axiom were true as a biological fact, even if the most extensive scientifically acquired evidence showed it to be true—as true, for example, as the sociobiologists claim it to be, and that is a very strong position—the point remains that culture, even were it to do no more than recognize biological facts, still adds something to those facts. The problem remains of just what the sociocultural aspects are, of what meaning is added, of where and how that meaning, as a meaning rather than as a biological fact, articulates with other meanings. If any biological fact wholly and completely determined every facet of a social fact then there would still be the need to describe what the cultural formulation, value, meaning, conception was in the total configuration of cultural meanings. But even in such a limiting case, that a sociocultural aspect is present makes that part of it something different from the biological part, places it in relation to other sociocultural elements, and therefore poses the sociocultural aspect as problematic.

But the axiom that Blood Is Thicker Than Water does not hold water even for the sociobiologists. I need offer no more evidence for that statement than to call attention to the fact that even the sociobiologists do not claim to be able to account for the so-called extension of kinship. They only claim to account for *some* aspects of *some* of the relations between very close kin. This leaves a good deal to be accounted for.

Let us assume that my criticisms of the study of kinship are generally not far off the mark. What, then, is to be done? One way in which this question has been put to me is: "Well, if you don't like the way we are doing it, how do you suggest we study kinship?" This presupposes kinship, that it is still out there to be studied and that all we have to do is to study it differently. I cannot take this position, but I can see where others might wish to.

The one ground on which they might proceed is to take kinship as an empirical question, not as a universal fact. One must start with a working hypothesis about what kinship is or how it is to be defined for purposes of such an inquiry. The paradigmatic construct of kinship is that of European culture as this is embodied in the second axiom. This, then, would be the working hypothesis. But it would be necessary to strip away the most troublesome parts of the conventional wisdom about kinship. Specifically, it could no longer be assumed that the genealogical grid is universal or has the same value and meaning in all cultures, nor that functionalist baggage which tries to account for the necessity of kinship while at the same time allowing for its variable forms. Instead, such questions should be set aside for future study. The immediate and salient questions are: Given this definition of kinship, do these particular people have it or do they not? If so, detailed ethnographic evidence must be presented to substantiate that position; if not, specific ethnographic evidence should be presented showing wherein they differ. In the field we must not translate or gloss every relationship between a woman and what appears to be the child she has borne as a mother-child relationship until that translation or gloss has been fully explored by examining in detail how the natives themselves conceptualize, define, or describe that relationship and their construction of just where it stands in the context of their culture. The same goes for the father-child and the marital and all other presumed kinship relations. To repeat, this means that the genealogical grid cannot be assumed but only held as a possible hypothesis. This in turn means that the idea of primary meanings as reflecting the assumed primacy or high value attached to engendering must be treated as a question and not taken as universally true. In other words, the assumption of primary meanings and extensions must either be held in abeyance until it can be shown just which meanings are indeed primary and which are demonstrable extensions for the particular culture being studied, or the whole presumption that there are universal, primary meanings from which all others derive must be set aside. For example, as in the Yapese case, we must find out what *citamangen* means in all its usages and in all contexts in which it occurs. Only then can we ask if any of those meanings are primary, and if so, in what sense, and what is the evidence for that conclusion. It may well turn out (as I believe) that even what is called "referential meaning" is not primary and that primary meaning cannot be ascribed to any particular form of signification.

One more point is important. Value and meaning in the total cultural configuration must be added to the formulation, so that omission of these important variables does not lead the field-worker into the kinds of difficulties I have described. To some extent this will be taken care of by avoiding the assumptions of universality and the genealogical grid. But more than that is needed. If the culture contains the assumption that sexual intercourse is necessary to human reproduction one cannot just stop there as Scheffler and Lounsbury suggest. This is clear for the older literature, such as Van Gennep (1906) and Durkheim (1913). It is also clear from the Yapese example. The Yapese regard that fact as of relatively minor cultural value and of limited meaning. To merely establish that the culture postulates that one person engenders another is insufficient: is the relationship held to be significant for that very reason or is that just one of the facts of life that are not really important, in terms of which social action is regulated?

There would be a considerable change in the way in which kinship studies proceed if this solution were accepted. It might turn out that European culture does provide a nice model, but that that model does not prove to be very generally applicable. Kinship might then become a special custom distinctive of European culture, an interesting oddity at worst, like the Toda bow ceremony. I think that such a way of dealing with kinship would teach us a great deal.

It might seem that a more radical road would be a general overhaul of the aims and methods of anthropology, but this is not so. The aims and methods of anthropology have always been and are always being sharply criticized and generally overhauled. Structural-functional analysis is not as popular as it was forty years ago. Structuralism has a number of converts, but others who have tried it have already abandoned it for some higher form of hermaneutics or lower functionalism. Various forms of "materialism," some dialectical and others not, are practiced now here and now there. Some anthropologists have been doing "symbolic anthropology," which is very close to, if not identical with, "interpretive anthropology." The differentiation of anthropological aims, approaches, methods, and theory is much greater than it was fifty years ago, and so too is the number of people doing anthropology. But revision, innovation, criticism have been constant throughout the history of anthropology.

The lines along which a general overhaul might be undertaken, then, depend very much on the guiding outlook. But it is at this point that the task of this book is finished. The aim of this book has been to say that the way in which kinship has been studied does not make good sense. Indeed, it is quite unreasonable in certain ways that I have tried to explicate. If that case has been presented my job is done. The case I have presented can be generalized to any anthropology which invokes universals on functionalist grounds or which employs any or all of the four privileged institutions of kinship, economics, religion, and politics. But that is another book.

References

Alexander, R. D. 1979. *Darwinism and Human Affairs*. Seattle: University of Washington Press.

Barnes, J. A. 1955. Kinship. *Encyclopedia Britannica*. 14th ed. Vol. 13, pp. 403–4. Chicago: Encyclopedia Britannica.

———. 1961. Physical and Social Kinship. *Philosophy of Science* 28:296–99.

———. 1964. Physical and Social Facts in Anthropology. *Philosophy of Science* 31:294–97.

———. 1967. Agnation Among the Enga: A Review Article. *Oceania* 38:33–43.

———. 1974a. Genitor: Genetrix: Nature: Culture. In *Character of Kinship*, edited by J. Goody, 61–73. Cambridge: Cambridge University Press.

———. 1974b. Kinship. *Encyclopedia Britannica*. 15th ed. Vol. 10, pp. 477–85. Chicago: Encyclopedia Britannica.

Beattie, J. H. M. 1964a. Kinship and Social Anthropology. *Man* 64:101–3.

———. 1964b. *Other Cultures*. London: Cohen and West.

Boon, J. A., and Schneider, D. M. 1974. Kinship Vis-a-Vis Myth; Contrasts in Lévi-Strauss' Approaches to Cross-Cultural Comparison. *American Anthropologist* 76:799–817.

Broder, C. R. 1972. Medical Theory: The Yapese Approach. M.A. thesis, Department of Anthropology, University of Chicago.

Chagnon, N. A., and Bugos, D. E. 1979. Kin Selection and Conflict: An Analysis of a Yanomamo Ax Fight. In *Evolutionary Biology and Human Behavior*, edited by N. A. Chagnon and W. A. Irons, 213–88. North Scituate, Mass.: Duxbury Press.

Derrett, J. D. M. 1971. Virgin Birth and the Gospels. *Man* 6:289–93.

Durkheim, E. 1898. Review of Kohler . . . *L'Année Sociologique* 1:306–19.

———. 1913. Review of Hartland . . . *L'Année Sociologique* 12:410–14.

Evans-Pritchard, E. E. 1940. *The Nuer*. London: Oxford University Press.

Fallers, L. A. 1957. Some Determinants of Marriage Stability in Busoga: A Reformulation of Gluckman's Hypothesis. *Africa* 27:106–23.

Firth, R. 1936. *We, The Tikopia*. London: George Allen and Unwin.

Fortes, M. 1945. *The Dynamics of Clanship Among the Tallensi*. London: Oxford University Press.

———. 1949. *The Web of Kinship among the Tallensi*. London: Oxford University Press.

———. 1959a. Descent, Filiation and Affinity. *Man* 59:193–97, 206–12.

———. 1959b. Primitive Kinship. *Scientific American* 200:146–58.

———. 1963. The "Submerged Descent Line" in Adhanti. In *Studies in Kinship and Marriage*, edited by I. Schadgra. Occasional Papers of the Royal Anthropological Institute, No. 16. London: Royal Anthropological Institute.

————. 1969. *Kinship and the Social Order*. Chicago: Aldine.

Fortes, M., and Evans-Pritchard, E. E., eds. 1940. *African Political Systems*. London: Oxford University Press.

Frazer, J. G. 1910. *Totemism and Exogamy*. 4 vols. London: Macmillan and Co.

Freedman, M. 1958. *Lineage Organization in Southeastern China*. London School of Economics Monographs on Social Anthropology, No. 18. London: Athelone Press.

Fustel de Coulanges, N. D. [1864] 1956. *The Ancient City*. New York: Doubleday Anchor Books.

Gellner, E. 1957. Ideal Language and Kinship Structure. *Philosophy of Science* 24:235–42.

————. 1960. The Concept of Kinship. *Philosophy of Science* 27:187–204.

————. 1963. Nature and Society in Social Anthropology. *Philosophy of Science* 30:236–51.

Goodenough, W. H. 1955. A Problem in Malayo-Polynesian Social Organization. *American Anthropologist* 58:71–83.

————. 1970. *Description and Comparison in Cultural Anthropology*. Chicago: Aldine.

Goody, J. 1961. The Classification of Double Descent Systems. *Current Anthropology* 2:3–26.

Hamilton, W. D. 1964. Genetical Evolution of Behavior. *Journal of Theoretical Biology* 7:1–52.

Jensen, J. T. 1977a. *Yapese Reference Grammar*. Honolulu: University Press of Hawaii.

————. 1977b. *Yapese-English Dictionary*. Honolulu: University Press of Hawaii.

Kirkpatrick, J. T. 1977. Person, Hierarchy, and Autonomy in Traditional Yapese Theory. In *Symbolic Anthropology*, edited by J. L. Dolgin, D. S. Kemnitzer, and D. M. Schneider, 310–28. New York: Columbia University Press.

Kirkpatrick, J. T., and Broder, C. R. 1976. Adoption and Parenthood on Yap. In *Transactions in Kinship*, edited by I. Brady. Honolulu: University Press of Hawaii.

Labby, D. 1976a. *The Demystification of Yap: Dialectics of Culture on a Micronesian Island*. Chicago: University of Chicago Press.

————. 1976b. Incest as Cannibalism: The Yapese Analysis. In *Incest Prohibitions in Micronesia and Polynesia*, edited by V. Carroll. *Journal of the Polynesian Society* 85:171–80.

La Fontaine, J. 1974. Descent in New Guinea: An Africanist View. In *The Character of Kinship*, edited by J. Goody. Cambridge: Cambridge University Press.

Lawrence, W. E. 1937. Alternating Generations in Australia. In *Studies in the Science of Society*, edited by G. P. Murdock, 319–20. New Haven: Yale University Press.

Leach, E. 1961. *Pul Eliya, a Village in Ceylon; A Study of Land Tenure and Kinship*. Cambridge: Cambridge University Press.

————. 1966. Virgin Birth. *Proceedings of the Royal Anthropological Institute for 1966*, pp. 39–49.

Lévi-Strauss, C. 1963. *Structural Anthropology I*. New York: Basic Books.

―――. 1969. *The Elementary Structures of Kinship*. Boston: Beacon.

Levy, M. J., Jr. 1952. *The Structure of Society*. Princeton: Princeton University Press.

―――. 1965. Aspects of the Analysis of Family Structure. In *Aspects of the Analysis of Family Structure*, edited by J. Coale et al. Princeton: Princeton University Press.

Lingenfelter, S. G. 1975. *Yap: Political Leadership and Culture Change in an Island Society*. Honolulu: University Press of Hawaii.

Linton, R. 1936. *The Study of Man*. New York: Appleton-Century.

Lounsbury, F. G. 1965. Another View of the Trobriand Kinship Categories. *American Anthropologist* 67:142–85.

Maine, H. S. 1861. *Ancient Law*. London: J. Murray.

Makarius, R. 1977. "Ancient Society" and Morgan's Kinship Theory 100 Years After. *Current Anthropology* 18:709–15, 724–29.

Malinowski, B. 1913. *The Family among the Australian Aborigines: A Sociological Study*. London: University of London Press.

―――. 1929. Kinship. *Encyclopedia Britannica*. 14th ed. Vol. 13, pp. 403–9. London: The Encyclopedia Britannica Co.

―――. 1930a. Kinship. *Man* 30:9–29.

―――. 1930b. Parenthood—The Basis of Social Structure. In *The New Generation*, edited by V. Calverton and S. D. Schmalhausen, 112–68. New York: Macaulay.

―――. 1932. Culture. *Encyclopedia of the Social Sciences*. 1832 edition. Vol. 4, pp. 621–45.

Marksbury, R. A. 1979. Land Tenure and Modernization in the Yap Islands. Ph.D. diss., Tulane University.

Maybury-Lewis, D. 1965. Durkheim on Relationship Systems. *Journal of Scientific Study of Religion* 4:253–60.

McLennan, J. F. [1865] 1970. *Primitive Marriage*. Chicago: University of Chicago Press.

Monberg, T. 1975. Fathers Were Not Genitors. *Man* 10:34–40.

Montague, S. 1971. Trobriand Kinship and the Virgin Birth Controversy. *Man* 6:353–68.

Morgan, L. H. 1870. *Systems of Consanguinity and Affinity of the Human Family*. Smithsonian Contributions to Knowledge, No. 17. Washington, D.C.: Smithsonian Institution.

―――. 1877. *Ancient Society*. New York: Holt and Co.

―――. 1901. *League of the Ho-de-no sau-nee, or Iroquois*. New York: Dodd, Mead and Co.

Murdock, G. P. 1940. Double Descent. *American Anthropologist* 42:555–61.

―――. 1949. *Social Structure*. New York: Macmillan.

Needham, R. 1960. Descent Systems and Ideal Language. *Philosophy of Science* 27:96–101.

―――. 1971. Remarks on the Analysis of Kinship and Marriage. In *Rethinking Kinship and Marriage*, edited by R. Needham. London: Tavistock.

Parsons, T. [1937] 1949. *The Structure of Social Action*. Glencoe: The Free Press.
————. 1951. *The Social System*. Glencoe: The Free Press.
————. 1955. Family Structure and the Socialization of the Child. In *Family, Socialization and Interaction Process*, edited by T. Parsons and R. R. Bales. Glencoe: The Free Press.
Parsons, T., and Shils, E. 1951. Values, Motives and Systems of Action. In *Toward a General Theory of Action*, edited by T. Parsons and E. Shils, 247–75. Cambridge: Harvard University Press.
Powell, J. W. 1884. On Kinship and the Tribe. Third Annual Report of the Bureau of American Ethnology for 1881–1882. Washington, D.C.: Government Printing Office, pp. xxxviii–xlv.
Radcliffe-Brown, A. R. 1950. Introduction. In *African Systems of Kinship and Marriage*, edited by A. R. Radcliffe-Brown and C. D. Forde. London: Oxford University Press.
————. 1952. *Structure and Function in Primitive Society*. London: Cohen and West.
Rivers, W. H. R. 1900. A Genealogical Method of Collecting Social and Vital Statistics. *Journal of the Royal Anthropological Institute* 3:74–84.
————. 1904. *Sociology, Magic, and Religion*. Reports of the Cambridge Anthropological Expedition to the Torres Straits, edited by A. C. Haddon, vol. 5. Cambridge: Cambridge University Press.
————. 1907a. On the Origin of the Classificatory System of Relationships. In *Anthropological Essays Presented to Edward Burnett Tylor*, edited by N. W. Thomas, 309–23. Oxford: Clarendon Press.
————. 1907b. Review of N. W. Thomas. *Man* 7, no. 56:90–92.
————. 1908. Some Sociological Definitions. The Report of the Seventy-Seventh Meeting of the British Association for the Advancement of Science, pp. 653–54. London: John Murray.
————. 1910a. The Father's Sister in Oceania. *Folk-Lore* 21:42–59.
————. 1910b. The Genealogical Method of Anthropological Inquiry. *Sociological Review* 3:1–12.
————. 1914. *The History of Melanesian Society*. 2 vols. Cambridge: Cambridge University Press.
————. 1915. Kin, Kinship. In *Encyclopedia of Religion and Ethics*, edited by J. Hastings. Vol. 7, pp. 700–707.
————. 1924. *Social Organization*. New York: Knopf.
Roth, W. E. 1903. *Superstition, Magic and Medicine*. N. Queensland Ethnographic Bulletin No. 5. Brisbane: Vaughan.
Sahlins, M. D. 1968. *Tribesmen*. Englewood Cliffs, N.J.: Prentice-Hall.
————. 1972. *Stone Age Economics*. Chicago: Aldine.
Scheffler, H. W. 1970. Kinship and Adoption in the Northern New Hebrides. In *Adoption in Eastern Oceania*, edited by V. Carroll, 369–89. Honolulu: University Press of Hawaii.
————. 1972. Systems of Kin Classification: A Structural Typology. In *Kinship Studies in the Morgan Centennial Year*, edited by P. Reining. Washington, D.C.: Anthropological Society of Washington.

————. 1974. Kinship, Descent, and Alliance. In *Handbook of Social and Cultural Anthropology*, edited by J. J. Honigman, 744–93. Chicago: Rand-McNally.

————. 1978. *Australian Kin Classification.* Cambridge: Cambridge University Press.

Scheffler, H. W., and Lounsbury, F. G. 1971. *A Study in Structural Semantics: The Siriono Kinship System.* Englewood Cliffs, N.J.: Prentice-Hall.

Schneider, D. M. 1953. Yap Kinship Terminology and Kin Groups. *American Anthropologist* 55:215–36.

————. 1955. Abortion and Depopulation on a Pacific Island. In *Health, Culture and Community*, edited by B. D. Paul, 211–35. New York: Russell Sage Foundation.

————. 1957. Political Organization, Supernatural Sanctions and the Punishment for Incest on Yap. *American Anthropologist* 59:791–800.

————. 1958. Typhoons on Yap. *Human Organization* 16:10–15.

————. 1962. Double Descent on Yap. *Journal of the Polynesian Society* 71:1–24.

————. 1964. The Nature of Kinship. *Man* 64:180–81.

————. 1965. Kinship and Biology. In *Aspects of the Analysis of Family Structure*, edited by H. J. Coale. Princeton: Princeton University Press.

————. 1968. Virgin Birth. *Man* 3:126–29.

————. [1968] 1980. *American Kinship: A Cultural Account.* Englewood Cliffs, N.J.: Prentice-Hall. (2d ed. with a new chapter, University of Chicago Press.)

————. 1972. What is Kinship All About. In *Kinship Studies in the Morgan Centennial Year*, edited by P. Reining. Anthropological Society of Washington.

————. 1976. Notes Toward a Theory of Culture. In *Meaning in Anthropology*, edited by K. Basso and H. Selby, 197–200. Albuquerque: University of New Mexico Press.

Seligman, B. 1928. Asymmetry in Descent, with Special Reference to Pentecost. *Journal of the Royal Anthropological Institute* 58:533–58.

Service, E. R. 1966. *The Hunters.* Englewood Cliffs, N.J.: Prentice-Hall.

Silverman, M. G. 1970. Banaban Adoption. In *Adoption in Eastern Oceania*, edited by V. Carroll. Honolulu: University Press of Hawaii.

Smith, W. R. 1885. *Kinship and Marriage in Early Arabia.* Cambridge: Cambridge University Press.

Spencer, B. and Gillen, F. J. 1899. *The Native Tribes of Central Australia.* London: Macmillan and Co.

Spiro, M. 1968. Virgin Birth, Parthenogenesis and Physiological Paternity: An Essay in Cultural Interpretation. *Man* 3:242–61.

————. 1972. Virgin Birth. *Man* 7:315–16.

————. 1977. *Kinship and Marriage in Burma. A Cultural and Psychodynamic Analysis.* Berkeley: University of California Press.

Thomas, N. W. 1906. *Kinship Organizations and Group Marriage in Australia.* Cambridge: Cambridge University Press.

Tonkinson, R. 1978. Semen Versus Spirit Child in a Western Desert Culture. In

Australian Aboriginal Concepts, edited by L. R. Hiatt. New Jersey: Humanities Press.

Van Gennep, A. 1906. *Mythes et Legendes d'Australie.* Paris: Guilmoto.

Westermark, E. 1891. *The History of Human Marriage.* London: Macmillan and Co.

Wilson, P. S. 1980. *Man, The Promising Primate: The Conditions of Human Evolution.* New Haven: Yale University Press.

Worsley, P. M. 1956. The Kinship System of the Tallensi: A Revaluation. *Journal of the Royal Anthropological Institute* 86:37–75.